A River Runs ' True Tales of the Rio Abajo

Edited by
Richard Melzer and John Taylor
A Valencia County Historical Society Publication

April 2018

To Kelly Fajardo —

Thanks for your great service to our community and state!

Richard Melzer.

Published by Rio Grande Books
Los Ranchos, New Mexico

© 2015 Richard Melzer and John Taylor
All rights reserved.
Rio Grande Books
Los Ranchos, New Mexico
www.RioGrandeBooks.com

Printed in the U.S.A.
Book design by Paul Rhetts

No part of this book may be reproduced or transmitted in any form, or by any means, electronic or mechanical, including photocopying, recording, or by any information retrieval system, without the permission of the publisher.

Library of Congress Cataloging-in-Publication Data

A river runs through us : true tales of the Rio Abajo / edited by Richard Melzer and John Taylor.
    pages cm
"A Valencia County Historical Society publication."
Includes bibliographical references and index.
ISBN 978-1-936744-50-3 (paperback : alkaline paper)
ISBN 978-1-936744-56-5 (ebook)
1. Valencia County (N.M.)--History, Local. 2. Rio Grande Valley (Colo.-Mexico and Tex.)--History, Local. 3. Valencia County (N.M.)--Biography. 4. Rio Grande Valley (Colo.-Mexico and Tex.)--Biography. 5. Valencia County (N.M.)--History, Military. 6. Rio Grande Valley (Colo.-Mexico and Tex.)--History, Military. 7. Valencia County (N.M.)--Social life and customs. 8. Rio Grande Valley (Colo.-Mexico and Tex.)--Social life and customs.
I. Melzer, Richard. II. Taylor, John M. (John McLellan), 1947-
III. Valencia County Historical Society (N.M.)
F802.V3R58 2015
978.9'92--dc23
                    2014048868

Cover: "River's Edge," photograph courtesy of Bill Tondreau, bill@unit16.net.

To Jim Boeck (April 7, 1945 – February 14, 2014), friend, colleague, and longtime stalwart of La Historia del Rio Abajo.

Acknowledgements

The editors wish to acknowledge the assistance provided by dozens of helpful individuals, including Eric Baca, Filomena Baca, Mary Ann Baca, Matt Baca, the late Rupert Baca, Jean Ballagh, Assunta Berry, Dante Berry, Ricardo Berry, Dylia Castillo, Leo Castillo, Leonard Castillo, R. Robert Castillo, Tibo J. Chavez, Jr., Pete V. Domenici, Robert Duck, the late James Fernandez, Jim Foley, the late Eva Glidewell, Rico Gonzales, Bill Gore, the Hesselgren family, the Isleta elders, Valentino Jaramillo, Ted Jojola, David Kadison, Paul Lujan, Lloyd Pancho, Jr., Theresa Pasqual, Dr. David Phillips, Frances Romero, Rita Padilla-Gutierrez, Bennie Sanchez, Irene Sanchez, Corrine Sedillo, Esther Shir, Francisco Sisneros, Lorraine Spradling, Ruth Tondre, Ramon Torres, Van Dorn Hooker, Dr. Henry Walt, and the late Anne T. Williams.

We also wish to thank the editors of the *Valencia County News Bulletin*, formerly Sandy Battin and now Clara Cano Garcia, as well as the paper's publisher, David Purdu, for publishing the Valencia County Historical Society's "La Historia del Rio Abajo" monthly series since 1998. Many of the chapters that appear in this anthology first appeared in "La Historia del Rio Abajo."

Finally, we wish to thank the faithful readers of "La Historia del Rio Abajo." Your enthusiasm for this series encouraged our authors to continue discovering intriguing new stories with the ultimate goal of one day collecting these tales in book form. Thank you, our neighbors and friends, for your interest in our Rio Abajo.

Contents

Introduction

The Rio Grande flows through the Rio Abajo, bisecting the region from north to south. It's called the Rio Grande because it's so long: 1,896 miles from its headwaters in Colorado to its mouth in the Gulf of Mexico. It's certainly not called the Rio Grande because it is wide. In fact, the river is so narrow that most of us travel over it by bridge nearly every day and never notice, much less think of its importance in our lives.

The Rio Grande is the lifeblood of our fields, the sustenance of our wildlife, and the center of our ecology. It can be beautiful or, in flood stage or in drought, it can be devastating. It can be full and robust or it can be largely empty and mostly full of sand. It can change course or remain steady for years. But, regardless of its condition from day to day, from season to season, and from year to year, it continues to flow.

The same can be said of our history. Like the river, time passes through our lives, although we hardly notice the people, places, and events that were once so vital to our community and its existence. Our history is full of beauty, but is sometimes marred by evil and turbulence. Our history can suddenly change course or remain on the same steady course for years. But, regardless of its condition from day to day, from season to season, and from year to year, it continues to flow.

A River Runs Through Us is an attempt to help us remember the history of the Rio Abajo. It is not a comprehensive history, but rather a reminder of various people, places, and events that have helped shape the Rio Abajo over many centuries. It is as if fishermen (historians) have cast a wide net to catch a few valuable fish (people, places, and events) so we can appreciate their importance before releasing them to the ever-moving river (the flow of time).

A River Runs Through Us is the Valencia County Historical Society's second anthology. The society's first collection, *Murder, Mystery, and Mayhem,*

1

introduced readers to forty-one stories from the rich history of the Rio Abajo. *A River Runs Through Us* continues to document the region's legacy with thirty-three true tales, focusing on people, places, wars, and mysterious events from the pre-Columbian era to the recent past. As with *Murder, Mystery, and Mayhem,* many of these tales have been published as part of "La Historia del Rio Abajo" series, written by Valencia County Historical Society members since 1998. Be it through articles or books, we strive to appreciate and preserve our history with as much determination and commitment as we strive to appreciate and preserve the Rio Grande that flows through us.

People

El Padre Eterno:
Father Jean Baptiste Ralliere

Richard Melzer

Jean Baptiste Lamy, New Mexico's first Catholic bishop, was named to lead the newly-created Vicariate Apostolic (later Diocese) of Santa Fe in 1850. Born and raised in France, Lamy returned to his native land several times to recruit French priests and nuns to serve in the distant parishes of New Mexico. By 1867, there were 51 active priests in the territory, 31 of whom had been recruited from France and six of whom were natives of other European nations.

Traveling to New Mexico

Twenty-one-year-old Jean Baptiste Ralliere was one of six young French seminarians recruited to serve in New Mexico in 1856. An honor student at Mont-Ferrand, the same French seminary that Lamy attended, Ralliere had been receptive to the new bishop's plea that New Mexico represented a worthy mission field for those with the true devotion and energy to serve.

Bishop Lamy had not mentioned that Ralliere and his five French colleagues would need bravery and good, seafaring stomachs as well as devotion and energy to simply travel to far-off New Mexico. All six Frenchmen suffered early bouts of seasickness while en route to the United States. A storm

3

tossed their ship, the *Alma*, over high waves in violent winds. Despite these hardships, the group enjoyed at least one "splendid" dinner marked by "the explosions of champagne corks and many hilarious toasts," in the words of a grateful priest at the scene.

Upon landing in the United States, Ralliere and his fellow recruits toured New York City by horse and buggy and witnessed what they called the "really overpowering" grandeur of Niagara Falls in western New York. Moving westward via Sandusky, St. Louis, and Kansas City, the group prepared for the longest leg of their land journey: across the Great Plains on the Santa Fe Trail.

New to the plains, the six were troubled by the haunting cries of coyotes at night and the possibility of hostile Indian attacks by day. But the coyotes were often drowned out by the singing of Latin hymns, and the visits of Indians seemed peaceful enough. According to one Frenchman, most natives were "satisfied with a little sugar, wheat, and some biscuits." When the travelers' morale dipped, their leaders reportedly opened "some good wine that brought our spirits back like a charm." The Frenchmen also made good use of their time by learning Spanish. They practiced their newly acquired language skills on the Mexican workers who accompanied their small wagon train west.

Jean Baptiste Ralliere and his fellow religious travelers arrived in Santa Fe on November 10, 1856. They were greeted with a solemn Mass celebrated at the Santa Fe cathedral. The six seminarians were officially ordained as priests in a ceremony conducted by Bishop Lamy a month later. Each was assigned a parish in New Mexico. Father Ralliere was dispatched to parishes in Santa Fe and Pecos before receiving his final assignment in Tome. Carrying a chalice he had brought with him from France, Ralliere assumed his new duties in the Rio Abajo on June 13, 1858. He was 23 years old.

Early Years in Tome

Father Ralliere needed all his youthful energy and devotion to face the hard work that lay ahead in Tome. Tome was the mother church of a parish that eventually included as many as fourteen *visitas* and mission churches in the Rio Grande Valley and on the eastern slopes of the Manzano Moun-

Father Ralliere as a young man

tains. Officially, his parish extended as far south as the Rio Bonito in Lincoln County. Ralliere rode on horseback (and later by buggy) to the distant corners of his parish. He said Mass in churches, in chapels, and even in a dance hall across from a saloon in La Constancia. Unaccustomed to French-sounding names, some of his parishioners preferred to call their new pastor Padre Rael.

Father Ralliere endured many hardships as he rode his circuit to the scattered settlements. Once, while gathering wood for a camp fire, he noticed

Indians peering at him from behind some bushes. Bravely, he continued to gather wood, but gradually wandered farther and farther from his camp and eventually slipped into the darkness to escape. Thereafter, his advice in dealing with potentially hostile Indians was, "Don't stand still and pray to the Santo Niño when you see Indians. Beat it!"

Safely back in Tome, Father Ralliere served his parishioners well, administering the sacraments and improving the local church. Although Tome was a farming community, its Immaculate Conception church lacked a *bulto* (statue) of San Ysidro, the patron saint of farmers. Father Ralliere took up a collection to purchase such a statue. Although the acquired image was not made in Tome, its two carved oxen—that always appear with San Ysidro—were the work of a local artisan, Teresita Z. Sedillo. Tome's Immaculate Conception church had been completed in 1750, but it lacked a wooden floor until Father Ralliere had one built over the old clay surface. A new pulpit, a new main altar, a new confessional, and a new choir loft were added

Tome's Immaculate Conception Church, circa 1915

6

with the help of a skilled French carpenter, François D. Foulenfant.

The church also needed a new bell. Church bells served many important functions in a village like Tome: to call the faithful to Mass, to announce the death of a church member, to signal the hours of the day, to warn of danger, and even to call residents to *fandangos* (dances). Each bell had its own distinct tone, or voice, recognized and admired by everyone in small, close-knit Catholic communities.

In 1863, Father Ralliere persuaded several families to contribute money for a bell to be placed in the church's south tower. With funding from Manuel A. Otero and other wealthy parishioners, Ralliere ordered the bell to be cast at a foundry in St. Louis. When it arrived, the bell's raised letters listed the city where it had been made, the year (1863), the church's name, and the names of its donors or *padrinos* (sponsors), since all church bells were officially baptized by the church. In 1892, a bell was purchased for the north belfry and was given the name Jesus Maria Jose, in honor of the holy family. Bells for the missions in Peralta, Valencia, and Manzano were also purchased with local contributions by the end of the century. The one in Peralta weighed no less than 975 pounds.

When not raising funds for church improvements, Father Ralliere worked to enhance religious services with fine music. The priest organized two church choirs in Tome, one for men and one for women. It was said that when members of a choir sang particularly well, the priest would reward them with some of his best homemade wine. We can only speculate whether the wine made his choirs perform better—or perhaps worse—as their evenings wore on.

Ralliere not only trained these church choral groups, but also wrote arrangements for their songs and composed many songs of his own. Over a hundred of these arranged and composed songs appeared in a book compiled by Ralliere, titled *Cánticos Espirituales*. Printed in thirteen editions from 1884 to 1956, *Cánticos Espirituales* was probably the most widely used hymnal in the Catholic churches of New Mexico and Texas in the late nineteenth and early twentieth centuries.

Within months of his arrival in Tome, Father Ralliere ordered a church organ from St. Louis, the first instrument of its kind in the area. Five more organs were later ordered: three for the missions of Valencia, Peralta, and

Casa Colorada, one for children's lessons, and one that was loaned from house to house. Ralliere taught Estevan Zamora to play the organ so well that Zamora played music for thousands of Masses, holy days, and other special occasions over a 50-year period. After Estevan died in 1903, his son Julian played for an estimated 8,000 Masses over the next 53 years.

Father Ralliere also encouraged the music performed in Tome's two most important religious plays of the Catholic calendar: *Los Pastores* at Christmas and the Passion Play during Holy Week before Easter Sunday.

The French priest owned, played, and taught at least seven musical instruments, including a flute, a clarinet, a violin, a trumpet, a cornet, drums, and, of course, the organ. Enjoying secular music almost as much as religious songs, Ralliere collected local folk songs, hosted musical events on winter nights, and even organized a brass band in Tome.

The Importance of Education

But Father Ralliere taught much more than music to the people of his parish. Realizing the importance of education for the young, he taught both religious and academic courses in a school he opened north of the church soon after his arrival in the 1850s. Teachers, paid by Ralliere, taught children Bible studies, arithmetic, geography, history, health, and music. Agriculture, animal husbandry, blacksmithing, rope-making, carpentry, and weaving were also taught at various times. But the subject that received the most attention (other than religion) was English. Although the vast majority in his parish still spoke Spanish on a daily basis at home and at work, Ralliere realized that learning to read and write in English was essential to the future success of community residents under U.S. rule.

Patriotism was likewise emphasized. The priest was said to have led his students to the top of Tome Hill on April 15, 1862, to see as much as they could of the Battle of Peralta, the last confrontation of Union and Confederate forces in the Civil War in New Mexico. Unable to observe much of the battle from this vantage point and distance, they at least sang litanies and prayed for the Union's success in combat. Their prayers were answered as the Confederates fled from the battle scene and, eventually, back to Texas.

In another effort to encourage loyalty to the United States, Ralliere went so far as to translate "America" into Spanish:

> *País mío y Libre*
> *Tierra muy noble*
> *Te canto a Ti.*
> *Patria de mi Padres*
> *País del peregrino*
> *Que de lejos vino*
> *Siempre a cantar.*

Impressed by the priest's success with his school in Tome, Valencia County leaders asked Father Ralliere to serve as the county's first superintendent of schools in 1887. Accepting the post, the priest displayed his usual enthusiasm by personally inspecting all 22 schools in his charge. His report to the County Commission described the schools as "very flourishing," with 1,165 children attending. Teachers included graduates of Ralliere's own school in Tome.

Unfortunately, the priest's enthusiasm soon waned when faced with the seemingly insurmountable problem of funding. Without sufficient funding, equipment could not be purchased, English could not be taught adequately, separate schools could not be opened for girls, and teachers could not be paid regularly, much less well. Distressed, Father Ralliere resigned his position on January 25, 1888, explaining that he could "not suffer the pain and the unhappiness" caused by this desperate financial situation.

An Active, Productive Life

Ralliere refocused his attention on his parish and his growing household in Tome. His household included several families who helped maintain the church, its *camposanto* (cemetery), and its *convento* (priest's quarters). Abandoned or runaway children were also taken in. One such boy reportedly traveled all the way from El Paso to Tome on a tame ram of great size. Later, Ralliere adopted a Navajo orphan named Juan Andres, giving the boy his own surname and sending him to St. Michael's School in Santa Fe for a good education and a good start in life. With so many mouths to feed, the *convento* used as much as 10,000 pounds of flour per year.

Helped by his parishioners and his considerable household, Father Ralliere farmed large tracts of land that he had personally acquired over the years. Much of this land was used to grow alfalfa, while tracts south of Tome Hill were used to grow as many as 2,500 grape vines by the late nineteenth century. In 1906, his winepress produced a dozen vats of wine, seven of which he sold and five of which he gave away to community leaders. Ralliere felt compelled to assert, "I have drunk nothing."

The priest's orchard produced additional fruit, and his flower garden included thorn trees grown from seeds he had brought with him from France. Ralliere used the trees' long thorns to make Christ's crucifixion crown, given to parishioners on Good Friday each year. Strong believers claimed that the touch of these thorns could cure various ailments, especially headaches. Other fields were used to raise the cattle, sheep, and hogs that were often contributed to the church as tithes collected from loyal parishioners.

Father Ralliere never grew wealthy from his farming and ranching activities, but he hardly led a life of poverty. Old records show that he paid $27.85 in property taxes in 1892, compared to most residents of Valencia County who paid less than $5.00 per year. The vast majority of his personal income went into the church and community activities he felt most strongly about, including the purchase of musical instruments and the daily operation of the parochial school he'd created for the youth of his parish.

Father Ralliere truly appreciated the general poverty of his flock and helped the poor in many ways. During crises, he refused to burden his parishioners by collecting tithes. And, when grooms could not afford rings for their brides at their weddings, Ralliere allowed his own gold ring, set with a jewel, to be used throughout the sacred ceremony.

Father Ralliere clearly enjoyed an active, productive life in the Rio Abajo. Most of his parishioners showered their devout priest with great praise, as did Bishop Lamy himself. In 1868, only twelve years after Ralliere's arrival in New Mexico, the bishop listed his fellow French countryman as one of his top three choices to serve as the first bishop of the newly-created Diocese of Tucson. In recommending the parish priest, Lamy succinctly described Ralliere as "a most successful missionary in New Mexico; speaks French, Spanish, English, Latin, Greek; efficient pastor of souls; excellent health; honest, discreet, prudent; never anything in his actions against moral principles; built several churches and schools." Ralliere was not appointed as the first bishop of Tucson, but he undoubtedly appreciated Lamy's evaluation of his labor as a vote of great confidence and respect.

Confronting Problems

But Father Ralliere's life in the Rio Abajo was far from perfect. Although Indian raids had subsided (the last local victim of an Indian attack died in 1866), smallpox, epidemics, droughts, and periodic floods continued to plague the valley, as they had for centuries.

Of all the terrible floods that destroyed life and property in the Tome area, the flood of 1884 is remembered as the worst. Breaking its banks near Isleta in May 1884, the Rio Grande inundated the valley as far south as La Constancia. At least two local residents drowned in the rushing waters. Survivors fled to higher ground, carrying as many supplies and salvaging as many valuables as possible. At Father Ralliere's request, villagers helped remove all the *bultos* (statues of saints) from the Tome church. But, according to legend, when the men attempted to carry the *Santo Entierro*, it miraculously became so heavy that it could not be moved. Witnesses explained that Christ made himself so heavy because he did not want to leave his church unprotected. Although much of the rest of the church later had to be rebuilt due to damage caused by the flood, the section where the Christ figure lay remained safely intact.

Meanwhile, villagers camped under cottonwoods or stayed in the *ranchitos* of friends and relatives on the mesa. A locally-composed *corrido* (ballad) told of the anguish and suffering that followed. Father Ralliere joined his destitute parishioners, setting up a makeshift altar beside a salt cedar tree. Hitching a red-speckled stallion to an improvised craft, the priest inspected the flooded plaza and the damage done to his parish as a whole. Help arrived in the person of John Becker, Belen's most successful German merchant. Although not a Catholic, Becker demonstrated his respect for Father Ralliere by bringing ten sacks of flour for the flood victims and urging the priest to go to Belen to seek additional relief.

The French priest traveled as far as La Constancia, but seeing how fast the river ran, he soon turned back. Before returning to Tome, Ralliere wrote pleas for help to residents of Belen. Becker dutifully carried these small cards to their destinations on the west bank of the Rio Grande.

The response to Ralliere's pleas for help was mixed. While some contributed generously, the priest noted that Don Felipe Chavez, known as *El Millonario*, gave him "only a lot of free advice and sent not one pound of flour." Other much-appreciated aid arrived from Ralliere's fellow clerics in Las Vegas, Bernalillo, and Santa Fe.

Father Ralliere conscientiously distributed the newly-arrived supplies up and down the valley. But he later wrote that the people "were not content with the distribution" and even accused him of keeping many of the provisions for his own use. Stung by such criticism, he vowed never to manage the sharing of provisions in future crises. Ralliere was forced to conclude that "I did not really know my own people."

Ralliere wrote of growing increasingly "sad and depressed" when he faced three additional crises. While described as an honest, intelligent man who saw humor in every situation, Ralliere was also called a passionate man and an idealist who, in historian Florence Hawley Ellis's words, "never flinched from a position taken." As a result, the priest alienated many in his parish. His enemies considered him hot-tempered, hard-headed, and sometimes unfair. In part, their animosity also stemmed from a perception that Ralliere, with his interest in teaching English and modern ways, was a representative of the *Americanos* and never truly a part of the local community.

Additionally, Ralliere enforced the collection of tithes, despite the protest of those who insisted that the poor could ill-afford this church tax. For these several reasons, Ralliere had his share of enemies and allies, with some moving from one side to the other in disagreements, depending on the current issue and their personal stake in it.

One such issue involved the cutting of an *acequia* (irrigation ditch) belonging to Don Juan Salazar. Father Ralliere claimed that the decision to cut the *acequia* to help drain stagnant ponds had been made by the community as a whole at a public meeting on March 8, 1877. When the *acequia* was cut on March 14th, Don Juan accused Ralliere of initiating the action and insisted that the priest repair the damage. The Frenchman refused, to which Don Juan replied, "There will be dead people here." "Then kill me at once," answered Ralliere. Rather than carry out his threat, Don Juan told the priest

12

that his "unjust behavior would have to be explained in another place," implying on Judgment Day.

Upset, Father Ralliere retreated to his church, later writing that he "wept to see that a thing so simple and so beneficial" had caused such a reaction. The priest did not set foot in Don Juan's house for two years. Taking sides in the dispute, most residents of Tome refused to go to confession during Lent "out of anger or shame," according to Ralliere. Two priests arrived at Ralliere's request, staying ten days and hearing 500 confessions made by what the Frenchman called "my rebels." Only time and the drainage of the stagnant pools brought peace. Years later, Ralliere philosophically concluded, "all is well that ends well."

Two Major Disputes

In 1877, Father Ralliere became embroiled in a dispute with an even more powerful member of his church, Manuel A. Otero. Otero claimed that the priest and others were using water for their fields upstream and depriving Otero of the water he needed to operate his mill downstream in La Constancia. Although Otero did not name Ralliere in a suit against those he accused of hoarding the water, hard feelings developed between the priest and the *rico* (wealthy landowner).

The Otero-Ralliere conflict culminated when Don Manuel's wife died in February 1877 and was buried in the Tome cemetery. Father Ralliere suggested that instead of using cash to pay for Doña Dolores's plot in the *camposanto*, Otero might contribute money for the purchase of a second church bell for the Immaculate Conception Church. Don Manuel responded in a letter that, having already helped with the purchase of bells in Tome and Manzano, he had decided "not to throw my money away by ringing into the wind."

The dispute continued for the next three years. Reflecting his anger, Father Ralliere even had the Otero name (as well as the other donors' names) removed from the bell the padrinos had purchased for the church fourteen years earlier. Dramatically, each stroke of the chisel was timed to sound like the tolling of bells customarily rung to announce a death.

The bitter conflict finally ended when Don Manuel remarried in September 1881. Without giving additional details, Father Ralliere later wrote that Don Manuel came to see him before the wedding and "a perfect reconciliation" resulted. Of course, it was too late to salvage Don Manuel and his fellow contributors' names on the old church bell.

Father Ralliere's last major dispute with members of his parish came in 1909, just two years before the aging priest's retirement. The original Tome land grant of 1739 had designated the property on the east side of the plaza to be used for the building of a church, a cemetery, and a house for the priest. No one disputed this fact until 1909 when the Archdiocese of Santa Fe requested a deed to prove its ownership of the land it had occupied for over a century and a half.

While the Tome land grant's Board of Trustees seemed ready to act affirmatively on the church's request, many local residents were not. Over 130 people signed a protest letter in July 1909, and an estimated 200 attended a mass meeting in August. According to the protestors' July 3rd letter to the Board of Trustees, the church's property and cemetery were "known to be properties belonging to the people of Tome. Never have these been placed under the priest and ... the Board of Trustees ... has managed them just as it has managed any other type of common land."

Angered by this statement and the behavior of those who signed it, Father Ralliere went so far as to close the church, saying Mass in his schoolhouse rather than on the disputed land. Defending the church's right to the property as well as Ralliere's extreme action, Bishop Jean Baptiste Pitaval (who had become bishop in January 1909) responded to the Catholics of Tome in writing. The bishop scolded all those who had signed the July 3rd letter for their "insubordination and rebellion" when there existed "all the reason in the world for you to treat your old pastor with more love and with the greatest respect possible in an effort to sweeten with good conduct the little life which is left to him instead of making more bitter his last journey."

To stress his point, the bishop concluded that the local residents' conduct "would justify my ... changing the parish headquarters from the village of Tome to another village ... but this I will not do out of consideration for Father Ralliere."

Properly chastised, several of the 132 residents who had signed the July 3rd letter asked that their names be removed from the controversial document. The protest movement failed and the deed of property ownership was finally given to the church. According to local legend, the leader of the frustrated movement soon suffered a great headache, leaving him permanently blind. He nevertheless survived and served as a leader of *velorios* (wakes for the dead) for many years.

Journey's End

And what became of the aging Father Ralliere? In 1908, he celebrated his 50th year of service as the pastor of Tome. Old disputes were set aside in what was described as a "gala program" filled with songs, dance, and orations, many of which were performed by the members of his parish for

Father Ralliere in later years

whom Ralliere cared the most—the school children.

Burdened with poor health, the pastor retired in 1911. Rather than return to his native France, Ralliere chose to remain in Tome. For three years, he lived in his old house next to the church, poverty-stricken and often bedridden with illness. Old timers recalled that he grew a long white beard, reminding many observers of Biblical patriarchs like Moses or Abraham. In age and appearance, he had clearly earned the name he was now respectfully called: *El Padre Eterno.*

As the end drew near, he wistfully remembered the first time he had met Bishop Lamy at his French seminary in 1854. Thirty-four years later, the bishop had died in Santa Fe. Ralliere wrote that "I hope to see him again soon." Father Ralliere's last journey was to a hospital in Albuquerque, at the insistence of Bishop Pitaval. But, missing home, Ralliere returned to Tome within days. He died at 9:00 p.m, on July 18, 1915. He was 80 years old.

Placed in a simple, homemade coffin, Father Ralliere was buried to the left of the altar in the same church where he had said thousands of Masses, had baptized hundreds of children, had married scores of couples, and had presided over seemingly countless funerals. But now it was his turn to be buried in holy—and properly deeded—land. He was laid to rest with the same French chalice he had brought with him from Europe so many years before.

It rained on July 20, the day of Father Ralliere's funeral, reminding the eleven priests and others in attendance of the many floods the priest had faced with courage and dedication. The rain fell so hard and the ground became so drenched that his coffin had to be weighted down with rocks.

But Father Ralliere would not have wanted his parishioners to think of the rain as tears of sorrow. Father Ralliere was a farmer as well as a priest, and he would have been glad for the rain to moisten the soil and water the crops. He would have been glad that life went on and crops and children and whole communities still thrived and grew.

It rained for an entire week in Tome.

Cracks in the Pope's Armor:
Protestantism Comes to the Rio Abajo

John Taylor

When Francisco Vasquez de Coronado came into New Mexico in 1540, he brought with him several Franciscan friars. For the next 300 years, Catholicism was quite literally "the only ecclesiastical game in town." Certainly the Native Americans worked hard to preserve their religious traditions, and, without question, there had been some divergence in Catholic religious practice—priests like Padre Antonio Jose Martinez in Taos who decided not to adhere to strict dogma and the rise of the Brotherhood of our Father Jesus the Nazarene, better known as Los Hermanos or the Penitentes.

The Rio Abajo was home to several Catholic parishes—St. Augustine at Isleta, Immaculate Conception in Tome, Our Lady of Belen, San Miguel in Socorro, and numerous missions from Los Pinos (now Bosque Farms) on the north to Luis Lopez on the south. Within these parishes and their scattered mission communities, the priests were extremely powerful and often found themselves at odds with members of the prominent families and with civic leaders.

Despite these challenges the Catholic Church reigned supreme from Mexican independence from Spain in 1821 until the election of Benito Juarez in 1855. In fact, the 1821 Plan de Iguala, promulgated by the newly formed government in Mexico City, declared that "The Roman Catholic Church would be the only one tolerated in the country" and the Mexican Constitution of 1824 required the Republic to prohibit the exercise of any religion other than the Roman Catholic and Apostolic faith. Nevertheless, the winds of change began to blow in New Mexico in the mid-1840s.

The Protestant Invasion Begins

The Santa Fe Trail between Independence, Missouri, and Santa Fe, New Mexico, had opened in 1821. This brought traders from the United States, mostly Protestant, if they were religious at all, into the solidly Catholic Mex-

17

ican province of New Mexico. Most of these men were nomads in the sense that they brought their goods or money, exchanged their goods, and returned to their homes in the United States. The Mexican War, from 1846 to 1848, changed that pattern. Now, responsibility for the security of the citizens of New Mexico rested with the United States, and the United States Army in particular.

Before Colonel Stephen Watts Kearny led his troops into New Mexico in 1846, he had been given strict orders to respect the existing ecclesiastical structure and traditions. There was great concern in Washington, D.C., that the war with Mexico, already being criticized both internationally and internally as an "aggressive, unholy, and unjust war," would also be perceived as a "war of impiety" against the Catholic Church. Therefore, when Kearny informed the citizens in Santa Fe that they "no longer owed allegiance to the Mexican government," he added,

> My government respects your religion as much as the Protestant religion, and allows each man to worship his Creator as his heart tells him is best. Its laws protect the Catholic as well as the Protestant.

Despite these assurances, it was clear that the ecclesiastical monopoly of the Roman Catholic Church was no longer operative. In fact, now that New Mexico was governed by the U.S. Constitution, freedom of religion was guaranteed.

The soldiers themselves, as well as the civilians that supported their forts and outposts, were largely Americans and many were Protestant by background. What's more, unlike the more nomadic Santa Fe Trail traders, these men were permanently or semi-permanently stationed in New Mexico, and Protestant church organizations recognized the need for providing spiritual guidance to these individuals. In addition, it was realized that the Mexican and Native American populations of New Mexico would be a fertile ground for evangelization and for fighting what many Protestants viewed as the scourge of Popism.

Challenges to the Catholic Monopoly

Cracks began to appear in the Roman Catholic monopoly in the Rio

Abajo in 1845, even before the outbreak of the Mexican War. Father Nicolas Valencia, newly arrived from the Diocese in Durango, Mexico, was dissatisfied with his assignment as assistant pastor at Sandia Pueblo. His complaints and requests for a more prestigious position were rebuffed by the bishop's vicar in Santa Fe. As a result of his complaining, he was assigned to a probationary position at Our Lady of Belen Church.

Valencia was glib and charismatic, and he soon began to act rather independently in Belen. In addition, he adopted a distinctly pro-American stance in the conflict that was now underway between the United States and Mexico. As a result of these "transgressions," Valencia was suspended by

Father Jose Antonio Zubiria, Bishop of Durango

Bishop Zubiria, a suspension that Valencia completely ignored. In fact, he persuaded the local civic authorities to remove the current priest from the parish of Our Lady of Belen and make him pastor. This, of course, did not go over well with Bishop Zubiria in Durango!

In the summer of 1849, another apostate Catholic, Fray Benigno Cardenas, appeared in Tome. Cardenas was a Franciscan from Mexico City who had fled north after having gotten crosswise with his superiors and having his priestly functions "removed." An articulate and charismatic priest, Cardenas convinced the local magistrate to allow him to take over the Tome church at the expense of Father Cabeza de Baca, the assigned priest. Cardenas appears to have been someone who genuinely questioned some of the dogma and regulations of the Catholic Church, although his superiors in Mexico accused him of various crimes including murder, embezzlement, and the use of forged documents (only the last of these was probably true).

There was a long-standing tradition under Spanish rule that permitted civil authorities to involve themselves in church operations. Needless to say, the church authorities were not pleased with this approach and appealed to the new American authorities to help them restore the rightfully assigned priests to their positions. However, the new U.S. representatives were not interested in becoming directly involved with church politics, noting the constitutional separation of church and state. In addition, despite the assertions of Kearny and others, if the truth be told, many of the Americans probably thought that the "Romanists" were finally getting their just deserts. Thus, the local civic leaders, some of whom had chafed under the priests' control of things like water rights and land ownership, were left in control.

In 1850, Jean Baptiste Lamy, a French-born priest currently serving in the Diocese of Cincinnati, Ohio, was assigned as Vicar Apostolic of New Mexico. Suddenly, the local priests who were used to an absentee landlord 1,500 miles away in Durango, had their boss just up the road in Santa Fe. Many of them elected to return to Mexico. Father Nicolas Valencia, however, managed to ingratiate himself with Lamy and was reassigned to churches in San Felipe, Jemez, and eventually back in Socorro, all apparently none the worse for his insubordinate behavior.

Benigno Cardenas was another matter entirely. He, too, tried to win Lamy's favor, but was rebuffed as soon as the new bishop found out about his

Father Jean Baptiste Lamy, Archbishop of Santa Fe

heretical escapades. Cardenas left New Mexico and traveled to Rome where he appealed to the Franciscan Minister General and to Pope Pius VI to be released from his holy orders. He was incarcerated for a short time before his request was granted. He traveled to France and then to England where he applied to be a minister in the Anglican Church. The Anglicans turned him down, but the Methodists accepted him with open arms and gave him a license to preach on their behalf.

With this "certification" and a stipend of $3,000, Cardenas returned to New Mexico in 1853. He preached his first Methodist sermon in front of the Cathedral in Santa Fe. In an attempt to discredit the new Methodist minister, the editor of the Catholic newspaper *Revista Catolica* declared that his conversion was neither a "gain for Protestantism nor a loss to Catholicism." According to a later report by Father Jean Baptiste Ralliere, the longtime priest in Tome, one of the first Hispanics to be "seduced from the true faith" by Cardenas was a wealthy Peralta farmer/rancher named Jose Maria Chavez.

Cardenas eventually settled in Peralta and continued to preach in Tome, Valencia, Belen, and Socorro, attracting a small cadre of followers devoted to his message. We will leave Cardenas for the moment, but we are certainly not finished with him.

Protestant Missionaries Arrive

Hiram Walter Read, a 30-year-old Baptist evangelist from Wisconsin, was assigned as the chaplain of Fort Marcy in Santa Fe in 1849. In addition

Reverend Hiram Read

22

to ministering to the soldiers, he began missionary work up and down the Rio Grande Valley. His focus was two-fold—passing out Spanish-language Bibles in the villages along the river and working to establish schools.

Read was forced to leave New Mexico in 1851 due to his wife's illness, but he returned for another two-year missionary stint from 1852 to 1854. On New Year's Eve 1854, Read baptized Jose Maria Chavez by immersing him in the icy Rio Grande just west of Peralta, making Chavez the first Hispanic to be baptized in New Mexico.

Read was followed in 1850 by George Nicholson, the first Methodist missionary. In 1853, during one of his trips down the valley, Nicholson met a Peralta man named Ambrosio Gonzales and gave him a Bible. Gonzales converted shortly thereafter, and, since Jose Maria Chavez was not baptized until 1854, Gonzales is widely regarded as the "first Mexican Protestant" in New Mexico.

In 1852, the Baptists initiated an outreach program to the Native Americans by assigning John Gorman as a missionary to the Laguna Indians. Also in 1852, Methodist minister John M. Shaw and his wife Harriet started a small school at the Los Pinos home of Henry Connelly and his wife Dolores. Shaw and his wife, while accepted by the Connellys and some of their wealthy neighbors, were not uniformly accepted by other residents. In an 1852 letter to her mother, Harriet wrote:

> The new Bishop [Lamy] and Vicario [Machebeuf] are very intolerant and are exerting their influence against us … but the Bishop and Vicario have many enemies and the parents of these we have will not submit to their authority.

In another incident in 1859, while preaching in Socorro, Shaw reported that

> I was attacked by a mob set on by the priest and driven from my stand amid shouts and stones and firing of guns. I received several shots from the guns, but only one did me any harm.

Despite the efforts by Lamy and his priests, by 1855, the Baptist church was solidly established in Peralta with Ambrosio Gonzales as a resident Bible school leader. The congregation set up a building committee and constructed a church on land just south of the present-day location of Our Lady of Guadalupe Catholic church in Peralta. (Note that the Peralta Catholic church itself was not built until the late 1880s.) By 1861, when their new church was completed, the Baptist congregation in Peralta and the surrounding area totaled one hundred members. In addition to the Peralta congregation overseen by Ambrosio Gonzales and Jose Maria Chavez, there were small Protestant congregations in Jarales, Polvadera, and Socorro. This four-church "circuit" was overseen by a Reverend Hansen. In 1860, another Methodist evangelist, Thomas Harwood, arrived in New Mexico. One of the first things that he did was certify Ambrosio Gonzales as a licensed Methodist preacher.

Eighteen sixty-two proved to be a challenging year for the Methodist community. During the Confederate invasion of New Mexico, two of their local stalwarts, Spruce Baird from Albuquerque and Jose Maria Chavez from Peralta, sided with the Confederates. When the Confederates retreated from the territory after their setbacks at Valverde, Glorieta Pass, and Peralta, Chavez and Baird fled with them. Neither man returned, and their property was taken by the government under the Confiscation Act of 1864.

By the late 1860s, the Baptists were struggling to provide missionaries and ministers. On the other hand, the Methodists were "going strong." In 1874, the Methodists purchased the Baptist church in Peralta and assigned a Reverend Steele as the pastor. In 1876, the Methodists held their first annual statewide conference at the Peralta church.

Methodist (formerly Baptist) mission in Peralta, New Mexico

24

Generating conflict between the Protestants and Catholics was not an exclusive property of Lamy and his priests. Stories are told of the Methodists ringing the bell in their mission while Father Ralliere was saying Mass at the Catholic church next door!

Cardenas's Return

As promised, we now return to one of the first Rio Abajo Protestants—apostate Franciscan turned Methodist minister Benigno Cardenas. When we left him, he was living in Peralta and preaching under a Methodist license from Peralta south to Socorro, assisting George Nicholson, Ambrosio Gonzales, Jose Maria Chavez, and the others in their attempts to evangelize the residents of the valley. One day in 1855, he was lying ill in his Peralta home when, as the story goes, he was dragged outside by a hog in full view of several individuals. Cardenas took this as a sign from God, and, after he had recovered, he went to Albuquerque and threw himself at the feet of Bishop Lamy's Vicar, Father Machebeuf, asking to be forgiven and readmitted to the

Ambrosio Gonzales's grave marker in the old Methodist Cemetery in Peralta

Catholic church. After consulting with Lamy, Machebeuf flogged Cardenas before the altar in Albuquerque's San Felipe de Neri church, then reinstated him to priestly service by vesting him with a cassock. After a period of time with Lamy in Santa Fe, Cardenas was reassigned to Havana, Cuba, where he lived out his years in service to the Catholic Church.

And so, with some challenges, Protestantism was established in the Rio Abajo. Interestingly enough, two of the first "converts," Nicolas Valencia and Benigno Cardenas, recanted their conversions and rejoined the Catholic ministry. However, the momentum that their schism started in the late 1840s was magnified by the arrival of ordained ministers such as George Nicholson, John Shaw, and Thomas Harwood, described by some as a "one man army of the Lord." The process that they had initiated achieved a permanent foothold.

Over time, the animosity between Catholics and Protestants would diminish as the ties of family, neighborhood, and common problems like flooding and drought became higher priorities. Although most of the American preachers left after a period of time, Ambrosio Gonzales continued to preach in the Rio Abajo until his death in 1884. He is buried in the old Methodist cemetery in Peralta.

Don Felipe Chavez: El Millonario

Jim Boeck

Don Jose Felipe Chavez was the richest, shrewdest businessman in Belen and most of New Mexico during much of the nineteenth century. Rancher, farmer, merchant, retailer, wholesaler, investor, large landowner, and mine owner were just some of his many business roles. He was, in fact, known in his day as *"El Millonario."*

Don Felipe Chavez

Born in Los Padillas in 1835, Don Felipe was a member of one of the oldest, most powerful families in New Mexico history. His father, Jose Chavez y Castillo, had served as an acting governor of New Mexico in the 1840s. His mother, Manuela Armijo de Chavez, was a member of the eminent Armijo family and a cousin of Manuel Armijo, the controversial frequent governor of New Mexico under Mexican rule. Already born with a proverbial silver spoon in his mouth, Don Felipe grew even richer when he inherited most of his father's business interests upon Jose Chavez y Castillo's death in 1858.

Don Felipe married his first cousin, Josefa Chavez, about 1860. Although the Catholic Church prohibited the marriage of such close relatives, the church granted a special dispensation to the young couple. Such dispensations were not unusual; many elite Hispanic families attempted to keep their status, power, and wealth by marrying close relatives.

Diverse Business Ventures

Don Felipe and his bride moved to Belen after a terrible Rio Grande flood. A natural born businessman, Don Felipe launched his first business venture in Belen, building a mercantile store where Walgreens now stands on North Main Street. His large store was famous for its many goods and for its long counter in which hundreds of Mexican silver coins were embedded.

The Chavez family had long been involved in the highly profitable trade on the Santa Fe Trail. The family's wagons shipped raw materials from Old and New Mexico and hauled manufactured goods from Missouri and beyond in the eastern United States.

Don Felipe soon entered this lucrative trade, hiring Antonio Castillo of Belen to be the wagon master of the caravan Chavez regularly financed and sent back East. Returning west, Castillo filled Don Felipe's wagons with such diverse commodities as coffee, sugar, canned goods, gingham, calico, boots, machinery, plows, hand tools, and building nails. All items were bought in bulk. His 1860 invoice was valued at $36,000, worth over a quarter million dollars in today's money. In 1865, his purchases filled seven five-ton wagons.

Don Felipe expanded his business operations by raising herds of nearly 5,000 sheep, using the *partido* system of labor. In this system, workers agreed to raise a number of sheep for a set number of years, with compensation based on a percentage of the new sheep born during the period of labor. The *partido* system generally worked well for the livestock owner, in this case Don Felipe, but badly for sheepherders, who usually ran up large debts over many years.

By 1870, Don Felipe was listed as the second richest Hispanic in the territory of New Mexico. Eager to invest and diversify his fortune, Don Felipe knew that New York City was the financial and commercial center of the country. Working through Peter Harmony & Nephew, a well-trusted Spanish firm in New York, Don Felipe soon expanded his business portfolio to include both commercial and residential real estate in the big city. He also invested heavily in the New York Stock Exchange. In fact, his son, Jose, became the first New Mexican to ever sit on the New York Stock Exchange.

Don Felipe and Josefa made at least one trip to New York to inspect Chavez's numerous investments. The couple traveled the first leg of their journey by horse-drawn carriage on the Santa Fe Trail. From Kansas City they traveled in far greater comfort by train. Once in New York, they stayed in the Barcelona Hotel, where they enjoyed a most cordial Spanish atmosphere.

A Military Foe and an Economic Ally

In probably the most exciting moment of his life, Don Felipe played unwilling host to Confederate General Henry H. Sibley during the American Civil War. Although Sibley's soldiers had defeated the Union forces in the Battle of Valverde south of Socorro, the Confederate army was woefully short on food and supplies. Having served as a U.S. army officer in New Mexico before the Civil War began, Sibley might have known of Don Felipe's great wealth and assets.

Upon entering Belen, Sibley confronted Chavez and demanded $5,000 in cash (equal to about $100,000 today) and many sheep and cattle to feed the general's over 2,000 hungry soldiers. Though hardly a Southern sympathizer, Don Felipe had little choice but to comply. Sibley gave Chavez IOUs, but never paid his large debt. Within weeks, the rebel commander and his army had been turned back after the Battle of Glorieta Pass and, while they traveled through Belen in their hurried retreat back to Texas, they had far less money and supplies than when they had first appeared at Don Felipe's door.

In 1869, a young German immigrant named John Becker arrived in Belen to work in his uncle's local mercantile store. Becker's uncle, Louis Huning of Los Lunas, was so impressed by John's energy and ambition that he soon promoted him to serve as the manager of his Belen operation. The German's hard work and vitality also impressed Felipe Chavez. When Becker asked Don Felipe for financial assistance so he could open his own store, Chavez gladly loaned him the money in 1877.

Frequently asked for loans, Don Felipe willingly lent money to other businessmen and even to friends and relatives, although he charged everyone the going interest rate.

Don Felipe had made a typically wise business investment when he lent money to young Becker. The John Becker Store prospered and grew, expanding into a large department store which served the Belen community for over a century. Don Felipe hardly saw Becker's local retail operation as great competition because most of Chavez's commercial business

Felipe Chavez house, Belen, New Mexico

transactions were in wholesale rather than retail operations.

Don Felipe contributed much to Belen's economy in the nineteenth century, but it was not until his twilight years in the early twentieth century that he made his most lasting contribution to his small town's fortunes. As a major stockholder in the Atchison, Topeka and Santa Fe Railway, Chavez was privy to insider information about the company's plans to build a new route through New Mexico. Rather than go north-to-south, as with its original route through the territory, the Santa Fe planned an east-to-west cutoff that would make travel to the West Coast much faster and more efficient.

Don Felipe knew that he could change the economic dynamics of his community—and make a handsome profit for himself—if he could convince the Santa Fe to locate its cutoff tracks through Belen. Don Felipe and John Becker teamed up as a self-appointed Chamber of Commerce to promote Belen's cause against competing towns in the Rio Grande Valley.

While Don Felipe lobbied the railroad, Becker and his able nephew, Paul Dalies, acquired the land needed not only for the new tracks, but also for a roundhouse, shops, and other essential railroad buildings. Nearby farmers were convinced to exchange their land for more distant property, with cash as an added incentive. Acquiring the needed land and offering it to the railroad, Chavez and Becker were successful in wooing the Santa Fe. The new route which passed through Belen on its way through Abo Canyon was, in fact, forever known as the Belen Cutoff; and with the north-south, east-west railroad intersection, Belen became known as the Hub City. Unfortunately, Don Felipe did not live long enough to see his dream come true.

Thanks to the vital roles played by Don Felipe and John Becker, Belen's economic future was assured. "There are two periods in the history of Belen," according to Jose Dolores Cordova. The first period was "when we had no money and the local people bartered in agricultural produce or livestock. There was no public education and people had a hard time making a living. There was a lot of misery." But then, wrote Cordova, "We have the era when money started getting into circulation. This was made possible by the Santa Fe Railroad coming to Belen." There was still considerable poverty, but there were many new opportunities not only for local residents, but also for the hundreds of workers who moved to the area with the completion of the cutoff in mid-1908.

Don Felipe also had a philanthropic side to his nature. Aware of the importance of education in a community's development, he established a private school for girls. Known as the Felipe Chavez School, the non-sectarian institution taught high moral standards as part of its standard curriculum.

The father of Belen's business community died in his home of a cerebral hemorrhage on April 11, 1905. He was buried in a marble mausoleum he had built outside Our Lady of Belen Catholic Church.

The Chavez store is now the site of a modern drugstore. His once-elaborate carriage house is now an empty lot (to the north of Walgreens). His school is long closed, and even his mausoleum was moved (in 1946) and finally dismantled to make room for a modern parking lot in 1973. Today only a wall made of the original marble remains in the cemetery, marking the burial place of Chavez, his wife (who died in 1898), his daughter Manuela (who died in 1920), and a popular parish priest, the Reverend Juan Picard (who died in 1918). Only Don Felipe's grand adobe mansion, well maintained by its current owners, the Leroy Baca family, remains of the vast Chavez estate.

But Don Felipe's legacy lives on and should be remembered whenever we hear a train whistle on each of the nearly one hundred freight trains that pass through Belen each day. Don Felipe's wise business voice is silent, but his impact in the Rio Abajo remains loud and clear.

Joe and Ruth Tondre:
A Los Lunas Love Story

Richard Melzer

Ruth Powers was an attractive, bright young woman when she worked at the front desk of the Plaza Hotel in Las Vegas, New Mexico, in the early 1920s. She had not been working at the hotel very long when a lawman from Valencia County registered as a guest.

Joe and Ruth Tondre

Immediately taken by Ruth's charm and beauty, Sheriff Joseph Tondre told Ruth that she would someday be his wife. Ruth hardly took Joe's words seriously; she had been flattered by admiring males before. But this admiring male was far more insistent than most, especially after the couple met again at a dance during one of Las Vegas's famous Rough Rider reunions and rodeos. Ruth began to notice that Joe Tondre was an "awfully handsome" man.

Joe visited Ruth every chance he got, volunteering to transport prisoners to the state mental hospital in Las Vegas whenever such transfers were ordered by the court. Joe also wrote daily letters to Ruth. In fact, Joe wrote so many letters from his home in Los Lunas that the station master at the Los Lunas train depot suggested that Joe write a whole bundle of letters and let him (the station master) mail them one letter at a time. It would at least save Joe a trip to the depot each day!

After several months, Joe and Ruth fell in love, and in the fall of 1921 Joe asked Ruth to marry him. She accepted. But not everyone approved. Ruth's father was especially leery because Joe was twenty years older than his 18-year-old bride-to-be. Joe and Ruth nevertheless married on October 10, 1921, exchanging vows at the Catholic Church west of the plaza in Las Vegas. Appropriately, their wedding meal was at La Castañeda, the Harvey House where the couple had first dined together. The newlyweds enjoyed a ten-day honeymoon in El Paso where they saw several minstrel shows and crossed the border to eat at good restaurants in Juarez.

Returning from west Texas, Joe and Ruth traveled to Los Lunas to start their married life. Always insisting on the best for his family, Joe had had a fine house built and furnished before Ruth's arrival. He had also hired a cook and others to help around the house.

The Tondres' house was located on Los Lentes Road, just south of the intersection of Main Street and Los Lentes Road. Although made with traditional *terrón* bricks, the house was built in a modern style for the 1920s. As his family grew in the following years, Joe added two bedrooms upstairs in a converted attic.

Ruth found Los Lunas of the 1920s to be much different from the Las Vegas of her childhood. Years later she recalled that Los Lunas was a small village with no paved roads, no sidewalks, and no streetlights, making her surroundings "pitch black at night." Los Lunas was so small that everyone

34

knew everyone else. In fact, Ruth remembered a day when she called a friend by phone and was told by the local operator (whose switchboard was nearby), "I think she's on the way to your house. She just passed by going in that direction."

Accustomed to having a Carnegie Library in Las Vegas, Ruth also noted the lack of a public library in Los Lunas. And there were few stores or restaurants. The largest stores were Huning's Mercantile and Simon Neustadt's, where Joe had worked since he was a boy and where he was now the manager when he was not busy with his duties as a lawman.

The only restaurant in town was a one-room adobe place on Main Street. For just 60 cents a person could buy a meal of beans, two fried eggs, fried potatoes, and steak, with canned peaches for dessert. Unfortunately, Ruth declared that it was "the worst food you ever saw in your life." It certainly did not compare to the food Ruth had enjoyed at La Castañeda in Las Vegas or, more recently, in Juarez.

Despite her initial culture shock, Ruth soon settled down to her new life with her devoted husband. The couple's first child, Joseph, Jr., was born at home in 1924 with the help of an Albuquerque nurse, who stayed ten days, and Dr. Samuel Wilkinson of Belen, who stayed overnight. Four other children, Patricia, Ruth, Katy, and Anne, followed. Ruth always considered Los Lunas to be "a good place to raise children."

Los Lunas remained a quiet small town, but there was occasional activity at Simon Neustadt's, at the old courthouse, along old Route 66, and on poor country roads. Ruth recalled that the road between Los Lunas and Belen was especially dangerous, requiring the crossing of the Santa Fe Railway tracks no less than four times. Several men were killed at these crossings and, while Joe went to deal with the accident scenes, Ruth often went to comfort the victims' grieving widows.

Ruth also recalled the Great Depression when countless homeless families from the nation's Dust Bowl traveled through Los Lunas on Route 66. The Simon Neustadt Store provided each family with bread, milk, and a gallon of gasoline to help them on their way west to California.

As a Republican leader (known locally as Mr. Republican), Joe was always busy with political campaigns and elections. Over the years he was elected sheriff, appointed U.S. marshal, and served on the local school board—the job he said was most satisfying and worthwhile for his community. Looking back, Ruth asserted that she must have fed every politician in Valencia County at one time or another. When Joe added a sunroom to the south side of their home, Ruth insisted that it have a cement floor, because politicians were always dropping ashes on her rugs, and a fireplace, so tobacco chewers would have a place to spit into.

Remembering her parents' love of reading (her father had favored the *Saturday Evening Post* and her mother could recite every Rudyard Kipling poem), Ruth taught her five children to appreciate good books. Missing the library she had enjoyed in Las Vegas, Ruth started Los Lunas's first public library. The library started with 300 old books donated by the Belen Women's Club. Thirteen years later the library had 6,000 books and was open three days a week.

The Tondres also traveled, especially when Joe's work took him out of town. Ruth accompanied Joe when he, as a U.S. marshal, took federal prisoners to trials as far away as Washington, Nebraska, and New York. Ruth always felt safe as long as she was with Joe. She even received $2.00 a day for "guarding" female prisoners on such trips.

The Tondres persevered during hard times as well as good. During World War II, Joe, Jr., served in the military for over two and a half years, but found time to write 230 letters to his worried folks back home in New Mexico. He returned home safely from Europe in early 1946.

The Tondres' least happy days came when Joe was appointed warden at the state penitentiary in Santa Fe in 1951. This was an important job and a testimony to Joe's fine work in law enforcement, but it required the family to relocate to Santa Fe and live in the warden's quarters just outside the prison's walls. Ruth remembered the year and a half her family spent in Santa Fe as the worst period of their lives. Joe worked long, hard hours, dealing with the many problems that plagued the prison. And there were problems at home. A prisoner was assigned to cook, while a second trustee did the yard work and a third drove the Tondres' daughters back and forth to school in Santa Fe. Not trusting a convicted criminal alone with her teenage daughters, Ruth went along on the daily trip to Santa Fe to protect her girls. With few other chances to leave the family's isolated quarters, Ruth said she felt that she was "as much like a prisoner as the prisoners themselves."

36

The Tondres were pleased to return to Los Lunas after their time in Santa Fe had ended. Going home was a welcome relief. A weaker marriage could not have withstood the long ordeal.

Joe Tondre retired from his many duties in business and politics in 1960. After about eight years of retirement, he suffered a stroke at breakfast one morning and spent the last four months in an Albuquerque nursing home. Ruth visited Joe as often as possible. She later remembered that during those visits, Joe would say, "Ruth, I loved you from the first moment I saw you." Recalling that first moment at the Plaza Hotel and the wonderful life and friendship they had shared since 1921, Ruth would weep all the way home to Los Lunas.

Joe Tondre passed away on February 3, 1968, at the age of 84. To honor his memory and many contributions to Valencia County, Ruth appeared before the county commission to request that a road be named for her late husband. The commission approved the request, but for political reasons refused to put up a road sign with the Tondre name on it. Devoted as ever, Ruth went out, hired a painter for $7.50, and got the sign painted herself.

Ruth graciously agreed to share her memories of her marriage to that "awfully handsome" fellow she had met in Las Vegas so long ago. This author simply took notes when he interviewed her in January 1988. Fortunately, Dr. Howard Leach videotaped his more extensive interview with Ruth in September 1989.

Ruth passed away on August 3, 1993, rejoining Joe for eternity. They are buried side-by-side in the Los Lentes Cemetery, fittingly at the end of Tondre Road. Their marriage had been one of true romance, loyalty, and devotion, surrounded by loving family and friends in the place they admired and thrived in most, the Rio Abajo.

Senator Dennis Chavez:
El Defensor *of Minority Rights*

Jim Boeck

Valencia County has produced many famous New Mexicans. But of them all, Dennis Chavez was undoubtedly the most famous and politically powerful. During his 32 years as a congressman and senator, Chavez rose to become the highest-ranking Hispanic in the federal government. In many ways, he served as a cultural and political bridge between New Mexico's territorial past and its more urban, modern present.

Early Life and Career

Born in Los Chavez on April 8, 1888, Dennis Chavez spent the first years of his life in Valencia County. Dennis Chavez's family history in New Mexico dates back to Pedro Duran y Chavez, who arrived in the region with the Spanish colonizer, Don Juan de Oñate, in 1598. Following the Pueblo Revolt of 1680, Don Diego de Vargas reconquered New Mexico with a new group of settlers, including a Chavez ancestor, the bold Fernando Duran de Chavez. For his honorable service to the Crown, Duran de Chavez received the Atrisco Land Grant.

Dennis's formative years were much like most Hispanic children raised on small farms and ranches. Working side-by-side with his four siblings, he grew to love the land of his forefathers.

Dennis's parents, David and Paz Chavez, made a difficult but sound decision in 1895. Realizing that educational and job opportunities were poor in Los Chavez, they decided that it would be best for their children if they moved to Albuquerque.

Dennis did well in the schools of Albuquerque, learning to speak English and excelling in all his studies. Sadly, he had to drop out in the seventh grade in order to help his family financially. Dennis worked as a delivery boy for the Highland Grocery Store from 6:00 a.m. to 7:00 p.m., five days a week, and to 11:00 p.m. on Saturdays. He was paid $2.75 a week—less, he

38

noticed, than Anglo boys doing the same work. Somehow he managed to find time to read and continue his education at the Albuquerque Public Library. Dennis's favorite books were about George Washington, Thomas Jefferson, and Andrew Jackson, early presidents who helped shape the nation's character. Dennis was especially interested in Jefferson's ideas about equality, ideas that helped Dennis mold his own ideas regarding fair play and equality.

Dennis's high ideals cost him his job at the grocery. When his employer told him to deliver groceries to a group of strike-breakers, 18-year-old Dennis took a brave stand. Convinced that poor workers had a right to make a decent wage, Dennis refused to make the delivery and was promptly fired.

But when one door closes in life, another one often opens. Dennis's new

Dennis Chavez as a young man

door came in the person of Jim Gladding, a young Albuquerque engineer, who saw great promise in the Hispanic boy. Encouraged by Gladding to become an engineer, Dennis studied higher and higher levels of math and engineering at night. He soon qualified as a surveyor, working for the City of Albuquerque and, later, for the State Highway Department. This first-hand knowledge of New Mexico roads was most helpful when Dennis later sponsored important highway legislation for the state in the U.S. Congress.

Romance entered Dennis's life when he met Imelda Espinosa, a strikingly pretty girl from a prominent Spanish family. Unfortunately, Imelda's parents objected to Dennis's proposal of marriage because he was uneducated and still quite poor. An independent soul, Imelda defied her parents' wishes and married Dennis on November 9, 1911.

Now 23 and with family responsibilities, Dennis began to think about a career in politics. He had been working in Democratic campaigns since before he could vote, giving speeches in both Spanish and in English and often serving as an interpreter. The Chavez family had always been staunch Republicans. As a Democrat, Dennis had heated arguments with his father, David. As Dennis saw it, Republicans were part of the old *patrón* system, where the poor simply served as peasants for their quasi-feudal lords. The down-trodden had to be defended, and Dennis believed that the Democratic Party was best suited to protect the rights of the "little guy."

Meanwhile, Dennis and Imelda's family grew with the arrival of a son, Dennis, and a daughter, Imelda. Life was good for the ever-ambitious Dennis, Sr., who decided to move to Belen to work for the local newspaper, run by Ed Otero. All went well until Dennis wrote a decidedly Democratic editorial that irritated Otero, a strong Republican. The two men parted company with Dennis realizing that life as a Democrat in a predominantly Republican state was not going to be easy. He was nevertheless determined to remain faithful to the philosophies of Jefferson and Jackson, as opposed to the values and interests of the rich.

Returning to Albuquerque, Dennis landed a job with Jim French, formerly New Mexico's territorial engineer. Under French's supervision, Dennis and his work crew built the first highway in Rio Arriba County, connecting Española to Abiquiu. Based on his good work on the Española-Abiquiu highway, Dennis was hired to help construct New Mexico's exhibit building

40

at the Panama-California Exposition in San Diego, created to celebrate the opening of the Panama Canal in 1914. The New Mexico exhibit received awards as the best at the San Diego exposition. Most importantly, the exhibit gave thousands of visitors the opportunity to learn about the southwestern state and its encouraging future.

Democratic Party leaders could not help but notice Dennis's energy and zeal. In 1917, New Mexico's U.S. Senator, A.A. Jones, asked Dennis to serve as his assistant legal clerk in Washington, D.C. Working for Senator Jones gave Dennis the great opportunity to work in a political capacity during the day while attending law school at night. Cramming late into the night, Dennis completed his legal studies and graduated from Georgetown University's prestigious law school in 1920.

Moving his family back to New Mexico, Dennis opened a law practice in Albuquerque where he frequently fought courtroom battles for his "little guy" clients. In 1922, when Santa Fe Railway workers went out on strike, Dennis offered them legal advice in his ongoing efforts to defend the rights of working men and women. That same year, Dennis ran for and won a seat in the New Mexico State Legislature, serving from 1923 to 1924. Representing Bernalillo County, he knew that this was his chance to act on his long-cherished beliefs of equality and fairness.

Chavez was particularly upset with the rate of illiteracy in New Mexico, arguing that children who could not read could never compete for good jobs and enjoy better lives. Blaming the Republicans for the poor state of education in New Mexico, Dennis recalled his own youth in Los Chavez, declaring that "in Los Chavez, there were no schools, no books, and only Spanish was spoken. I saw that under Republicans, English-speaking communities had schools, while Spanish-speaking communities had none."

Dennis promptly introduced legislation to provide free textbooks for all New Mexico school children. His bold proposal did not become law in a short legislative session that ended in a fistfight on the House floor, but the seeds of the idea were planted and later bore fruit.

Impressed by this rising star in their party, Democratic leaders chose Dennis as the obvious candidate to oppose Congressman Albert Simms, the Republican incumbent, for New Mexico's only seat in the U.S. House of Representatives in 1930.

Having campaigned for many Democrats in the 1920s, Dennis mobilized support from unions like the American Federation of Labor (AF of L), the United Mine Workers, and the Railroad Brotherhood. With union members and many Hispanic residents as his base, Dennis beat Simms by the impressively wide margin of over 18,000 votes.

The Chavez family packed bags for yet another move, although this time their stay in Washington, D.C., was to last 32 years. Tragically for the United States, the Chavez family's arrival in the nation's capital coincided with the onset of the Great Depression, which spread across the land like a plague.

The New Deal

New Mexico was particularly hard hit by the Great Depression. Many railroad workers and agricultural laborers lost their jobs. Farmers and ranchers could not find markets for their crops and livestock. Small rural communities suffered with little income, no electricity, dirt roads, and no hope of conditions improving soon. Eager to help alleviate this misery, Dennis was re-elected in 1932, campaigning not only for himself, but for the Democratic candidate for the presidency, Franklin Delano Roosevelt. Like a large majority of the American people, Dennis was convinced that FDR could help the country pull itself up by the bootstraps through public works projects in what was called the New Deal.

A loyal New Dealer, Dennis supported FDR's plans for national economic recovery. When Republicans criticized him as nothing more than a rubber stamp for New Deal proposals, Dennis proudly replied, "If a vote for Social Security legislation, for home ownership laws, for the Federal Housing Administration, for the Security Exchange Bill, for conservation of natural resources, and for larger relief and works appropriations deserves the name 'rubber stamp politician,' then I am proud of the designation."

Dennis wanted New Deal programs for not only the nation, but also New Mexico. He fervently sought a rural electrification program, especially for small communities like Los Chavez. He also sought funding for the Middle Rio Grande Conservancy District to assure water for irrigation and flood control measures.

As an effective congressman, Dennis was able to bring many New Deal projects, dollars, and jobs to New Mexico. The Works Progress Administration (WPA), Public Works Administration (PWA), Civilian Conservation Corps (CCC), and other New Deal programs built hundreds of needed public structures and over a thousand miles of new roads in the state.

Dennis prepared for the toughest political campaign of his life in 1934. Dennis had set his sights on the U.S. Senate seat held by Senator Bronson Cutting since 1927. Everyone knew that it would be a steep, uphill battle against Cutting. Cutting was a wealthy Easterner who had originally come to New Mexico to restore his poor health. Once recovered, he had served as an officer in World War I and had purchased the state's most powerful newspaper, the *Santa Fe New Mexican*. A liberal, progressive Republican, Cutting was very popular among Hispanic voters because of his philanthropy and because he had learned to speak fluent Spanish. Experts gave Chavez no more than an even chance to beat this formidable foe.

The two political titans stumped New Mexico from one end of the state to the other. Chavez won the endorsement of not only President Roosevelt, but also—and ironically—conservative Republicans who wanted to unseat the maverick progressive Cutting. On election night, voting returns showed Chavez and Cutting in a neck-in-neck race. But when the final vote was tallied, Cutting had pulled off a victory by the narrow margin of only 1,261 votes out of a total of 150,257 votes cast. The vote was so close that Chavez called for a recount, with both sides crying foul play. In the end, the New Mexico State Canvassing Board approved the official election results; Bronson Cutting was sworn in for another term as Senator.

Senator Cutting was no sooner back in office than he was killed in a tragic air crash en route from New Mexico to Washington on May 6, 1935. Democratic Governor Clyde Tingley appointed Dennis Chavez to fill Cutting's now-empty Senate seat. With much compassion, Chavez expressed his sorrow for Cutting, who had fought like a lion to win probably the most famous election in New Mexico history.

Dennis had to face a new election to retain his Senate seat in 1936. This time he faced Judge Miguel A. Otero, Jr., the son of a former territorial governor. Despite endorsements for Otero from both the *Santa Fe New Mexican* and the *Albuquerque Journal*, Chavez soundly defeated the judge in November. Chavez's supporters had been most impressed by his ability to bring New Deal funding, jobs, and projects to New Mexico. In Chavez's words, "We needed the help, and I was never ashamed to ask for it." Hispanics and other minorities were impressed by Chavez's ability to work on their behalf. They often turned to Chavez with problems, especially in cases involving discrimination. Chavez investigated each case and succeeded in resolving many of them fairly. He soon earned the richly deserved title of *El Defensor*, the defender.

Defending Civil Rights

Senator Chavez never forgot the civil rights of all Americans. With his strong belief in equal opportunity regardless of race or gender, he had supported the creation of an Equal Rights Amendment to the U.S. Constitution in 1937. During World War II he demonstrated his commitment to fair employment for women in particular. As the chair of the powerful Armed Services Appropriations Subcommittee, Chavez discovered that female officers in the armed forces were being paid less than half of what their male counterparts earned. This discrepancy had helped to cause a great shortage of women nurses in the military. Upset by this inequality and the nursing problem it helped create, Chavez persuaded the War Department to change its policy. A fairer standard of pay was created, and nursing recruitment improved substantially.

Chavez used his political clout to help in another just cause closer to home. The senator learned that a young girl had not been allowed to swim in a public pool in Roswell because she was of Hispanic descent. Infuriated, Chavez called the mayor of Roswell and, in a strong voice, declared, "Open the swimming pools and all the public facilities to everybody in Roswell or Walker Army Air Base will not be financed." The swimming pool, golf course, and other public facilities were soon open to all residents of Roswell.

Shortly after World War II, retired General Patrick Hurley tried to unseat Senator Chavez in the election of 1946. In yet another bitter campaign, Chavez accused Hurley of being a carpetbagger who knew little about the people and problems of New Mexico. When the votes were counted, Chavez held a slim 4,000 vote advantage. Hurley ran against Chavez a second time in 1952, with the same results. An essential part of the senator's campaign had been his strong stance on civil rights. Recalling his youth, he once declared, "I have been fighting for the so-called underprivileged all my days because I was one of them." Later, in a radio address, he asserted, "I cannot reconcile myself to the possibility of a really solid American lifting a finger, raising a hand, penning a word, or voicing a thought in conscious support of the hideous forces of intolerance, the poisonous fangs of which our fathers came here to escape."

On March 27, 1947, the opening day of the 80th Congress, Senator Chavez introduced a bill to prohibit discrimination in employment based on

Senator Dennis Chavez

45

race, religion, color, national origin, or ancestry. Chavez's proposal, known as the Fair Employment Practices Bill, was far ahead of its time. Although defeated by Southern conservative senators in 1947, it would become a key part of the Civil Rights Act of 1964 at the height of the civil rights movement of the 1950s and 1960s. Sad to say, Dennis Chavez is seldom given credit for having helped lead the civil rights movement in its earliest, post-war stage.

In the days following World War II, America and the world became aware of the atrocities committed by Hitler against the Jews. Senator Chavez was particularly moved by the Jewish people's losses and suffering. In the late 1940s, thousands of Jews wandered aimlessly, trying to return to their ancestral homeland of Palestine. As early as 1945, Chavez and a small group of congressmen and fellow senators felt that the Jews deserved their own homeland where they could somehow begin life anew. But Palestine was a hotbed of political intrigue, filled with never-ending enmity between Muslims and Jews. Oil was a major concern, as it remains today. Seeking to appease oil-rich Arab nations, Great Britain did little to help create a Jewish nation. As depicted in the famous movie, *Exodus*, British naval patrols turned back steamers carrying war-ravaged Jews in their attempt to return to their Promised Land.

Chavez and his allies in Congress and the Senate vowed to oppose this policy of ruthless British imperialism, supported by the U.S. Department of State. On May 13, 1948, Chavez gave the keynote address at a rally in New York's Madison Square Garden. With eloquence worthy of Winston Churchill or Abraham Lincoln, Chavez said, "The honorable role that Americans can play in Palestine is to recognize the sovereignty of the Hebrew nation over that land. We should aid in moving displaced Jews of Europe to Palestine. ... We must help them to establish a free and democratic country, offering equal rights to, all citizens. ... This is a task worthy of America; it is consistent with our traditions, it serves American interests, and it will reflect our everlasting honor and glory." With the help of persistent leaders like Senator Chavez, Israel was established as an independent country and a worldwide haven for Jews on May 14, 1948.

Personally, the senator was facing his own battle for survival in 1948. When doctors discovered stomach cancer, Chavez checked into St. Joseph Hospital in Albuquerque where surgeons removed two-thirds of his stomach. Fortunately, Senator Chavez recovered quickly and was soon back at work. Continuing his fight for the "little guy" and remembering his meager wages as a grocery boy, Chavez labored to raise the national minimum wage. His efforts resulted in a raise in the minimum wage to 75 cents an hour in the late 1940s.

In 1949, Senator Chavez was appointed chair of the Senate Public Works Committee. In this powerful position he was able to create legislation and fund a series of federal highways in the West, vastly improving the nation's infrastructure. Chavez improved New Mexico's modern infrastructure as well. By the early 1960s, he had seen to the construction of more than 2,000 miles of surfaced highways in the state, helping it to keep pace with other progressive states in the West.

Fighting McCarthyism

Internationally, the Cold War divided the United States and its democratic allies from the Soviet Union and its communist bloc. Americans feared the spread of communism abroad, especially when the Soviet Union tested its first atomic bomb in 1949, and when North Korea invaded South Korea in 1950. Americans also feared the spread of communism in the United States. In this era of paranoia, a little-known senator from Wisconsin emerged as the leader of what amounted to an American inquisition to identify suspected communists at work in the federal government and elsewhere. Senator Joseph R. McCarthy conducted a series of hearings investigating the so-called un-American activities of public officials and private citizens, many of whom worked in the movie industry.

Senator Chavez saw these sensational hearings as nothing but a political witch-hunt. While most politicians feared to speak out against McCarthy for fear of being called communists themselves, Chavez bravely insisted that it was wrong to accuse people of misdeeds with little or no evidence. His 1950 speech in the Senate drew national attention. Other politicians eventually joined Chavez in opposing McCarthyism and its attack on American rights and freedoms. When the Senate finally censured McCarthy in 1954, his unjust, inflammatory hearings came to an end at last.

Senator Chavez's stand against Joe McCarthy should not be confused with a weak position on the Cold War. On the contrary, Chavez worked to improve our country's weapons system, especially through the establishment or expansion of scientific labs, missile ranges, and military bases in New

Statue of Dennis Chavez in the National Statuary Gallery, Washington, D.C.

Mexico. With millions of federal dollars pouring into the state, Walker Air Force Base in Roswell, Cannon in Clovis, Holloman in Alamogordo, and Kirtland in Albuquerque played critical roles in the nation's defense. Federal spending was a great boon to the New Mexico economy, then and now.

Failing Health

Tragically, Senator Chavez's health began to fail in the early 1960s, with a recurrence of cancer, now in his throat, and other complications. Despite these health issues, he continued to work hard for New Mexico, the country, and his party, campaigning for John F. Kennedy in the Southwest and Hawaii during the presidential election of 1960.

Chavez remained one of the most popular, powerful members of the U.S. Senate. He was, in fact, the most powerful Hispanic senator in American history. To the end, as throughout his long, distinguished career, Senator Chavez worked to guarantee civil rights, workers' rights, and a strong national defense during World War II, the Korean Conflict, and the Cold War. In the words of Judge Tibo J. Chavez, Sr., *El Senador* was responsible for bringing New Mexico "from the adobe age into the atomic age."

Dennis Chavez died in Washington, D.C., on November 18, 1962, at the age of 74. Hundreds attended his funeral and lined the streets of Albuquerque as a hearse carried his remains to his final resting place at Mount Calvary Cemetery.

Every state in the Union can honor two of its greatest leaders with statues placed in the National Statuary Gallery. New Mexicans honored Senator Chavez by placing a statue of him in the gallery in 1966. Until recently, he stood alone as New Mexico's strong, proud leader, just as he had stood in countless important struggles in his lifetime.

Dennis Chavez once said, "I like to think I've repaid New Mexico in some small measure for the favors she did for me as a child in Los Chavez and Albuquerque." Perhaps it is all New Mexico who owes the greater debt to this tireless defender of his home state and all the "little guys" he represented.

Tibo J. Chavez:
Historian, Judge, and Politician

Richard Melzer

Tibo J. Chavez, or simply Tibo, as he was known to most, was born in Belen on June 10, 1912, just six months and four days after New Mexico achieved its statehood. His parents were 37-year-old Ignacio Rodrigo Chavez and 34-year-old Emilia Vigil Chavez. He was the fifth of seven children born in the Chavez family.

The Chavez family dated back to the Spanish conquest of New Mexico under Don Juan de Oñate in 1598. Don Pedro Gomez Duran y Chaves, born in Extremadura, Spain, was a soldier in Oñate's small colonial army. By 1626, Don Pedro commanded all Spanish troops in New Mexico. Famous Chavez ancestors included the fabulously rich Belen merchant, Felipe Chavez, known as "The Millionaire," and Dennis Chavez, the most powerful Hispanic senator in U.S. history. Tibo belonged to the eleventh generation of Chavez genealogy in New Mexico.

On Tibo's mother's side, the family was especially proud of Francisco X. Vigil, a Valencia County deputy sheriff who lost his life in 1898 while bravely pursuing William "Bronco Bill" Walters, the most famous train robber in local history.

Tibo acquired his lifelong thirst for history as a boy learning about his heroic ancestors. His interest in history only grew as he read books and spoke to men and women across New Mexico. But, unlike most of us who admire the past, he not only studied history, but also made it, preserved it, and shared it with countless others.

Traditional and Modern Worlds

Tibo Chavez grew up in a very traditional Hispanic home. Spanish was his first language. His mother used herbs for many purposes, including as beverages and for cures. *Curanderas*, or experts in the use of herbs and other traditional cures, were respected members of his community. *Dichos*, or

50

folk sayings, were used to teach values from one generation to the next. The Catholic Church played a central part in Tibo's life, especially once he became an altar boy at Our Lady of Belen Church.

But Tibo lived in two worlds: the traditional and the increasingly modern. He learned English and was introduced to Anglo ways in public school and in the Boy Scouts, where he become Belen's first Eagle Scout. From the time he was twelve to the time he graduated from Belen High School in 1930, he worked part-time at the Becker-Dalies Store, earning money and learning about the business world. Tibo also learned about business from his father who owned a farm, ran a construction business, and operated a liquor store and bar on Main Street. Ignacio Chavez may have given his son his

Tibo J. Chavez, Sr., as a young man

first lessons in politics when he served on the Valencia County Commission.

Tibo was always an overachiever. In addition to the Boy Scouts, work, and activities at church, he found time to play four high school sports: baseball, basketball, football, and track. Using savings from his job at Becker-Dalies, he bought his own violin and paid for private lessons.

Upon graduation from Belen, Tibo attended the University of New Mexico, earning his bachelor's degree in four years at the height of the Great Depression. He managed to afford his college education by working three jobs, including as a salesman. Somehow he found time to belong to the UNM debate team and Foreign Service Club.

With help from Senator Dennis Chavez, Tibo entered the prestigious Jesuit institution, Georgetown University in Washington, D.C., to study law and earn his law degree by 1939. He passed the New Mexico bar exam and, in a short article published in the *Belen News* on October 5, 1939, announced his intention to practice law in his hometown. Tibo practiced law in Belen until the beginning of World War II when he served the United States as a diplomatic attaché in the American Embassy in Santiago, Chile. He returned to Belen and his law practice at the war's end in 1945.

And then he began his incredible public service in New Mexico. The list of organizations he belonged to and often led seems endless, but included the UNM Board of Regents, the UNM Alumni Association, the New Mexico State Police Board, the New Mexico Heart Association, the Belen Rotary Club, the Belen Lions Club, the Organic Gardeners Club in Albuquerque, the New Mexico Bar Association, and the American Bar Association.

Entering politics, Tibo became a leader of the Valencia County Democratic Party by the late 1940s. Elected to the New Mexico State Senate from District 29, he served in the legislature from 1948 to 1950 and from 1956 to 1974, including eight years as the senate's majority party leader. In the intervening years, 1951 to 1955, he served as the state's lieutenant governor under Governor Edwin Mechem. In June 1979, Governor Bruce King appointed him state district court judge in the newly established 13th Judicial District, a position he held for the rest of his life. Tibo was one of only a handful of people in New Mexico state history to serve in all three branches of state government in the course of his long political career.

Making History

Tibo Chavez made history in each of these roles. It would be difficult to find a major piece of legislation of the 1950s, 1960s, and early 1970s that did not bear the imprint of his influence. He was, of course, aided by his many political friends and allies in the state legislature, including Fabian Chavez, Jr., and Bruce King. It appears that he was most proud of two groundbreaking laws in particular: the Fair Employment Practices Act of 1949 and the state's first DWI law, passed in March 1971.

Minorities had long faced discrimination in securing good, high-paying jobs in New Mexico. For example, Hispanics were hired by large railroad companies like the Santa Fe, but only on track crews and as mechanics. Even the state police had unreasonable requirements, such as the requirement to be 6' tall, a thinly veiled method to discriminate against most Hispanics. While U.S. Senator Dennis Chavez battled discrimination in hiring on the national level, Tibo fought against these practices in New Mexico. The result was the passage of the Fair Employment Practices Act, enacted before most other states and long before the national Civil Rights Act of 1964.

Tibo was also largely responsible for New Mexico's first DWI law, introduced in the state senate as Senate Bill 1 in 1971. According to this law, drivers were required to submit to a breath test to measure the alcohol level of their blood system when arrested by a police officer who had reason to believe that they were driving while under the influence of alcohol. In signing the bill in March 1971, Governor Bruce King declared it to be "the most important highway safety measure ever passed in New Mexico."

Disappointments and Tragedy

Tibo enjoyed many victories in election campaigns and in state government. But he also suffered several major setbacks, both personally and politically. Although his Fair Employment Practices Act helped many men and women in their search for job opportunities, discrimination continued to afflict minorities, women, and others. And while the 1971 DWI law was an admirable start, DWI accidents continued to plague New Mexico at alarming rates.

53

Tibo was also disappointed by the defeat of a safety bill he introduced in 1973. Tibo sought to make wearing motorcycle helmets mandatory in New Mexico. Many bike riders objected that such a law would infringe on their personal freedom. Members of the Hells Angels and Banditos protested so strenuously that the state police had to be called in to maintain order at the capitol in Santa Fe. The bill did not pass and the issue remains volatile to this day. Meanwhile, many have died or have suffered severe injuries without proper protection.

In another setback, Tibo lost to Jerry Apodaca in the Democratic primary of June 4, 1974. Believing that the time was right, Tibo had thrown his hat in the ring in the gubernatorial election, but faced stiff competition in a six-man primary. He won 24 percent of the vote to Apodaca's 31 percent, with the rest of the field dividing the remaining 45 percent of votes cast. Apodaca went on to narrowly defeat Joe Skeen, becoming the first Hispanic governor of New Mexico since 1921, an honor that would have been Tibo's if he had prevailed.

A Tibo Chavez campaign button

Tibo told reporters that he had "no regrets or ill feelings" about the campaign which he said he had run at a "high level." He made himself available with advice for Willie Chavez, his successor in the senate, but only if the new senator wanted it. Using an appropriate *dicho,* Tibo said, "Advice not sought is given by busy-bodies."

Unfortunately, Tibo's wise counsel was not taken eight years later when the citizens of western Valencia County sought to create a separate county based on the enormous profits created by the uranium boom near Grants. As early as 1958, Tibo had addressed the Grants Chamber of Commerce, contending that Valencia County's rich traditions and strength would be compromised if it were divided. Cibola County was nevertheless created on June 19, 1981. Sadly, the uranium boom ended shortly thereafter.

In a personal tragedy, Tibo lost his law partner, Denis Cowper. An Englishman, Cowper had migrated to the United States and had finished UNM law school in 1950. Coming to Belen, he joined Tibo's law firm where he worked for the next 24 years. Although very different, Tibo and Cowper became close friends and colleagues. While Tibo was well organized and punctual, Cowper was brilliant but less organized and seldom on time. When Filomena Baca, their efficient legal secretary, asked Tibo if she could help with one of his campaigns, he replied, "I'll take care of the campaign if you take care of Denis and the firm."

In addition to law, Cowper was fascinated by three interests: cacti, butterflies, and Mexico. He was on a trip to Mexico to observe unusual butterflies when he disappeared in the wilderness in November 1974. His badly decomposed body was found in the jungle eight days later. Hearing the news, Tibo said he was stunned by the tragedy. All of Belen agreed. The mystery of Cowper's death has never been solved.

Preserving and Sharing History

When not making history, Tibo Chavez was busy preserving and sharing it. Tibo helped preserve history as a member of the National Trust for Historic Preservation's board of advisors and the Museum of New Mexico's board of regents. As president of the latter board, he was especially interested in preserving the deteriorating Spanish mission ruins at the ancient pueblos of Abo, Quarai, and Gran Quivira in Torrance County. Working with Senator Pete Domenici, Tibo secured federal funding to save the missions and make them part of what is now the Salinas National Monument.

Tibo also hoped to preserve Valencia County history through the creation of a local history museum. His dream was realized when the Belen Harvey House was saved from demolition in the early 1980s. A large part of the building soon became a museum. With the help of dedicated people like Marion Herlihy, Suzie Baca, Maurine McMillan, Margaret McDonald, Ronnie Torres, and Mike Moreno, the museum has preserved and displayed artifacts contributed by hundreds of people in the county.

Tibo helped preserve history through oral histories as well as artifacts. As a politician, he often visited people in their homes to learn their needs and ask for their support in elections. Tibo told author Daniel Gibson in 1983 that "when you go into homes, you become acquainted with people. And when you become acquainted…they take you into the kitchen and they give you the family secrets," in the form of stories, herbs, *dichos*, and documents. Tibo interviewed hundreds of old-timers in this manner, including Felicita Montaño, Jose Dolores Cordova, Boleslo Romero, Cresencio Marquez, Toribio Chavez, Jose Ignacio Chavez, and Luis Lockhart.

Tibo shared what he learned in books, plays, and speeches. He authored two books, including *El Rio Abajo*, which he co-authored with fellow attorney and historian Gilberto Espinosa. Published in 1973, this book remains one of the main sources of information about the mid Rio Grande region of New Mexico. Long a rare publication, it is now available online.

Five years later Tibo published *New Mexican Folklore of the Rio Abajo*. The book includes some ninety *remedios*, or herbal remedies, complete with illustrations and descriptions of how each herb can help cure various ailments. Tibo enjoyed collecting herbs from his garden or in the wild, storing them in glass jars that covered an entire table in his office. Remedies ranged from the most popular herbs, like *yerba buena*, said to be able to cure almost all ailments, to dog skull, said to help heal broken bones when it is ground up, baked, and applied to damaged bones.

Of course, Tibo never claimed to be a *curandero*. "I never recommend that anybody take an herb or tea," he told an interviewer. "It's up to them. I only tell them of the cultural uses of them. I tell them what the old-timers used them for. If they want to use them, they're on their own. In the first place, I'm not a doctor; I'm a judge. In the second place, I don't have malpractice insurance!" As a lawyer, he knew that this disclaimer was important because he ran the risk of being sued if a person consumed the wrong herb, like the poisonous *garbancillo*.

The second part of *New Mexican Folklore of the Rio Abajo* lists 81 of Tibo's favorite *dichos*. Three examples suggest the wit and wisdom of these sayings:

Dicho: *De lo dicho a lo hecho, hay mucho trecho.*
Translation: From talk to reality there is a great distance.

Dicho: *No será el Diablo, pero apesta asufre.*
Translation: He may not be the Devil, but he sure smells like sulphur.

Dicho: *Díme con quién andas, y te diré quién eres.*
Translation: Tell me who your friends are, and I will tell you who you are.

Tibo and his family traveled around the world, often discovering that similar traditional remedies and *dichos* are shared by many cultures, suggesting that people are often more alike than different no matter where they reside.

In the early 1980s Tibo became a moving force in a huge project to preserve the histories of local families in a 352-page book titled, *Rio Abajo Heritage*. Tibo wrote the book's introduction and, with Carter Waid, Marion Herlihy, Austin Lovett, Aubrey Notman, Gertrude Delgado, and many others, helped compile hundreds of short family histories.

Tibo was also a major force in the organization and performance of "The Legend of Tome," a huge bilingual undertaking created as Valencia County's main contribution to the bicentennial year of 1976. All work was voluntary, so it took a true mover and shaker to not only lead the effort, but also make sure everything was done well and on time. Only a person with Tibo's persuasive personality and perseverance could have managed such an enormous project. The author remembers Tibo's handshake, a firm shake in which he looked you straight in the eye, held your arm with his other hand, and refused to let you go until you had agreed to whatever he wanted you to do on this or any other project. He clearly used his political skills and salesman's experience to get things done in the interest of preserving New Mexico's history and culture.

Tibo also shared history through the Valencia County Historical Society, which he organized and led as its first president in 1968. Many of these projects, from the museum to *Rio Abajo Heritage*, were sponsored by the historical society with Tibo as its leader. The historical society supported many other events, including field trips (led by "wagon masters") and "show and tell" events where residents described unusual artifacts handed down in their families from one generation to the next.

Finally, Tibo gave countless speeches about history. In January 1975, for example, the *News-Bulletin* reported that Tibo had just spoken to 74 men and women at the Belen Senior Citizens Center. Enthralled, the crowd heard him describe New Mexico's colorful past, including the four flags that have flown over the state since 1598: the Spanish, the Mexican, the Confederate, and the U.S.

On other occasions, Tibo liked to speak to groups about the alliance and cooperation of Hispanic settlers with Pueblo Indians in the later Spanish colonial period, in contrast to the earlier friction and violence that divided the two groups. He also liked to emphasize important, often forgotten contributions made by Hispanics in American history.

Tibo was perhaps most famous as a speaker for his herbal "roadshows," as his family called them. Tibo and his wife, Betty, would load up a great variety of herbs before each speech. Tibo would describe them as Betty handed them to him, one by one, as appreciative audiences looked on.

The last time I remember seeing Tibo was at one such presentation performed at the Harvey House Museum on a Sunday afternoon. I recall trying to take notes, but was soon overwhelmed by all the herbs he described. Betty could hardly keep up with him. By the end of the presentation, a table was piled high with herbs. I was exhausted, but was sure that with his energy and enthusiasm Tibo could have kept going if there were more samples to share and more hours left in the day.

Legacy

Tibo J. Chavez, Sr., died of heart failure at the Lovelace Medical Center on Monday, November 25, 1991. He was 79. A huge funeral was held in his honor at Our Lady of Belen Catholic Church, the same parish he had grown up in and where he had been an altar boy as far back as the 1920s. Hundreds of friends and neighbors filled the church to capacity. In reporter Sandy Battin's words, "They came dressed in expensive suits and windbreakers, elegant hats and blue jeans…. There were babies and judges, rich and poor, Spanish and Anglos." All admired Judge Chavez and came to show their respect. A riderless horse (his own Bronco), with empty boots turned to the rear, followed the hearse to the nearby cemetery.

Tibo left a great legacy in his political and personal lives. But I think he would most like to be remembered for the history he made, preserved, and

Judge Tibo J. Chavez, Sr.

shared with others. His legacy continued through his sons, Chris, Reggie, David, and Tibo, Jr., and especially through his wife Betty.

After Tibo's death, Betty, whose own family dates to before the American Revolution, became active in creating Founders' Day celebrations to help celebrate the first Spanish settlers in New Mexico. She opposed the use of a statue of Po'pay, the leader of the Pueblo Revolt of 1680, to represent New Mexico in the U.S. capitol. She worked at the Belen Harvey House Museum as an active member of the Valencia County Historical Society that Tibo had help found. She was the Belen Chamber of Commerce's Citizen of the Year in 1998 and was honored with the prestigious Doña Eufemia Award, given by the New Mexican Hispanic Culture Preservation League, in 2002.

The Chavez family has also used proceeds from the sale of Tibo's books to establish the Tibo and Betty Chavez History Scholarship at the University of New Mexico's Valencia Campus. Tibo had always hoped that courses on New Mexico history would become required subjects in the state's public schools. Inspired by him and other historians, these courses are now required at the 4th grade, 7th grade, and high school levels.

There's a *dicho* in Tibo's book on New Mexico folklore that I think of when I think of his life and accomplishments. In Spanish, the *dicho* says, "*Semos como los frijoles, unos para arriba y otros para abajo.*" Translated, it means, "We humans are like beans boiling: some are going up and some are going down."

By respecting and recording Spanish culture and history in New Mexico, Tibo always tried to help others "go up" with renewed self-esteem and determination. We are all better off for his tireless work and inspiration.

Judge Filo Sedillo: El Jefe

Richard Melzer

The date was Wednesday, October 29, 1980. It was 5:00 p.m. when 71-year-old District Court Judge Filo M. Sedillo left the Los Lunas courthouse after another busy day on the bench.

We can only imagine what Judge Sedillo was thinking on that fateful afternoon as he got into his 1976 Monte Carlo and began his usual trip home to Belen. He might have been thinking about the things he enjoyed most, including his cabin up in the Jemez Mountains. He and his sons, Filo, Jr. (Bobo), and Raul, spent many summers at the cabin, hunting and horseback riding through the countryside.

Or Judge Sedillo may have been thinking about his own father, Antonio A. Sedillo. The judge truly admired his father, a man who had worked hard as a laborer, a store clerk, and a teacher while studying law and entering the bar in 1900. A Republican, Antonio Sedillo held many important political offices, from a local school board member to a member of the University of New Mexico's Board of Regents and speaker of the state House of Representatives. Most importantly, he served as one of a hundred delegates to the 1910 convention that wrote New Mexico's state constitution on the eve of statehood in 1912. Coming from a political family, it was as if politics were in Judge Sedillo's DNA.

Early Life and Career

Thinking of his father, Judge Sedillo might have reflected on his own political career. Born on December 14, 1908, to Antonio A. and Donaciana Sedillo, he was one of five children, including two brothers (Juan and Rufino) and two sisters (Mela and Tula). From an early age he was known simply as "Filo" (short for Filomeno), a nickname used by his family, friends, and even his political adversaries over the years.

Young Filo went to school in Albuquerque, graduating from Albuquerque High School in 1928. He attended St. Louis University, the University of Virginia, and George Washington University, where he earned his law

61

Filo Sedillo and his father, Antonio A. Sedillo

degree in 1933. His education completed, Filo headed home to Albuquerque to hang out a shingle and begin to practice law. But Albuquerque had more lawyers than clients during the Great Depression. Filo made up his mind to move to El Paso to offer his legal skills in new surroundings. His father might well have suggested this option, having passed the bar in Texas in 1899, and having begun his own successful legal career at age 23.

As he drove south toward El Paso, Filo stopped to visit Fidel Delgado in the small railroad town of Belen. Delgado told Filo that Belen lacked lawyers and a good young attorney like himself would be wise to move in and start a practice. Filo took his friend's advice, opened his office the next day, and began a legal career in Valencia County that would span over four decades.

Entering Politics

Filo Sedillo was not in Valencia County long before he entered local politics. He and a small group of like-minded friends created an independent political organization called the Native Sons of New Mexico, with Filo as its leader. Filo joined the Valencia County Democratic Party in 1935 and soon rose in leadership roles. Although his family had long been Republicans, Filo said that seeing long bread lines in Washington, D.C., made him change his political affiliation. He was disappointed that Republicans in the Herbert Hoover administration were not doing more to help the poor and end the Great Depression. He hoped that Democrats, led by Franklin D. Roosevelt, might act to help create new jobs and restore economic prosperity.

Filo remembered how small the Democratic Party in Valencia County had been when he first joined its ranks. Only six party members attended Filo's first meeting. Elected the group's secretary, Filo claimed that the party had been so inactive that its "records were delivered to me in a match box."

Republicans, led by powerful men like Solomon Luna and J. Francisco Chaves, had dominated Valencia County politics for so long that Democrats seldom won elections and didn't even bother to run candidates in some campaigns of the early twentieth century. But the political winds had begun to shift with the rise of Democratic leaders like Dennis Chavez, Clyde Tingley, John E. Miles, and, nationally, Franklin Roosevelt, in the 1930s. Riding these shifting winds and impressing all who knew him, Filo entered politics, first serving as the president of the Valencia County board of education and then as an assistant district attorney by 1937.

In 1938, Filo won his party's nomination for state attorney general, drawing praise from many sources. A newspaper in Las Cruces admired his fluency in English and Spanish, a skill that clearly helped him win his "political spurs" at such a young age. A letter writer in Santa Fe added that Filo was "the smartest young politician in the current campaign." The writer suggested that New Mexicans "Keep your eye on that boy. He should be senator someday."

Twenty-nine-year-old Filo Sedillo beat his Republican opponent, James McCall, 85,220 votes to 67,727, making him the youngest attorney general in New Mexico history. He had only been a lawyer for four years. His mercurial rise in state politics was unprecedented.

Filo returned to his private practice in Belen at the end of his 2-year term as attorney general. He would serve in various appointed positions and run unsuccessfully for public office (a judgeship in 1942), but by the late 1940s he had become more and more focused on politics back home in Valencia County.

Becoming *El Jefe*

Filo Sedillo was elected the chairman of the Democratic Party in Valencia County in 1941. With the exception of a few months, while working temporarily in Washington, D.C., he remained chairman until 1971. Already powerful in the 1940s, Filo's control of his local party increased steadily through the 1950s. New Mexico's politics were still structured to allow the dominance of individual party bosses, or *jefes*, in many counties of the state. Emilio Naranjo dominated Rio Arriba County politics. George Baca dominated Socorro County. And Filo rose to become the political boss of Valencia County.

As *El Jefe*, Filo controlled party politics, deciding who received political appointments and who ran for office, from the smallest job to the most prominent positions in Valencia County. Once nominated, candidates could count on Filo's unwavering support. On election day, they were almost guaranteed election. From 1952 until 1964, at the height of Filo's power, Democrats, facetiously known as "Filocrats," won every major election in Valencia County. Some said that Filo ran nothing less than a political machine.

Filo claimed that there were three main keys to success in winning campaigns: discipline, teamwork, and hard work. Of these three, discipline was most important. Party loyalty must be absolute. Those who wavered in their loyalty could never be trusted—or politically favored with jobs or benefits—again. Abe Peña, a Republican who ran for the state legislature in 1962, remembers a good example of how loyal Filo's Democrats could be to their leader. During the campaign Peña went to two of his *primos* (cousins) to ask for their support. Both cousins refused, insisting that Filo would know if they voted for a Republican. Peña pointed out that it was a secret ballot

64

and Filo would never know how individuals voted. One cousin replied that secret ballot or not, Filo would know. "He'll look me straight in the eye and know I voted for you."

Filo worked side-by-side with his chosen Democratic candidates, going door-to-door through the day and holding political rallies at night. Most rallies were well attended, with plenty of *mariachi* music and good food. At a rally in October 1964, 1,500 turned out for a BBQ beef dinner in the new sheriff's posse building.

Filo insisted that Democratic candidates make their scheduled speeches even if only a handful of loyal voters attended. Party loyalty was to be rewarded in large and small ways. At political rallies he also advised candidates to keep their speeches short and to the point. As Peña noticed, Filo sat behind the podium so he could kick any speaker who went on too long. *El Jefe* instructed his candidates to avoid talking about their opponents in their campaign speeches. Instead, candidates should focus on their own positive messages and avoid the temptation of mudslinging. The odds were in their favor anyway. There was no need to fight in the mud if your team was far ahead.

Known as a "master politician," Filo's ability to coach and promote Democratic candidates was unequaled. Able to deliver the votes needed for victory, Filo could reportedly tell candidates how many votes they would get in a particular race. According to one admirer, "he was often off by only one or two votes."

Filo also enjoyed great power in state Democratic politics, especially at party conventions. *El Jefe* took pride in delivering Valencia County's thirteen delegate votes as a disciplined, solid block. Valencia County always had the "last say" because delegates cast their roll call votes by counties in the counties' alphabetical order. In other words, Filo often controlled the critical swing vote (or block); many deals could be made to benefit Valencia County at such critical moments.

Filo served as a member of the State Democratic Central Committee from 1936 to 1971. He was a delegate to several Democratic national conventions, and was proud to have been an early supporter of John F. Kennedy's campaign for the presidency in 1960.

By 1964 the *Valencia County News* called Filo Sedillo "the most talked-about man around." According to the *News*, "Some regard him as the champion of the little man, a sort of benevolent despot with a big heart for the underdog. Other people believe him to be a tyrant, and to others he is a legend."

Waning Power

But with all his clout and influence, Filo Sedillo's political power showed signs of wear by the mid-1960s. Politics in New Mexico were changing and with few exceptions old-time political bosses began to lose the absolute grip they had held at the state and local levels for so long.

In 1964, for example, Filo had his thirteen delegates to the Democratic Party's state convention ready to help select their party's candidate for governor. As always, Valencia County's delegates could be expected to vote as a group, with Filo controlling their final decisions. Filo delivered his thirteen delegates to a rising star in the party named Bruce King. King later recalled that he decided to withdraw his candidacy because he did not want it to look like he had made a deal with a political boss like Filo. Rather than being considered an asset, Filo's support had become a political liability for a new generation of leaders like King.

Five years later a state constitutional convention was called to write a new constitution to replace the outdated document of 1910. Filo was elected as a delegate, becoming one of only two delegates whose families were represented at both the 1910 and 1969 conventions. (H.O. Bursum, Jr., was the other delegate.) Filo had also hoped to be elected chair of the 1969 convention, but ran into opposition from the same man he had supported for governor in 1964. Bruce King won the coveted leadership role, but was wise to make sure that Filo was chosen as his first vice chair. Remembering Filo's good work at the convention, King later declared that "I never have worked with any man who showed more compassion for the people than Filo Sedillo."

Once the new constitution was written, King and his fellow delegates began the campaign to have it passed by the voters of New Mexico. Filo vowed to secure the important Hispanic vote by winning the support of key Hispanic leaders who could then deliver the votes of their followers. Such strategy may have worked in the past, but not by the late 1960s. The new constitution failed at the ballot box by about 2,500 votes. Filo delivered a slim 183 majority in his own county, an unheard of result a decade before.

A New Direction

Bruce King might not have gotten a new state constitution passed in 1969, but he was able to secure his party's nomination for governor in 1970. As in 1964, Filo supported King, who beat his Republican opponent, 38-year-old Pete Domenici. Remembering Filo's support in both 1964 and 1970, King appointed the aging politico to a whole new role, district court judge in the newly created 13th judicial district. Some observers were leery of the appointment, wondering if a partisan leader like Filo could administer equal justice when old political enemies stood before his bench.

Filo's supporters came to his defense. The *News–Bulletin* noted that while Filo had earlier believed that "to the victor goes the spoils," he did not seem to carry a grudge after an election "and eventually worked with those he may have earlier opposed." Filo pointed out that other politicians had made the transition and had become good judges, including former governor Edwin L. Mechem. Filo won the endorsement of all twelve lawyers in Valencia County, including several who were Republicans.

Filo Sedillo was sworn into office at the courthouse in Los Lunas at 5:00 p.m. on Saturday, June 26, 1971. Supreme Court Justice Paul Tackett administered the oath, and Filo's 7-year-old grandson, Antonio, led the pledge of allegiance. A reception, catered by Kotch's Cafe, followed at Our Lady of Belen parish hall. Among the nearly thousand people in attendance were such dignitaries as Governor Bruce and Alice King, State Senator Tibo J. Chavez, Speaker of the House Walter K. Martinez, and Representatives Dickie Carbajal and Fred Luna. Attorney Gilberto Espinosa gave the invocation. The new judge was surrounded by family members, including his wife Emily and his children, BoBo, Sonia, and Raul.

Judge Filo Sedillo and his wife, Emily

Speaking to the crowd, Judge Sedillo said, "A judge should divide himself completely from politics. I am happy to cap my career as a judge." Filo promised to protect the interest of society as a whole, upholding the rights of all defendants. Just as at his old political rallies, *mariachis* played their music at the reception, singing many of the judge's old favorites and even singing a new one, appropriately titled, "His Name Is Filo."

Cartoon representation of Filo Sedillo's move to the judiciary

Judge Sedillo served as a district court judge for nine years. He was known as a very fair judge, able to "temper justice with compassion," in the words of one observer. In his first seven years, he handled over 8,000 cases, with only 45 decisions appealed. Of those appealed, 90 percent were confirmed by the state appellate court.

Filo's daughter-in-law, Corrine G. Sedillo, served as his court reporter while he served on the bench. Corrine remembers many difficult trials, including a sensational first-degree murder case held in Deming in 1975. After two weeks of testimony, the jury took only about two hours to find Daniel DeSantos guilty of the 1974 Halloween night murder of 19-year-old Glennie McDonald in Silver City.

Judge Sedillo sentenced DeSantos to death in the gas chamber, but the verdict was overturned on a technicality. Judge Sedillo presided at DeSantos's second trial, held in 1977 with the same guilty outcome, but with a different sentence: 10 to 50 years in prison.

Clearly admired by the citizens of Valencia County, Judge Sedillo was reelected for 6-year terms in 1972 and 1978. Asked in 1978 if he ever thought of retiring, Filo replied, "I wouldn't know what to do if I retire. Besides, I enjoy the court work, even though we are very, very busy."

Last Trip Home

And so it was on Wednesday evening, October 29, 1980, that Judge Sedillo headed home. We'll never know for sure what he was thinking as he drove down Luna Avenue and made a right turn on Courthouse Rd. We only know that Filo crossed the railroad tracks and began to turn south onto old Hwy. 85. The sun was setting and might well have shown in his eyes, making it hard to see oncoming traffic. The judge collided broadside with a north-bound pickup. The pickup's 41-year-old driver was transported to Albuquerque's Presbyterian Hospital in serious condition. Arriving quickly from his office in the courthouse, Sheriff Bill Holliday believed that Filo had died almost instantly.

Hearing the news of Filo's death, the citizens of Valencia County were in "shock and dismay," according to one newspaper report. Condolences poured in from men and women throughout the state and across the nation. Longtime political friends and foes, including Bruce King, Tibo Chavez, Fred Luna, Ron Gentry, District Attorney Tom Esquibel, Lucy Brubaker, Walter Martinez, Frederick "Ted" Howden, Joe Fidel, and District Court Judge George Perez, expressed their sorrow and recalled their favorite stories about the judge.

Memorial resolutions were introduced in the State Senate by Willie M. Chavez and in the State House of Representatives by Fred Luna and Ron Gentry. Local resolutions were passed by the town council in Belen and the village council in Los Lunas.

Newspapers ran complimentary editorials and obituary notices. The *Albuquerque Journal* observed that Filo was "one of the last" great *jefes* in New Mexico history. The *Grants Beacon* called him Valencia County's "political patriarch." The *Santa Fe New Mexican* wrote that his passing left Valencia

70

County politics "less colorful and not nearly as interesting."

Over a thousand men, women, and children attended Filo Sedillo's funeral at Our Lady of Belen Catholic Church. Judge Tibo Chavez gave the heartfelt eulogy, praising Filo's years of service and lauding his ability to unite diverse groups. "Filo's name," said Judge Chavez, "is synonymous with Valencia County."

Judge Chavez might have agreed with a political observer who wrote that whatever his virtues or faults, none could dispute that Filo M. Sedillo was "a real political 'pro' and a genius with the common touch."

Gloria Castillo: Belen's Movie Star

Richard Melzer

A beautiful young actress took her place on stage moments before the curtain rose and the play, "Late Love," began at the Pasadena Playhouse on July 22, 1954. There was no need for Gloria Castillo to review her lines at this exciting moment in her acting career. At the age of 21, she had already starred in many plays and had always learned her lines quickly, usually in just one night. Gloria also knew her lines because she had performed them to rave reviews at the Albuquerque Little Theatre (ALT). In fact, "Late Love's" success in New Mexico had led to the invitation for the ALT troupe to perform the three-act comedy on a much larger stage in Pasadena.

Who was this talented New Mexican, and how had she become interested in acting and the stage?

Gloria Castillo had been born in Belen on March 3, 1933, to Richard C. and Mary Davis Castillo. Her family proudly traced its roots to the first Spanish settlers of New Mexico. Gloria's father had run several successful businesses in Belen, including a grocery store, a filling station, a motel, and a Pontiac car dealership. The family had lived next to their store east of Kuhn's Hotel until 1942 when they had built a beautiful new home on North Main Street. Richard Castillo was active in community affairs, having served as both the chairman of the Belen public school board and the chairman of the Valencia County Democratic Party.

Gloria had three older brothers, R. Robert, Leonard, and Leo. A year separated each sibling, making them close in age and spirit. As the only girl and youngest child, Gloria was everyone's favorite.

Richard and Mary Castillo encouraged their four children in all their ambitions and goals. The children were taught to think in smart, creative, organized ways. Mary in particular motivated her children, emphasizing the importance of a good education and making them comfortable with people from all walks of life. Guests in the Castillo home included a chief justice of the New Mexico supreme court, Senator Clinton P. Anderson, and the *grande dame* of New Mexico politics (and Mary's cousin), Concha Ortiz y Pino.

72

As a child, Gloria had enjoyed playing near her family's home and grocery store. Her best friends included Rosie Tabet, Helen Griego, and her beautiful cousin, Eva Garcia.

A Talented Girl

Born actors and imaginative children, Gloria and her brother Leo performed plays in their backyard, using the bed of their father's truck as a stage. Gloria later said that her first acting experience came at "about the tender age of three, in our backyard in my brother Leo's own drama school in the barn." Gloria's father often brought her to Belen's Central Theater (now the Hub Furniture store building) to watch newly-released movies. She had no favorite actors. She seemed to enjoy them all.

Gloria had gone to school at St. Vincent's Academy in Albuquerque for one year before returning to Belen, attending St. Mary's, and graduating from Belen High School in 1950. Gloria was popular and active in her teenage years in Belen. Always generous—and often the only girl with a car—Gloria taught several of her friends how to drive. Her school activities, as listed in the 1950 *El Aguila* yearbook, included three years as a cheerleader, two years in the drama club, and membership in the school band, where she played the oboe.

Gloria had roles in two high school plays, "Willie's Weekend" in her junior year and "The Man Who Came to Dinner" in her senior year. Everyone who watched her perform in these comedies recognized her acting potential. Gloria also displayed musical talents. In addition to playing the oboe in school, her parents paid for private piano lessons with a teacher from Belen.

No one was surprised that she majored in music at the University of New Mexico when she started college in the fall of 1950. She minored in education, planning to teach music to schoolchildren after graduation. But Gloria was drawn to the stage at UNM and landed the lead role as Cecile in the university's rendition of "The Importance of Being Earnest." She earned high praise from the drama department's Gene Yell and from John Donald Robb, the Fine Arts college dean.

Popular both on and off the stage, Gloria dated several young men while in college, including a future general, Leo Marquez, and a future U.S. senator, Pete V. Domenici. Domenici remembers Gloria as a "delightful, vibrant" young woman who always "loved acting and learning."

Gloria Castillo as a young actress

Building on her acting success in college, Gloria auditioned at the Albuquerque Little Theatre and got the lead role in "Gigi," one of the most popular Broadway plays of the early 1950s. Directed by the ALT's founder, Kathryn Kennedy O'Connor, Gloria made the perfect Gigi in this French comedy set in the late nineteenth century. And then there was "Late Love" at the Little Theatre, which was brought to Pasadena for a two-week run just weeks after Gloria's college graduation.

Discovered in Pasadena

As the curtain rose and the Pasadena audience fell silent on July 22, 1954, it is doubtful that Gloria was even nervous. Self-assured, she later recalled that she had a strong feeling that she would do well and, in performing well on this important night, it would change her life forever. Gloria was right. Unbeknownst to her, a Hollywood producer and casting director sat in the audience to see her act in "Late Love." Paul Gregory and Mildred Gussie were so impressed by Gloria's acting abilities that they agreed that she had a future on the movie screen as well as on the stage.

Paul Gregory arranged for Gloria to meet director Charles Laughton to discuss her acting in a United Artist movie titled "Night of the Hunter." Gloria seemed ideal for the role of Ruby, a 15-year-old girl, especially since Gloria always looked younger than her actual age. Gloria clearly remembered her initial meeting with Gregory and Laughton. "At first, I held my breath. I was scared. But Mr. Laughton just discussed the role with me, and what I thought of it and the kind of girl I thought Ruby was. There was no reading. I recall that Mr. Laughton said I had the part—but I was too happy, frightened, and trembling to know what anyone said next."

After a brief visit home to Belen, Gloria reported to RKO studios in Culver City, California, to begin work on the filming of "Night of the Hunter." Suddenly she was acting alongside such Hollywood stars as Robert Mitchum, Shelley Winters, and the legendary Lillian Gish. Observing Gloria at work with these famous actors, director Laughton told reporters that the 5'2", dark-eyed, blonde woman from Belen was one of the finest natural actresses he had ever seen. Always supportive, but also concerned about their daughter's safety in far-off California, Gloria's parents went so far as to hire an older woman named Sara Hearn to accompany Gloria to California and stay with her and her brother Leo in a little house while the movie was being shot.

Thrilled by her first movie-making experience, Gloria told reporters that she was "still on a cloud and I hope I never fall off." But she quickly added, "There's just one thing I really want to be always—whatever happens—and that's just myself." Her Hollywood experience was, nevertheless, exhilarating. Gloria first saw her name on a billboard advertising "Night of the Hunter" as a coming attraction. She recalled that "A friend called and told me and I went to the theater early in the morning to see the poster. It was exciting."

After completing work on "Night of the Hunter," Gloria returned to Belen in time for the movie's opening night in Albuquerque at the KiMo Theatre on Tuesday, October 4, 1955. Gloria's brother Leo remembers how proud his family was and how his father beamed when he saw his daughter's name on the marquee on Central Avenue in downtown Albuquerque. The premiere was front-page news in the *Belen News* on September 30, 1955. "Night of the Hunter" soon showed to large crowds at the Oñate Theater as well.

Richard Castillo was so proud of Gloria that he gave his daughter a new Pontiac from his dealership on North Main Street. Unfortunately, the new car was stolen while the family attended Mass one Sunday morning. Determined that Gloria be rewarded for her movie success, Richard simply gave her another car from his lot.

New Roles

Gloria's next movie opportunity came in 1955 when she played the role of a young Navajo woman named Yashi in "The Vanishing American." Based on a novel by Zane Grey and set in the 1920s, the movie was shot in Gallup, New Mexico, and St. George, Utah. Its cast included Jay Silverheels, best known for his role as Tonto in the Lone Ranger series. But few other opportunities came Gloria's way in Hollywood. Instead, Gloria acted in several television series, including episodes of the General Electric Hour, Alfred Hitchcock Presents, The Millionaire, Gunsmoke, Zorro, and Disneyland (in a show about New Mexico's Elfego Baca).

Gloria had hoped to land larger roles in such blockbuster movies as "The Ten Commandments" and perhaps "Gigi" when the Broadway hit was made into a movie in 1958. After all, Gloria had stolen the show when she appeared as Gigi at the Albuquerque Little Theatre. But it was not to be. Instead another young actress named Audrey Hepburn, who had played the part on Broadway, got the leading role as Gigi in the movie version.

When Gloria's agent, Gus Demling, found work for Gloria in the movies, it was in two new genres: teenage stories and science fiction films. Both

76

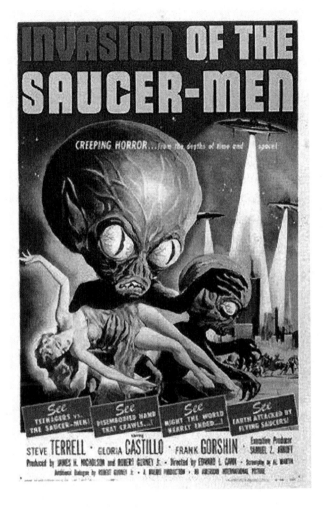

Poster for "Invasion of the Saucer-Men"

genres drew large movie crowds, especially among young drive-in fans of the late 1950s. Although now in her mid-20s, Gloria still looked much younger and easily played the roles of troubled teenage girls in "Runaway Daughters" (1956) and "Reform School Girl" (1957). These roles must have been difficult for a young woman who had enjoyed a virtually perfect childhood in Belen.

In 1957, Gloria also played a teenage girl confronted by alien invaders at a lovers' lane in "Invasion of the Saucer-Men." The sci-fi thriller was released as a double-feature with "I Was a Teenage Werewolf," starring Michael Landon, two years before he first starred as Little Joe Cartwright in the Bonanza television series. In 1958, Gloria played a conniving young woman in "Meteor Monster," a low-budget sci-fi film set in the old West. Teenage and monster movies of the 1950s helped launch the careers of actors like Michael Landon, but did little for Gloria's professional progress. Gloria's acting career had clearly stalled. What had caused this change in direction after such a promising start? Perhaps it was her youthful appearance or some poor advice by her agent. Or perhaps it was discrimination.

Gloria had faced discrimination before. At UNM she had rushed a largely Anglo sorority and had been rejected. Not discouraged, she had accepted membership in another, lesser-known sorority. By her senior year she had become a highly respected leader of her sorority, had landed the leading role in "The Importance of Being Earnest," and had been chosen UNM's homecoming queen. With few movie opportunities, Gloria did what she had done so well at UNM: She made her own opportunity.

In 1958, Gloria had married a successful Hollywood screenwriter, producer, and director named Ellison Kadison. The couple had started a family, with their oldest son, David, born on June 2, 1959, and their second son, Joshua, born on February 8, 1965. By the mid-1960s, Gloria and Ellison decided to write, produce, direct, and act in a movie of their own making. It was no easy endeavor; independent film making never is. The huge project required attention to every detail, from casting to financing the movie, originally called "Methuselah Jones." The multi-talented couple poured all of their energy and most of their finances into the project. It was finally released as "You've Got to Be Smart" in April 1967.

"You've Got to Be Smart" was a major gamble created to help launch Gloria's acting comeback. The romantic musical starred Gloria, cast as Connie Jackson, a young career woman. Veteran character actors Preston Foster and Mamie Van Doren co-starred, along with three little-known young brothers, Fritz, Jeff, and Mike Bantam. Gloria and Ellison attempted to appeal to a wide audience: independent young women (with Gloria's lead role), children (with the Bantams), men (with the voluptuous Mamie Van Doren), and movie musical fans (in a decade of musical hits like "The Sound of Music").

The Kadisons were so enthusiastic about "You've Got to Be Smart" that they spoke of future movie projects to be set in New Mexico. A Western, tentatively called "The Princess and the Maverick," was to be shot in the summer of 1967, while "Memories of Today," described as an "adult drama of the go-go generation," was to follow within two years.

As Gloria told an Albuquerque reporter, "I can't see why we can't do movies in New Mexico as well as in Hollywood. We have dependable weather here—better than Los Angeles with its smog—and there isn't the problem with jet planes going over all the time." Ellison even scheduled a meeting with Governor David Cargo to discuss the future of movie making in New Mexico. All of these plans depended on the box office success of "You've Got to Be Smart." Without profits from their first independent film, there would be no money for Ellison and Gloria to make later movies set in New Mexico, L.A., or anywhere.

But "You've Got to Be Smart" enjoyed little success. Opening in Albuquerque at the KiMo Theatre, followed by showings in Belen, Santa Fe, Gallup, and Los Alamos, the film received only faint praise in the press. An Albuquerque movie critic called it "a pleasant family musical without the pretense of greatness…and with little depth of acting," especially by the Bantams. Gloria was said to be at her best in the film's musical numbers, "featuring some excellent night scenes in Los Angeles."

Faced with this setback, Gloria may well have been discouraged and may have simply retired. After all, her husband was a successful screenwriter, producer, and director, and she had two young sons to keep her busy in their Westlake, California, home. Instead, as at UNM and at other times in her life, Gloria looked for new opportunities, if not in the movie business, perhaps somewhere else. Few predicted that her new venture would be in the fashion industry.

Chessa Davis Skirts

No one in the Castillo family recalls where Gloria got her idea to make a truly innovative style of women's skirts in the late 1960s. Perhaps seeing her husband's collection of long, colorful ties drew her attention and inspired her to sew them together as long, colorful skirts. To make them more appealing,

Gloria designed her skirts with elastic waistbands, meaning that one size fit all. Ellison applied his writing talents by adding a short story to each skirt. He called their first skirt "The Peddler's Cloak."

The couple named their fashion label Chessa (Gloria's nickname) Davis (her mother's maiden name). The skirts soon enjoyed tremendous commercial success, especially with the help of Gloria's resourceful brother Leo. Leo marketed the skirts in locations across the country, including in the Beverly Hills Hotel dress shop, I. Magnum, Saks Fifth Avenue, and Bloomingdale's. Full-page ads appeared in newspapers like the *New York Times* and in fashion magazines like *Vogue*.

The Kadisons' business grew so quickly that they opened a factory in Tarzana, California, and hired workers to help fill all the orders they received. Gloria spent countless hours at the factory and became involved in every aspect of the business operation. Gloria had grown up watching her father working hard to make his business ventures succeed in Belen. Now it was her turn to apply her talents and energy on a far larger stage, just as she had done earlier when she had taken her acting skills from a small stage in New Mexico to a larger stage in California.

Gloria and Ellison enjoyed personal as well as professional success by the early 1970s. Their son, David, recalls days of happiness, growing up in what he calls a "busy L.A. family." When not hurrying through their daily lives, the family enjoyed time together at the beach and, sometimes, skiing in the mountains of Switzerland. (David also remembers spending happy summers in Belen, visiting his relatives, driving on the mesa, attending early balloon fiestas, and hunting with his maternal grandfather, Richard.)

Fighting a Tumor

But then tragedy struck. Doctors discovered a malignant tumor in the back of Gloria's mouth. Her brother, Dr. R. Robert Castillo, and other physicians determined that Gloria suffered from an extremely rare form of cancer. Dr. Castillo says that he had never seen a similar case in his 45 years of practicing medicine. Adding to the medical mystery, Gloria had enjoyed good health and there was no history of such a disease in the Castillo family. Doctors could only conclude that the tumor had been caused by something

Gloria Castillo as Chessa Davis, the name of her fashion label

toxic in Gloria's surroundings. To this day, Dr. Castillo suspects that the cancer may have been caused by Gloria's frequent exposure to carcinogens used in the production of skirts at her factory.

As was her nature, Gloria was not about to surrender to her illness without a fight. Following her brother's advice, she visited specialists and explored possible treatments in hospitals as far away as Frankfurt, Germany. Seeking spiritual guidance, she stayed for a while with the Handmaidens of the Precious Blood, a devout order of Catholic nuns living in a secluded convent in Jemez, New Mexico. But nothing helped and, after a brief period of remission, Gloria's condition continued to deteriorate. Often traveling from

New Mexico to California, her devoted family members stayed by her side. After months of suffering, Gloria finally died in a Los Angeles hospital on October 24, 1978. Only 45-years old, she was buried at Forest Lawn Cemetery beside many great TV and movie stars.

Gloria's family was devastated. Each family member grieved in his or her own way. Her sons were 13 and 19 years old. Her younger son, Joshua, was so distressed that he eventually left home, traveled across the nation and tried to express his emotions in music, a talent he had inherited from his mother. Today a well-known singer and composer, one of his most popular songs is titled "Mama's Arms."

Going back to a tender age,
So full of confusion and rage,
Daddy says, "Boys, your Mama's gone."
There's a hand on your shoulder as...
Someone says, "Time heals all hurt.
Little man, you got to keep on keepin' on,"
But all you want is Mama's arms.

Gloria Castillo left an enduring legacy. Her talent, skills, and determination are an inspiration to her brothers, her sons, and all who knew her. A beautiful photo of Gloria hangs in the very center of the main room of the Castillo home on North Main Street—she remains in the very center of her family's heart.

Art Aragon:
Valencia County's Golden Boy

Richard Melzer

When Valencia County residents joined the millions of Americans who went to see the hit movie "Ali," some remembered that our county boasted its own great boxer long before Muhammad Ali became world famous in the 1960s and 1970s. In fact, Belen's Art Aragon, with all his charisma, color, and controversy, could be called the Muhammad Ali of the 1950s, when Art, known as the "Golden Boy," was in his boxing prime.

Boyhood in Barelas

Art Aragon was not always the famous Golden Boy. Arthur Benjamin Aragon was born on November 13, 1927, to Blasita and Desiderio "Desi" Aragon of Belen. With a family that eventually grew to 12 children (11 boys and one girl), the Aragons sent Art to live with his maternal aunt Nellie and her husband, Eddie Gallegos. Having no children of their own, Aunt Nellie and Uncle Eddie raised Art as an "only child" in their home at 1423 South Second Street in the Barelas neighborhood of southwest Albuquerque. The busy Santa Fe Railway yards lay directly east, across Second Street from the Gallegos home.

As a boy, Art and his pals attended the old West San Jose Elementary School and Washington Middle School. They went to the Sacred Heart Catholic Church and played at the Barelas Community Center, known locally as the Pink House. It was at the Pink House that an older man named Louie taught Art the fundamentals of boxing. A neighbor, Tom Wilson, gave Art his first boxing gloves.

Art had a good home life, albeit with few frills during the Great Depression. He had to chop wood for the fire, and there was no indoor plumbing. But Eddie Gallegos was a well-known singer in Albuquerque, and those who knew him say that Art became a showman largely by being around Eddie so much.

83

Art also had many good friends in Barelas. Eric Baca, who lived only yards from the Gallegos' home, became Art's best friend in a relationship that lasted their entire lives. Art described Eric as "just like a brother to me."

Art moved to Cincinnati, Ohio, with his aunt and uncle in the late 1930s and to Los Angeles with the outbreak of World War II. Nellie worked in the war industry, while Art went to high school. He graduated from Roosevelt High School in East Los Angeles in 1946.

Becoming the Golden Boy

While attending high school, 16-year old Art worked at a creamery owned by a man named Lee Bornen. One day at work, Art got into a fist fight with an older fellow employee. Rather than break up the fight, Bornen watched, becoming increasingly impressed by Art's power and raw fighting ability. Bornen took Art under his wing and became the young boxer's first manager.

Art became an amateur boxer, fighting 13 opponents and knocking out all 13. Although only 16 (when the legal age to get a professional boxing license in California was 18), Art began his professional career in 1944. Art continued boxing during a two-year stint in the Coast Guard immediately after World War II. Stationed near Boston, Massachusetts, Art won seven of his eight fights in "easy wins," as he recalls. Half of his victories were by knockouts scored in the first round.

Once out of the Coast Guard, Art returned to the West Coast. After a slow start, he rose quickly in success and fame in the late 1940s. By the early 1950s, he was a favorite in Los Angeles boxing circles, soon earning the nickname "Golden Boy." There are different stories about how Art became known as the Golden Boy. According to Art, sports writer Johnny Allen gave him the colorful moniker because so many of Art's fights were sold out, assuring "gold" in profits for his promoters and at the gate. Art claimed that he could have fought actress Grace Kelly and fans would have bought tickets to see him in the ring.

Art was also "gold" for sports writers and the newspapers they wrote for. With all his in-ring success, out-of-ring controversies, and quotable comments, sports writers could always count on Art for good copy. The *Los*

Angeles Times's file of Art's photos alone was said to be an inch thick by the mid-1950s. One of Art's wives (he had four) collected enough newspaper clippings about Art to fill 15 large scrapbooks.

Eric Baca told a different story about how Art became known as the Golden Boy. Eric recalled that actor William Holden had starred in a boxing movie called "Golden Boy," but after seeing Art in the ring, Holden declared that Art was the true Golden Boy.

Art Aragon

Whatever its origin, the name stuck, adding luster to Art's rapidly grow-ing public image. Art even became famous for the golden shorts he wore in each fight. Proud of his sobriquet, Art signed his mail "Golden Boy," had the initials "GB" put on his vanity license plate, and hung a sign over the door of his house that read *La Casa de Oro* (The House of Gold).

In a career that spanned seventeen years (1944-60), Art Aragon fought 114 professional fights, winning 77 percent of them and knocking out no fewer than 60 of his opponents. More than half (58 percent) of his KOs came in the first, second, or third rounds of his fights. In his busiest year, 1949, he fought 16 opponents, with at least one fight a month and with three fights in the month of September alone. Nine of his sixteen opponents in 1949 went down in knockouts.

Art fought in many cities, including San Francisco, Las Vegas, Phoenix, and El Paso, but the record books show that two-thirds of his fights were fought in his adopted home town of Los Angeles. Once well-established in the West, Art refused to fight in New York or anywhere else back East. In his words, "Why should I fight for peanuts back there when I get lettuce, whole great heads of it, out here?" This was true. But by limiting the range of his venues, Art remained a regional figure and never a national one, hurting his national ranking in the long run.

Art fought in Albuquerque four times, in 1949, 1952, 1958, and 1959, winning all four fights, including three matches by knockout punches. Belen merchants sometimes sold tickets for Art's Albuquerque fights.

Art fought at least one exhibition fight in Belen, at the old gym near Becker Avenue and South Main Street. Those who attended were disap-pointed because Art's opponent was described as "punch drunk" and not much of a challenge for the Golden Boy. Despite this, Art's older brother, Ambrose, refused to attend because he could never stand to see Art get hit.

In the course of his long career, Art became the winningest New Mexi-co-born fighter in state history and the first New Mexico boxer to fight for a world title, although he lost. In 1997, sports writer Carlos Salazar of the *Albuquerque Tribune* ranked Art among the top six fighters in all of New Mexico history.

Art's opponents were often second-rate, with names like Harold "Baby

Face" Jones, Danny "Bang-Bang" Womber, and Dickie Wong. But Art also fought some of the best boxers of his day, including "Wildcat" Phil Kim, Jimmy Carter, Lauro Salas, Vince Martinez, and Enrique Bolanos.

Art fought Enrique Bolanos, an extremely popular Mexican fighter, twice in 1950. The large crowds of mostly Bolanos supporters grew hostile when Art knocked out the Mexican favorite in the 12th round on February 14 and as early as the third round on July 18. The fans booed, but Art never seemed to mind. In fact, Art soon realized that the more people came out to boo him, the more tickets were sold at the gate. In Art's words, "every boo was a buck." As a result, Art packed L.A.'s 10,400-seat Olympic Auditorium 32 times in his career. Even when Art attended fights as a spectator, the boos and catcalls were sometimes so loud that the scheduled fight had to be stopped until the crowds calmed down.

Life Filled with Controversy

As with most athletes, Art had his share of defeats and controversy. In fact, controversy seems to have shadowed Art nearly everywhere he went in his personal and professional lives. This was certainly true in 1951.

Three months after beating lightweight champion Jimmy Carter in a non-title fight in August 1951, Art faced the black New Yorker in a rematch that Art called the biggest fight of his life. The 15-round scheduled match received great publicity and was broadcast on nationwide radio, including on station KFFM in Albuquerque. All of Valencia County listened, especially two of Art's brothers, Camilo and Tony, who still lived in Belen. Broadcast on national television, it was the first championship boxing match shown live on coast-to-coast TV.

But Art's November 14, 1951, fight against Jimmy Carter went poorly from the start. Art had difficulty getting down to lightweight status, having to nearly live in a steam bath to reach 135 pounds before weigh-in time. By fight time, Art was so weak that he claimed that he was the only fighter who ever had to be carried into a ring. The results were sadly predictable. A disappointed *News-Bulletin* reporter summarized the fight by saying, "A courageous Art Aragon, who fought valiantly but often wildly, lost an unanimous 15-round decision" as he was hit "unmercifully during much of the last five rounds" of the match. Borrowing from a famous baseball poem, the same reporter wrote:

> Ah, somewhere in this favored land the sun is shining bright;
> The band is playing somewhere, and somewhere hearts are light.
> And somewhere men are laughing, and somewhere children shout;
> But there is no joy in Bethlehem; Belen's Artful Art has lost out.

Art's other major defeat came three years later when he faced Vince Martinez of Paterson, New Jersey. On this occasion, 17,158 fans crammed into L.A.'s Gilmore Field on a warm summer evening. Referred to as the "Great Mouthpiece" by the press, Art confidently predicted, "I'll knock the bum out in four rounds." But Art was too optimistic. Art managed a solid left to Martinez's jaw in the fifth round, but that was the best he could do in the 10-round match. Simply put in the press, Art "was the victim of a hopeless, horrible beating." Both his eyes were damaged and his nose was broken as early as the second round. Sports page photos attest that his face was a "bloody mess" by fight's end. The decision against Art was unanimous. Martinez credited Art by saying, "he's got lots of heart and is real strong." Wearing dark sunglasses to cover his bruised eyes, the usually talkative Aragon said nothing as he exited Gilmore Field and drove away. Boxing experts predicted that Art's 1954 thrashing would end his career in the ring. It probably should have, as Art was the first to admit. "I should have retired five years before I did," he confessed.

Instead, the Golden Boy fought on, often surrounding himself with controversy, as much by what he said as by what he did. Once, when his bitter foe, Lauro Salas, tried to make amends in a popular L.A. restaurant, Art spurned the peace offering. Art recalled that an angered Salas "hit me several times while I was taking off my overcoat, and then we got going. The cops came in, and I invited them into the brawl, but they wouldn't join. Then I polished Salas off." The newspapers ran a far different account of the incident by interviewing Salas only.

Art was once described as "the straw that stirs the drink." In mid-1956, he "stirred" the boxing world by being charged with wearing an illegal eye patch in the late rounds of a fight he won in L.A. After another controversial fight, the Los Angeles City Council took the unprecedented step of taking

88

sides in the disputed outcome, voting against Art and creating new headlines for the press.

Art got into far more trouble in 1957 when he was accused of offering a boxer $500 to take a dive in the fourth round of their scheduled December 18 fight in San Antonio, Texas. Hearing the charges prior to the match, Art claimed that he was too ill to fight and went directly home to Los Angeles. He was, nevertheless, brought to trial, convicted, and sentenced to one to five years in prison. Still professing his innocence, Art won an appeal for a new trial. Hearing the appeal verdict, Art's manager wired the good news in a two-word telegram, "Justice triumphs!" Art reportedly replied with a two-word message of his own, "Appeal immediately." All charges against Art were eventually dismissed.

Art finally knew it was time to hang up his gloves when, in his last fight on January 21, 1960, "I hit the other guy on the chin and I went down." Acknowledging that boxing is an extremely dangerous occupation, Art admitted he was fortunate not to have suffered more injuries. Besides the broken nose he suffered in the Vince Martinez fight, Art's only other injury was a broken knuckle suffered in a June 1952 fight against Joey Barnum in Albuquerque. Knowing how lucky he was, Art said, "All my life, I was scared I'd kill somebody in the ring—me!"

Although he suffered relatively minor physical injuries, Art worried about the damage that countless blows to his head had on his memory. He often deferred to his friend Eric Baca for details about the past. He joked about his memory loss, telling one interviewer, "I have a great memory. Er, what's your name?"

Retiring at Last

When Art finally did retire, he considered new careers in real estate sales or professional golf. He even tried his hands at acting, with roles in a half a dozen movies filmed both before and after he left boxing. His biggest role was as a fighter in the movie, "A Street with No Name." But Art knew that his acting potential was limited. He claimed that he never could remember his movie lines anyway. In one movie, his two-word line was, "I will," but, after days of practice, he always said it came out, "Will I?"

At one point someone suggested that Art use his highly recognizable name to open a bail bond business. Art took the suggestion and opened Golden Boy Bail Bonds in Van Nuys, California. His business card featured a picture of himself in a boxing pose and the words, "I'll get you out of jail if it takes 10 years!"

In his 70s, Art all but retired from his business career, letting his son Brad run the bond business most of the time. He still went into the office once or twice a week to see how things were going, but spent more time with his fancy cars and with his good friend, Audrey. He liked to travel and was pleasantly surprised when someone overseas still recognized him as the famous Golden Boy of boxing history.

Although he realized that boxing was good to him over many years, Art had few fond memories of fighting. As early as 1954, he told a *Saturday Evening Post* reporter, "I don't like fighting. I don't like fighters. You can believe this or not, but I never watch a fight on television, never listen to one on the radio and never go to one unless I have a good reason to. I don't like fight-goers. I don't like fight writers. I don't like fight hangers-on. I don't like any of it. I only like the money—to support me in the manner to which I have grown accustomed." Years later, in retirement, he had the same feelings, although when pressed about what he missed most about fighting, he didn't mention money. By then, he said he simply missed "the broads."

In 1990, Art was proud to be inducted into the World Boxing Hall of Fame. The program at the induction ceremony acknowledged that Art never won a world championship, but "Art could punch." The program also noted that Art "always put on a show." As a result, "he could draw more fans and more money to a club fight than could most world champions in a title match."

The 1990 induction ceremony program could have added something more about Art's life that makes him a world class person. It could have said that Art was a loyal friend. He remained close to his lifelong friend, Eric Baca of Albuquerque, and the two talked by phone or visited often. Eight hundred of his friends came out to a dinner in his honor held in Albuquerque on December 30, 1990.

Art was particularly loyal to his friend Frankie Gallegos of Albuquerque. When Frankie was dying of heart disease in Albuquerque's Veteran's Hospital, he continuously refused to have an operation that could save his life.

90

Then Art and Eric appeared at Frankie's bedside. Art spoke to his boyhood pal and promised that he'd take him to New Orleans, Mexico, Europe, or anywhere else if Frankie agreed to have the needed operation. Frankie took Art's offer, had the operation, survived, and traveled with Art to all the places the Golden Boy had promised to take him. Frankie lived 15 more years, when the doctors had given him only hours to live if he had not had the heart operation in time.

Art Aragon on his throne

On a trip home to New Mexico in the early 1950s, Art told an Albuquerque newspaper reporter that boxing fans "come to see me get killed" because he was always cast as the bad boy, the villain in the press. "I have to work hard to be a villain and sell tickets to standing-room-only crowds." "Of course," he quipped, "underneath, all the time, I have a heart of gold." As with most of what he said, the Golden Boy was only half kidding.

Much has changed in the 40 years since Art retired from the ring. His boyhood home on Second Street in Albuquerque has been replaced by a fine new house, and the railroad yards across the street are largely silent. Legion Stadium in Los Angeles, where Art rose to boxing fame, is now a fitness center. And a colorful, often-controversial young Hispanic fighter named Oscar de la Hoya became known as the Golden Boy of California and the boxing world. But before there was a de la Hoya or an Ali or a Johnny Tapia or a Danny Romero, there was an Art Aragon who helped pave a wide, usually-lucrative path in sports. For this, and for his many other achievements, Art Aragon of Valencia County will always be the charmed Golden Boy of the professional ring.

The Duke of Ducks:
Robert Duck and the Deming Duck Races

Richard Melzer

Robert W. Duck of Bosque Farms was listening to his car radio while driving to work one morning in 1980. The radio host, Larry Ahrens, was interviewing an organizer of Deming's first Great American Duck Race, scheduled for August 23-24 of that year. Robert thought it would be fun to enter two ducks he had recently purchased at a feed store in Peralta. Who knew, maybe the Duck name would bring them good luck.

And so Robert Duck entered Deming's first duck race, held at the Luna County Courthouse Park, popularly known as Duck Downs. Robert remembers that no one believed that his name was really Duck when he went to enter his birds for the competition. Racing on land like a duck takes to water, one of his feathered friends finished third in a competition that began with 186 ducks. Not a bad start.

Becoming a Champion

Encouraged, Robert returned to Deming the following year. He entered seven ducks, calling them the Magnificent Seven. Four of his seven birds qualified for the final heat of the 400-duck competition. One of them, BFD Express, waddled to victory, winning first prize. In fact, Robert and his brood plucked first prize victories in each of the next three years. He bowed out for two years so others could enjoy winning, but, never a lame duck, he returned to win four more years in a row. After a timeout of three years, he and his ducks returned to win five straight championship races.

Robert's victories were especially sweet because each of them was won by a different bird. The Bosque Farms trainer showed his competition that he and his flock were all they were quacked up to be. Robert enjoyed the races and especially the fun he, his competitors, and the increasingly large crowds experienced each year. As Robert puts it, "You can't watch a duck race without smiling."

Training Champions

Robert Duck was never one to duck a challenge. Joining the U.S. Army when he was 20 and the New Mexico Army National Guard when he was 33, he played the saxophone as a member of the 44th Army Band for 21 years. He retired as a first sergeant. He learned business by completing a Masters in Business Administration and opening his own jewelry store in Albuquerque in 1979. He, his wife, Kathy, and their two children, Bryce and Sharon, moved to Bosque Farms in 1977. Their acre and a half of land gave them plenty of room to raise horses, dogs, and ducks.

Robert continued to have fun racing ducks, but began to take his new hobby a bit more seriously. After some experimenting, Robert concluded that Mallards were the fastest running ducks of all duck breeds. He ordered one hundred Mallard ducklings per year, usually from the Whistling Wings hatchery in Hanover, Illinois, known as the Mallard capital of the world.

Robert raised his animals with high protein feed mixes and lots of vitamins. He trained them each day, timing them to see which ones were the fastest. The fastest 25 made the cut. He released the remaining 75 into the wild along the Rio Grande.

License plate representing the Great American Duck Race

For many years, when people asked Robert the secret to his success he usually fed them a lot of quack. He told one inquisitive reporter that he fed his ducks a steady diet of green chile and placed ice cream at the end of the racetrack to inspire them. More open today, he says that one of his strategies was training his ducks to race on 24' tracks, knowing that actual tracks were only 16' long. Sixteen foot races seemed easy for birds used to racing 24'.

Race Days

Robert clearly remembers race days in Deming. Competitors came from throughout the Southwest. One team from Arizona even arrived in an 18-wheeler with an air-conditioned interior for their ducks. Duck owners sized up the competition before the races began. Robert says that race organizers held a Calcutta pool for the final race as a way for duck owners to bet on the outcome. This illegal practice was later stopped, although betting in the crowd continued. Robert recalls that some judges drank too much on race day, potentially marring the sport and its results. But no one dared cry "fowl" or resorted to "fowl" language if they lost.

Robert brought the fastest 25 ducks he trained each year. Heats were run throughout the weekend until the eight fastest birds competed in the finals. The excitement was thrilling. As Robert described his handling of his winning duck in 1982, "I just tickled his ribs to get him excited, said a prayer, and let him go."

It was over in a matter of seconds. In fact, one of Robert's ducks holds the world record for a 16' race: .83 seconds. Robert claims he inspired his flock with the slogan, "Be a winner or be dinner." Prize money was good: $50 for winning each heat plus $500 for third place in the finals, $1,000 for second place, and $2,000 for the top prize. With multiple ducks in the races, Robert won as much as $4,500 in a single year. He estimates that he feathered his nest with about $50,000 (before de-duck-tions) in all his years of racing.

Enjoying Success

Robert and his web-footed friends were so successful in Deming that

Robert Duck helping young racers in Virginia

some duck owners became discouraged and dropped out of the races. As a result, Robert agreed to hang up his wings for several years at a time. Racing officials went so far as to change the rules in 1997. Notified of the changes, Robert good-naturedly declared them to be "just ducky." He certainly didn't want to ruffle any feathers.

Now, instead of racing their own ducks, people of all ages are given birds to race on race day, meaning that anyone could be a winner. One year the big winners were a 9-year-old girl and a 14-year-old boy. Each took home $1,415.

Meanwhile, Robert and his animals received local, national, and even international attention. Robert had a lot to quack about. Locally, he was named an honorary citizen of Deming and Luna County. He and his charges appeared on TV shows like the "Tonight Show" and "Good Morning, America." He has been interviewed on radio stations broadcast from as far away as Canada and Australia. Associated Press and United Press International stories about his success appeared in newspapers throughout the country. Feature articles appeared in magazines like *People*, *Ducks Unlimited*, and *Sports Illustrated* (four times).

On the Road Again

Duck racing became such a part of Robert's life by 1999 that he got his ducks in a row, sold his jewelry business, and migrated with his ducks across the country. The only touring duck show in the United States, his traveling show has appeared at 265 state fairs, RV shows, and similar events as far east as Maine and as far west as California. That's an average of 22 events a year. Only logistics have prevented him from traveling to Alaska, Hawaii, the Bahamas, Australia, and China, although he's gotten invitations from all these places and more.

Robert keeps about 80 ducks and travels with about half of them (mostly females) in a specially designed, air-conditioned, well-insulated van. His favorite—and fastest—duck was named Baldy, although she had other stage names as well. His oldest duck lived to be 18; most ducks live only four to five years in the wild.

Maintaining a great sense of humor, Robert and his family have given their birds such appropriate names as "Duck Knipfing," "Grateful Duck," "Green Bay Quaker," "Michael Du-Quack-us" and "Sugar Ray Mallard." Robert calls himself the "Chief Quacker" and even has a WEB site on the internet: www.racingducks.com.

Robert chooses the fastest and least cranky (usually female) ducks for each of four daily shows held at events like the annual Waterfowl Festival in Kennett, Missouri. People in the crowd, especially children, get to temporarily name the ducks, race them, and win toy prizes. It's great fun for whole families, especially because everyone gets to participate and not just observe. Running the races is as easy as water off a duck's back.

Robert spends much of the year on the road, sharing fun and making others happy. And it's all because of Robert's last name. "If my name would have been Smith or something, I would never have done this," he realizes. "In my wildest imagination, I could not have imagined doing this in my life."

Even if our imaginations flew wild we could not image another career in which Robert Duck and his birds of a feather could have won so many well-deserved feathers in their collective racing caps.

PLACES

Pottery Mound:
The Premier Archeological Site
in the Rio Abajo

John Taylor

Let's invoke the magic of time travel and transport ourselves back to 1400 A.D. As we soar over the valley of the Rio Puerco in central New Mexico, we see a pueblo just southwest of the river. The pueblo has two large plazas, each bustling with activity. Surrounding the plazas are homes, some as high as two levels, containing perhaps 500 individual rooms. We count a number of *kivas* (eventually we would find 17), a surprisingly large number for the size of the pueblo. Up and down the river and along the mesa to the west and south are small plots where residents grow squash, beans, and maize. Men are working in the plots. Women, some with children alongside, are busy grinding corn in *metates* on the plazas. We do not know what these people called their home, although Isleta tradition recalls two possible names—*Ba'chi d'wei Te'ui* (Bubbling Water Place or Whirlpool Place) and *Te'di Te'ui* (Parrot Place). Today we call this unique location Pottery Mound.

First Surveys

Pottery Mound is an archeological site (Laboratory of Anthropology site number 416, LA 416 for short) about fifteen miles southwest of Los Lunas, on the southern bank of the Rio Puerco. It was noted by Adolf Bandelier in 1883 and first described in some detail by Thor Warner in 1926. It acquired the name Pottery Mound because of the abundance of pottery sherds that cover the area. Most specialists agree that it was occupied either continuously or in two periods between the middle of the fourteenth century (about 1350) to the late fifteenth century (about 1490).

99

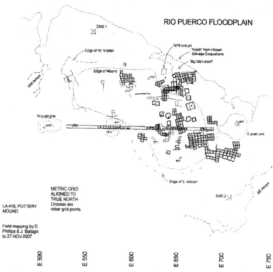

Top: An early survey of Pottery Mound. Bottom: An early archeological pap of the site

Frank Hibben, a charismatic and controversial professor of anthropology at the University of New Mexico from 1935 until 1977, led several summer-long field studies of Pottery Mound, starting in the 1950s. Hibben and his students surveyed the site and excavated dozens of rooms and burials. In addition, they excavated the 17 *kivas*, discovering hundreds of painted pan-

Dr. Frank Hibben

els in 11 of them. This *kiva* art, painted on plaster in multiple layers, would become the defining feature of the site.

In the fifteenth century, Pottery Mound was on a slight rise just south of the Rio Puerco. Since the location is near a bend in the river, lateral erosion over the centuries moved the river bed ever closer to the pueblo itself. The whirlpools and eddies that would naturally occur in this part of the river are a possible source of one of the names that still exists in the Isleta corporate memory. From the time Hibben was working at the site to the present day, the river has encroached within the pueblo boundaries, and some of the structures, including parts of at least one of its *kivas*, have fallen into the watercourse and been lost forever.

As if Mother Nature's destruction was insufficient, Hibben brought in a small bulldozer and cut a deep trench across the site in an attempt to discover (unsuccessfully, as it turns out) a postulated pyramidal structure. This highly unorthodox approach to archeology, not unlike that of Heinrich Schliemann's destructive 1865 trenching at Hisarlik, Turkey, in search of the fabled city of Troy, is considered by many to have been unnecessary and inappropriate.

Perhaps even more unfortunate than the bulldozer trenching, at least in retrospect, was Hibben's approach to documenting the kiva art. Although some of the existing techniques available to actually remove and preserve the layers without destroying them were employed for a few of the panels,

101

Eroding bank of the Rio Puerco near Pottery Mound

Bulldozer trenching at Pottery Mound

102

Removing overlay images in a Pottery Mound kiva

because of the large number of images and for reasons of time, cost, and logistics, Hibben elected to have his excavating crew photograph and draw the images and then scrape off the covering layer, revealing the next panel and so on through the entire set. This documented the images, but destroyed the originals so that modern analytical techniques cannot be applied to acquire even more information about the images and their artist-creators.

Origins

The origins of Pottery Mound, both in terms of where the residents came from and why they settled at this location, are complex. Starting in the 800s AD, a sophisticated civilization existed in what is now central New Mexico, centered on a set of great houses and large *kivas* in Chaco Canyon. This civilization, which we refer to today as either Anasazi or Ancestral Puebloan, continued to expand and develop for nearly 300 years. Plentiful rainfall produced agricultural surpluses that allowed elite classes such as religious leaders and merchants to emerge. Religious practices expanded, and major trade routes were established to the north, west, and south, including some to the vicinity of Pottery Mound, although that site was not yet occupied.

However, things began to deteriorate in the late eleventh century. A series of droughts meant that food supplies were threatened and there were periods of starvation. Raiding by other tribes who were also affected by the drought became more frequent, and the society that had developed around the religious and political center in Chaco Canyon unraveled. In fact, anthropologist David Stuart has stated, "The two centuries following the decline of the Chacoan society were the most violent and tragic in the Southwest's human history up to that time." This assessment is confirmed by skeletal remains that reveal severe malnutrition and evidence of violent deaths.

The farmers who were the most vulnerable and who provided the sustenance for the Chacoan culture were probably among the first to leave. Many of them moved north and established new homes in upland locations in northwest New Mexico and southwest Colorado, typified by Mesa Verde. No doubt because of the violence that bedeviled the late Chacoan peoples, these new villages were built in much stronger defensive locations, as well as being in areas that received more annual rainfall. Based on oral traditions of the modern pueblos, some Chacoan expatriots may also have migrated into the valleys of the Rio Grande and Rio Puerco.

Sometime in mid to late thirteenth century, there appears to have been another large-scale Anasazi migration, this time from Mesa Verde and the other upland locations south to the riverine areas of central New Mexico. These migrations were probably driven by similar causes—population pressures, raiding from nomadic tribes, unreliable rainfall, and salinizatiom in

104

fields. There may also have been residual cultural pressures associated with the end of the Chacoan culture that led the future residents of Pottery Mound to leave their former homeland.

A Melting Pot

In the two or three hundred-year period before the first European contact by the Francisco Coronado expedition (1540-1542), there were at least 27 settlements in the southern Rio Grande Valley—commonly referred to as the Rio Abajo. Pottery Mound lies in an area between the Southern Tiwa and Piro languages within the Tanoan family of languages, as well as being adjacent to the Keres speakers from Laguna and Acoma. The site's remarkable collection of pottery remnants includes sherds from Tiwa, Piro, and Keres Pueblos as well as pottery of Zuni and Hopi origin. This wide variety of pottery types suggests that Pottery Mound may have been something of a melting pot or ritual center where individuals from various tribes and cultures came together to share and develop new ideas. There may even have been people from the Tompiro pueblos east of the Manzano Mountains bringing precious salt to the pueblo. One can imagine conversations in Tiwa, Piro, Keres, Zuni, Tompiro, and Hopi filling the plazas as old acquaintances were renewed and as religious leaders from up and down the Rio Grande Valley and from the pueblos to the east and west shared new ideas.

It is also interesting to note that about half of the *kivas* at Pottery Mound face to the south and the other half face to the east. Kivas located at the

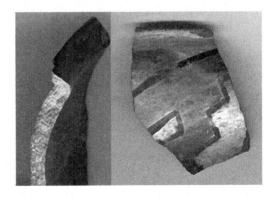

Pottery sherds collected at the Pottery Mound site

105

western pueblos (Hopi and Zuni) face south and those from the eastern and Rio Grande Valley pueblos face to the east. This, too, suggests a site where different religious traditions may have met and mingled.

Based on analysis of the layout and architectural features, some archeologists believe that Pottery Mound may have been occupied twice with a period of abandonment sometime between. Others believe that it was occupied continuously with two major periods of construction. In any event, it may seem surprising that a major location such as Pottery Mound with significant investments in infrastructure and art was only occupied for a short period of time (about 140 years). However, many settlements in Arizona and New Mexico had relatively short spans of occupation. In the case of Pottery Mound, this may have been partly due to a buildup of salts in the plots around the pueblo, gradually making them unsuitable for agriculture. This process of salinization is not uncommon when alkaline soils are cultivated over a long period of time. Regardless of the reason for its final abandonment around 1490, the occupants of Pottery Mound had been gone for decades before the first Spaniards arrived in 1540.

Kiva Art

The most remarkable features of Pottery Mound are hidden in its *kivas*. Pottery Mound had the richest collection of *kiva* art that has yet been identified. In fact, some of the *kivas* had as many as 31 separate layers, each painted on a plaster coating that covered the previous painting. Based on a detailed assessment by Helen Crotty, there were more than 800 drawings at Pottery Mound, representing about 300 murals. In this context, "mural" means the images on one layer of one wall. Research by Crotty and others has revealed that some murals covered more than one wall. In fact, they could wrap all the way around the *kiva*. This means that there were probably fewer than 300 murals when multi-wall murals are considered.

Sacred paintings in secret, remote, or restricted locations are not unique to the Pueblo culture. The famous cave paintings at Chauvet-Pont-d'Arc and Lascaux in France date to 30,000 BCE and depict animals that were pursued by Paleolithic hunters. The Egyptians decorated the sealed tombs of their pharaohs with complex drawings of gods, symbols, and hieroglyphs

Lascaux cave painting

Egyptian funerary art

designed to help the king on his journey through the next life.

The kiva art of Pottery Mound, as well as Kuaua (near present-day Bernalillo), Picuris, Kawaika-a, and Awatovi in the Hopi pueblos, and Gran Quivira east of the Manzanos consists of human-like entities along with symbols for rain, lightning, corn, animals, insects, and celestial bodies. These images are done in color with pigments obtained from natural minerals such as hematite (red) and copper carbonate (green). Many of the symbols resemble those found on petroglyphs throughout the Southwest, and some of the figures are similar to those found on pottery from the now-abandoned Hopi pueblo of Sikyatki.

Kiva *Image from Pottery Mound and a modern rendering of the image: "Elaborate depiction of rainmaking ceremony in a framing device. A masked figure with the hairdo of an Anasazi maiden dances with two parrots. On her head is a pottery bowl from which a lightning bolt extends to the hand of a 'mosquito man.' Surrounding the figures are numerous dragonflies. Both the mosquito and the dragonfly are symbols of rain"* (description from Hibben Center, University of New Mexico).

108

Additional renderings of Pottery Mound kiva images: "Elaborate kiva scene. On the shelf above are headdresses and other paraphernalia. The married Anasazi woman (hairdo) is apparently dead. She is lying on an altar carried on the back of a masked priest with a feather headdress. Other human figures hold bows, quivers of arrows, a shield, a club, and staffs decorated with feathers and rattlesnakes" (description from Hibben Center, University of New Mexico).

The human-like images all seem to be dressed in kilt- or skirt-like garments. Some are clearly male and others are clearly female. The figures usually hold ritual items in their hands and frequently have elaborate headdresses, necklaces, and earrings. Contemporary pueblo individuals have identified some of the figures as similar or ancestral to those used in present-day native rituals.

It is undisputed that the mural paintings at Pottery Mound were religious in nature, designed to appeal to various deities for assistance in day-to-day and season-to-season activities. Lightning depictions might have been a request for abundant rainfall during the summer monsoon season. Depictions of corn or gourds may have been a request for a bountiful harvest. Depictions of warriors may have been meant to provide assistance in battle or to dissuade tribes who might have been planning attacks on the pueblo. Other images may be entreaties for fertility or for freedom from disease.

There is some discussion about the uniqueness of the Pottery Mound murals. Anecdotal reports from early Spanish explorers note wall paintings in the Piro pueblos in the middle Rio Grande Valley. In 1581, Hernan Gallegos described one of the Piro pueblos along the Rio Grande as having

Insect images from Pottery Mound: "These human-headed insect figures, according to Acoma informants, represent a creation scene" (description from Hibben Center, University of New Mexico).

110

"mud walls, whitewashed inside, and well decorated with monsters, other animals, and human figures." These reports notwithstanding, the murals at Pottery Mound are by far the most extensive extant example of kiva art.

Human figure with insect head and wings: A "mosquito man," with feather headdress and gossamer wings, wears short trousers instead of the usual kilt. Photograph of the original appears at bottom.

111

Kachina **Religion**

The introduction of the *kachina* religion to the pueblos of New Mexico and Arizona was almost coincident with the initial occupancy of Pottery Mound in the early to mid-fourteenth century. *Kachinas* are spirit beings that can intercede with the gods on behalf of the people. These intercessions occur when men from the various *kachina* cults don special masks and costumes and perform sacred dances and rituals. The divine being portrayed in the mask and other accoutrements worn by the dancer is believed to temporarily enter into the dancer.

The word "*kachina*" comes from the Hopi word "*katsinum,*" a word that means spirit. This is the story of the origin of the *kachina* as told by Hopi artisan Sakhomnewa,

> There was a time of drought and starvation for many years. Slowly the food stores ran out and the people began to die. When all hope was lost, the *Kachinas* saw the people suffering and took pity on them. They decided to show themselves and materialized in human-like form to help them with their power to grow food,

Kachina *dancers*

bring rain, and heal the sick through prayers of song and dance.

The people were afraid of the *Kachinas*, never seeing them before and thinking they might be evil; gathered up arms and prepared to drive them away. The *Kachinas*, however, blessed the people through song and dance and produced gifts of food for the starving, helped heal the sick and brought rain for the thirsty crops [which they still do today].

So, thankful to the *Kachinas*, the Hopi people asked them to become a part of their tribe. It was in this village where they all lived side-by-side for many years. Over time, however, the people, no longer hungry and dependent on the weather, became lazy and began to neglect their way of life. Fields were choked with weeds, husbands and wives became promiscuous, and elders who could no longer care for themselves were forgotten. Children were left alone, crying and dirty, and the buildings of adobe began to crumble.

The *Kachinas*, seeing the results of living with the Hopi people, thought it best to leave because they had interfered with the Hopi way of life. The people, realizing what was about to happen, begged the *Kachinas* to stay ... but they refused. Before leaving, the *Kachinas* agreed to teach the Hopi people how to prepare offerings, the ceremonial dress, the songs and dances, and how to harness the power over the elements. Only when properly performed will the true spirits deliver their prayers to higher deities to bring rain, bountiful harvests, health, and happiness to all the people of the world.

One common anthropological theory of the origin of the *kachinas* in New Mexico is that this religious movement originated in the Aztec or Toltec cultures in Mexico and migrated north with traders or warriors. There are significant similarities between depictions of divine beings in both cultures, and it is widely accepted that there was considerable trade-based interaction between the Native Americans in Mexico and those in New Mexico and Arizona. For example, coral beads and feathers from tropical birds such as parrots and macaws have been found in pueblo excavations, and birds and feathers are depicted in the *kiva* art. Note also that one of the ancestral

113

names for Pottery Mound may have been Parrot Place and that there is a Parrot clan in present-day Isleta, attesting to a possible connection with Central America. In addition, the kilt-like garment shown on male figures in the images is very similar to garments shown in deity depictions in some Mesoamerican imagery.

Some specialists within the anthropological community suggest that *kachinas* first came via traders to the western pueblos (for example, the Hopi) from the large cultural center of Casas Grandes (also known as Paquime) in Chihuahua, Mexico. Helen Crotty suggests that the archeological records place Hopi mural art at Awatovi slightly earlier than that at Pottery Mound. Other scholars believe that the new religious tradition may have come north along the Rio Grande to the eastern pueblos and then spread to the western pueblos. This latter view has been supported by comparison of petroglyph images along the Jornada del Muerto with *kiva* mural images. In addition, it could be supported by the anecdotal reports of extensive *kiva* art in the Piro pueblos and at Pottery Mound.

Comparison of Mesoamerican and Pottery Mound figures

114

Regardless of the introduction pathway, the new religion quickly took hold in most of the existing pueblos from the Rio Grande west to the pueblos of the Hopis. (One identifiable exception to this is the Northern Tiwa pueblo of Taos.) One motivation for the shift from previous religious beliefs to the *kachina* cult may have been the period of droughts and crop failures in the late thirteenth century which the tribes may have attributed to a failure to properly appease the gods. This would also be consistent with Sakhomnewa's origin story from the Hopi perspective.

In fact, the Franciscan attempts to suppress the widespread nature and strength of belief in the *kachinas* would become one of the important causes of the Pueblo Revolt led by the Okay Owingeh (formerly San Juan) shaman Po'pay and others in 1680.

Given the wealth of and extreme variation in pottery at Pottery Mound, the extensive *kiva* art at the site, and the timing of occupation of Pottery Mound with the introduction of the *kachina* cult to the region, one might speculate that this site could have been an early center for the propagation of the new ritual system either east or west. Alternatively, it may have been a major ritual center where the eastern and western pueblos, the Tanoan and Keresan pueblos, the Piro pueblos to the south, and settlements such as Casas Grandes further to the south came together to share and enhance their religious and cultural traditions.

A speculative reconstruction of the Pottery Mound configuration in a paper by David Phillips and Jean Ballagh also suggests a melding of eastern and western traditions. As shown below, the back-to-back configurations with south-facing *kivas* from the western tradition on the western side and east-facing *kivas* from the eastern tradition on the eastern side, all along a common central core, would provide an ideal situation for both shared and separate rituals. Note also the loss of structure to the Rio Puerco in the northeast corner of the site and the macaw site nearby—perhaps suggestive of a Parrot Place name for the site.

In Dispute

In 2003, Frank Hibben, then 92, donated money to the University of New Mexico for a new archeology building. As a part of the structure's interior, a set of 20' x 40' paintings that depicted some scenes from the *kiva* art at Pottery Mound was commissioned. However, the mural commission was abruptly cancelled when objections were raised by residents of Acoma Pueblo. Damian Garcia, the Acoma cultural preservation director, said, "These murals depict some of our cultural icons or images. They were found inside a sacred chamber."

Frank Hibben disagreed. His wife Brownie said,

> He [Frank] told me that the ancient images of Pottery Mound belonged to no special interest group, religious, Indian, or otherwise. They belonged to the world of art and science, and to humanity as a whole, just as do the cave paintings of Lascaux or the wall murals of Pompeii.

However, Garth Bawden, director of the Maxwell Museum of Anthropology on the University of New Mexico campus, defended the university's decision:

> The Native American Graves Protection and Repatriation Act has brought into being a much heightened sensitivity to using

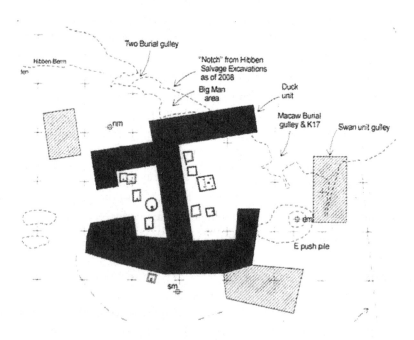

Speculative Pottery Mound layout

116

cultural heritage that belongs to the Native American tribes of the region. Although the Acoma tribe has no known link to Pottery Mound, we wished to consult with the tribes that had the closest relationship with the people who were there. ... There are a lot of things that are gray in this, and legally we could do anything we want. We are part of a broad constituency that includes numerous Indian tribes. If we are doing anything that pertains to their heritage, we will consult with them.

Today, Pottery Mound is surrounded by Pueblo of Isleta land, and in December 2012, after a period of negotiation, the University of New Mexico deeded to the pueblo the thirteen acres that contain the archeological site. Isleta Pueblo Cultural Affairs Committee Representative Valentino Jaramillo told the university's Board of Regents

> The Pueblo has a strong connection to what was uncovered and what still exists in my community and that connection has not vanished. This site remains a window to the Pueblo's past.

Jaramillo also noted that the area was of great significance to Isleta and to other tribes.

Transfer of ownership of Pottery Mound from UNM to Isleta Pueblo

The university retained the right to continue to analyze the extensive collection of artifacts from the site, to conduct research that will not disturb the site or require further collection of artifacts, and to continue to use the site for student training.

Present-day access to Pottery Mound is strictly controlled by Isleta Pueblo. As noted earlier, the site is slowly being eroded away by the encroaching Rio Puerco. Although studies are underway to stem this encroachment, financial and political pressures are limiting what may be possible.

Pottery Mound remains the premier archeological site in the Rio Abajo, if not in New Mexico as a whole. Its remarkably diverse pottery, its location at the nexus of a number of language groups, and its amazing *kiva* art combine to make this site unique. But questions remain. Was it a major cross-cultural ritual site? Was it a formative location for the propagation of the *kachina* religion? What language or languages did the residents speak? Why was it abandoned and when and where did the residents go? Helen Crotty probably said it best, "Pottery Mound, with its deliberate integration of separate traditions, has much to tell us yet."

Los Ojuelos or Comanche Springs

Richard Melzer

The time is the mid-eighteenth century. The place is a pair of springs located ten miles east of Tome, New Mexico, near the foothills of the Manzano Mountains. Comanche warriors are watering and grazing their horses. The Comanches have just completed a tiring ride over a high, narrow pass through the mountains.

For many years Comanche (and, later, Apache) Indians came from the eastern plains of New Mexico to trade peacefully with the Spanish communities and Indian pueblos of the Rio Grande Valley. At other times Indians came to raid villages like Tome, leaving as many as 30 dead in a single year (1778).

Many Uses

The springs where Comanche Indians stopped in preparation for their periodic appearances in the valley are now called Comanche Springs. Previously, and for most of their long history, they were known simply as *Los Ojuelos*, or The Springs. *Los Ojuelos* were often used as a staging ground for violent forays, but fortunately they were also used for many useful purposes as well.

Given their location, the springs were especially useful on a wagon trail that once ran more or less parallel to the base of the Manzano Mountains, from Abo Pass in the south to Tijeras Canyon in the north. As the main source of water for miles in each direction, the springs served as a virtual oasis for weary travelers and their livestock. Trees growing near the springs offered welcome shade from the hot New Mexico sun.

The springs were also used to water livestock owned by residents of Tome. Located on the Tome land grant (established in 1739), *Los Ojuelos* served as a convenient watering hole for goats, horses, cattle, and especially sheep raised on the *ejido*, or land shared jointly by community land grant heirs. And, like countless Indian travelers, Tome residents used the springs to rest on their trips coming and going over Comanche Pass in the Manza-

119

no Mountains. Spanish settlers of the Rio Grande valley traveled over the pass to hunt game and gather firewood on the more heavily wooded east side of the mountains. The pass also afforded access to Hispanic friends and relatives who lived in scattered east-side villages. Valley residents visited and often engaged in trade in places like Manzano and Chilili.

The Little Lion

Eager to exploit a ready source of water on an otherwise arid mesa, a few hardy ranchers went so far as to live near the springs. Manuel Antonio Chaves, a descendant of one of the 39 original recipients of the Tome land grant, was the most able rancher to attempt to make *Los Ojuelos* his home. By the time of his arrival at the springs, Chaves was well known as an intrepid

Manuel Chaves—The Little Lion of the Southwest

Indian fighter and as a trusted leader of men. From an early age he had clearly earned his nickname, *"El Leoncito,"* the "Little Lion." Accompanied by his wife Vicenta, their many children, and his brother-in-law Lorenzo Labadie, Chaves made *Los Ojuelos* his home from sometime in the 1850s.

According to historian Marc Simmons, Chaves built a formidable hacienda about midway between *Los Ojuelos's* two main springs. Digging ditches from the springs to nearby fields, Chaves planted several gardens, making his ranch as self-sufficient as possible. But not even *El Leoncito* was immune to danger at the isolated springs. On one occasion, his young son, Ireneo, was almost swept away by raiding Indians as the boy played near his home. Only Chaves's heroic action saved Ireneo from certain death or years in captivity. (During his rescue, Ireneo suffered a life-long head injury, but lived to the age of 90, dying peacefully in Albuquerque in 1946.)

On other occasions, Indians drove off thousands of Chaves's sheep and most of his cattle and horses while the rancher was away on business or engaged in the Civil War campaign to defend New Mexico against a Confederate invasion in 1862. These incidents forced Chaves to leave his family in Peralta or Albuquerque when he could not be home to protect his loved ones at *Los Ojuelos*. With all the dangers and uncertainty he encountered, it is understandable why Chaves abandoned his ranch by the springs and set off to start a new life with his family in the Pecos River Valley in 1864.

Theories

Los Ojuelos was thus famous as a valuable but dangerous watering hole over many centuries. But *Los Ojuelos* played a much larger role in the history of the Rio Abajo, if we are to believe certain archeologists. These archeologists have discovered the remains of big game near the springs, suggesting that prehistoric hunters regularly lay in wait for bison and other animals to drink from the springs before opening fire with their primitive weapons. Some archeologists also claim to have uncovered evidence of Spanish armor and weapons. These artifacts led University of New Mexico archeologist Frank C. Hibben to conclude that *Los Ojuelos* was once a well-fortified Spanish military outpost.

Following excavations of the *Los Ojuelos* site in the mid-1970s, Hibben

121

asserted that none other than Juan de Oñate, the Spanish conqueror of New Mexico, stayed at the springs for extended periods of time in the first decade of the seventeenth century. Hibben believed that Oñate and his men occupied *Los Ojuelos* because the Spanish had discovered a valuable silver mine in the Manzano Mountains and had used the springs as a convenient place for their smelting activities. Frustrated in his almost desperate search for gold or silver elsewhere in the Southwest, Oñate supposedly hoped that *Los Ojuelos* would be the *El Dorado* that had long eluded him and his fellow Spanish settlers.

Later archeologists and historians, including Ann F. Ramenofsky, Albert B. Ward, John P. Wilson, E. Boyd, Marc Simmons, former state historian Myra Ellen Jenkins, Fray Angelico Chavez, and the late Tibo J. Chavez, Sr., have disagreed with almost everything Hibben claimed about *Los Ojuelos*. Several of these experts acknowledged that while there may have been a military outpost at the springs, it would have been very small and very temporary. Albert Ward points out that Spanish records make no mention of Oñate visiting, much less spending extended periods of time at *Los Ojuelos*. Ann F. Ramenofsky states that Spanish artifacts at the springs date from the period 1650 to 1680, not from the decade 1600 to 1610. One historian went so far as to call Hibben's claims of a Spanish fort and smelter at Comanche Springs "little short of ridiculous." Another called them "pure, unadulterated nonsense."

The Legend of Juan Soldado

But what about stories of a mysterious mine in Comanche Canyon just east of *Los Ojuelos*? According to this legend, a former Spanish soldier, known only as Juan Soldado, worked the mine in colonial times, but kept its location a secret so he could hoard the mine's great wealth for himself. Years later, several Tome residents claimed to have found the mine's entrance while exploring or working in the foothills of the Manzanos. Cresenio Marquez recalled the day he was herding sheep and suddenly spotted the mine's obscure entrance. Peering inside, Marquez saw a shovel, a pickaxe, and other mining tools. Excited and hoping to later return to the source of potential wealth, Marquez left a red handkerchief at the mine's entrance and hurried

122

Los Ojuelos—Commanche Springs

home. He soon returned, but, despite an extensive search, could never find his red handkerchief, much less the elusive mine itself.

Charlie Sanchez, Jr., remembers his grandfather, Ramon de Chavez, saying that he too had found the entrance to a silver mine in the foothills of the Manzano Mountains. Chavez left his rifle to mark the location of his valuable find. But, like Cresenio Marquez's experience with his red handkerchief, Chavez could not find his rifle when he later returned to the area. The rifle was eventually recovered, but nowhere near the place where it had been left.

Others had similarly mysterious experiences. Many believe that Juan Soldado, or at least his spirit, is responsible for removing items left to mark the mine's location, thus preventing anyone from returning, let alone entering, working, and profiting from Juan's ancient claim. So far, Juan has been successful in his vigilant watch through the centuries.

Fortunately, *Los Ojuelos*, or Comanche Springs, still exist. In an effort to protect and maintain the property, the springs were placed on the New Mexico State Register of Cultural and Historic Properties in 1977. Thanks to the efforts of the Valley Improvement Association (VIA), they were entered on

123

Los Ojuelos—Commanche Springs

the National Register of Historic Places a decade later.

Watering hole, hunting field, rest stop, Spanish fort, smelting center, and ranch: these are the springs' multiple purposes, as identified by historians, archeologists, and local residents. Will we ever know the truth in all its details? While some identified purposes are clearly plausible, others are not, based on modern scientific and historical research. Perhaps the best we can do is join Judge Tibo J. Chavez, who, after much study and many interviews, concluded, "*¿Quién sabe?*" ("Who knows?") The legends, wrote Judge Chavez, "keep the imagination fired up" and interest in the site keen.

This is what makes history exciting. And this is what will undoubtedly make *Los Ojuelos* the center of attention, study, and intrigue for years to come.

La Joya: A Jewel in the Valley

Richard Melzer and Francisco Sisneros

La Joya was an exciting place to be in the late eighteenth century. Once a year, in late November, about 500 Spanish colonists gathered on the east bank of the Rio Grande 23 miles south of Belen to prepare for a 40-day journey to Chihuahua, the site of the largest annual trade fair in northern New Spain (now Mexico). Priests, soldiers, and whole families gathered at the rendezvous point. Soldiers were needed to escort the *conducta* (caravan), although the odds of Indian raids on such a large, well-armed group were slim.

New Mexicans gathered at La Joya with wagons full of local products to sell or exchange at the trade fair. Their cargo included deer hides, furs, salt, piñon, textiles, and, the greatest delicacy, buffalo tongues. Supplies filled whatever space remained. Oxen pulled the many wagons. Some men rode on horses or mules, but most people walked. Herders drove hundreds of sheep to sell at the fair or eat along the way.

Families usually journeyed together because it was often safer for women and children to travel south with the men of their families rather than to stay at home where they were vulnerable to Indian attacks. The colonists who gathered at La Joya shared news of recent Indian attacks, epidemics, floods, and other tragedies in various parts of New Mexico. Many mourned those who had died of natural or violent causes in the year since the travelers had last met. Colonists also shared much happier news. Proud friends and relatives announced engagements, weddings, and recent or anticipated births.

As if this hometown news was not enough, travelers collected additional information—as well as gossip and rumors—as they passed through large and small communities en route to La Joya. While they waited for their fellow travelers to arrive, colonists entertained themselves with traditional songs and dancing. We can imagine the good food they prepared, knowing that La Joya would be the last place they would stop for any length of time before reaching their destination in far-off Chihuahua.

But annual rendezvous in La Joya should not be confused with modern tailgate parties. There was much to do to prepare the caravan for the long

125

journey ahead. Did the travelers carry sufficient guns and ammunition? Had at least a hundred men been chosen to serve as sentries to guard the caravan at night? Had men been found to care for the *caballada* (herd of horses)? Had wagons been identified to travel at the head, the middle, and the rear of the caravan on an alternating basis? Did every man, woman, and child carry a travel permit, as required by Spanish colonial law? These details, and many more, had to be carefully arranged before the eager group could leave at last.

The brief gaiety at La Joya was also interrupted by the thought of potential dangers that lay ahead. Shortly after breaking camp at La Joya the caravan would enter the most treacherous 90-mile stretch of the Camino Real in New Mexico. Ominously known as the *Jornada del Muerto* (Journey of the Dead Man), the section of the *Camino Real* south of Socorro left the Rio Grande Valley to cross desert terrain largely devoid of water, fuel, or grass. Previous travelers through the Jornada had established *parajes*, or campsites, but there was no guarantee that these sites could satisfy the needs of hundreds of travelers, especially in the late fall in often winter-like conditions.

As the last wagon disappeared behind the hills, the lively activity at La Joya subsided as suddenly as it had begun. La Joya's normal serenity returned for at least another year.

Changing Roles

La Joya's role changed considerably by the early nineteenth century. By then colonists no longer traveled in one large annual caravan and there was less need to rendezvous at La Joya or any other place before continuing south on the Camino Real. La Joya's role also changed in 1800 when New Mexico's governor Fernando Chacon ordered the resettlement of three villages that had been abandoned prior to or after the Pueblo Revolt of 1680. Sevilleta, first named by Don Juan de Oñate in honor of Sevilla, Spain, was one of the three. Sevilleta's official name had become "La Joya de Nuestra Señora de los Dolores de Sevilleta" by 1802. The name was soon shortened to "La Joya de Sevilleta" and then simply "La Joya," meaning the hollow or, as proud residents would prefer, the jewel.

By mid-1800, a fortified plaza had been built and crops had been planted in the surrounding fields. By 1801, priests from Belen and Tome were baptizing children in La Joya's *oratorio*, or private chapel. Served by priests from Socorro and Sabinal for much of the nineteenth century, La Joya eventually became a separate parish with Our Lady of Sorrows Church as the center of Catholic religious life and culture.

As the small farming community continued to expand, an *acequia mayor*, or main irrigation ditch, was completed and operational by 1814. Five years later, 68 local residents petitioned and received a quarter million-acre land grant from the Spanish governor, Facundo Melgares. (Names of the 68 petitioners are listed in the original land grant document, now preserved in the New Mexico State Records Center and Archives in Santa Fe.) Most of the families that had answered Governor Chacon's call for the resettlement of La Joya had migrated from the Rio Arriba, or northern region of New Mexico, with fewer from the Rio Abajo, or southern region. The Mexican census of 1833 listed 133 families and a total of 524 residents living in *la plasa de la Jolla*.

Major Problems

But La Joya faced major problems in the nineteenth century. Despite precautions, the village suffered many Apache and Navajo attacks. In one instance, raiding Indians killed Esquipula Tafoya while the boy tended his family's sheep west of La Joya. Navajo raiders later captured and held Esquipula's uncle captive for 18 months. Another boy was captured, but was soon rescued after a fierce battle. Tomas Baca was so badly wounded in this rescue that his leg had had to be amputated to save his life. To help defend their vulnerable community, local men willingly served in the militia. But with no money for guns or ammunition, each foot soldier in the militia was issued a bow and a quiver (filled with 25 arrows) as his meager means of defense.

The residents of La Joya fell victim to white as well as Indian depravations. During the Civil War, as a Confederate army invaded New Mexico from Texas, nearly every able-bodied man in La Joya volunteered to join the Union army to help defend the territory against the dreaded *Tejanos*. Mustered into the army on December 12, 1861, La Joya's company of 63 men (plus another dozen who had joined a company organized in Socorro) served at Fort Craig during the Battle of Valverde. They were mustered out

Our Lady of Sorrows Catholic Church in La Joya

of the service just three days after the battle. (Lists of these volunteers are also preserved in the New Mexico State Records Center and Archives.)

Fortunately, the volunteers from La Joya suffered only one death during their brief military duty: Private Manuel Sais had been killed in an ambush by raiding Navajos. The raiders had captured Sais's $200 horse, a fact that seemed to upset army officers far more than the loss of the private's life.

Advancing north from the Valverde battlefield, rebel forces commandeered horses, saddles, sheep, mules, feed, cooking utensils, and even roof poles (for fuel) from villages up and down the valley, including from La Joya. Community members later filed claims for these damages, but were never fully compensated by the federal government. There is even some question about whether the men who had volunteered for the army were ever compensated for their service in the Civil War.

The residents of La Joya fought among themselves as well. In particular, they argued about the fate of their land grant. After many years of legal squabbles and discord, the villagers finally lost their grant to outside interests by 1936. Local poet Manuel Antonio Esquibel wrote *"La Trajeria de la Merce de La Joya"* ("The Tragedy of the La Joya Land Grant") which decried the shenanigans of those he held responsible for this sad loss.

128

Other residents of La Joya became divided on issues of religion. Thomas Harwood, an active Methodist missionary in the Rio Abajo, had established a Methodist church in Socorro in 1871. Starting with eight adults and two young girls, the church gradually grew to include members of extended families in several surrounding communities. While a majority of the families in La Joya remained Catholic, some joined the Methodist faith.

But there is little evidence of friction between Methodist families and their Catholic neighbors, as had occurred in other towns in New Mexico. In Peralta, for example, Methodist missionaries were said to ring their church bells to drown out Sunday sermons delivered by Father Jean B. Ralliere at the nearby Catholic mission of Our Lady of Guadalupe. Further north, Bishop Jean B. Lamy told Catholics in Santa Fe that they would suffer excommunication if they even looked at a Methodist missionary who had arrived to preach in the territorial capital.

In addition to those who joined the Methodist Church, other families in La Joya joined the New Jerusalem or Divine Catholic Church for at least a short period in the early twentieth century. Some families later joined the Pentecostal Church. Locally called the "*aleluyas*," these people were best known for the loud gospel music they often played outdoors.

Despite Indian raids, Civil War invasions, and the loss of its land grant, La Joya remains a "jewel in the valley," steeped in Hispanic tradition and largely content in its small size and isolation.

Anna Becker Park: A Gift of Love

Richard Melzer and Margaret Espinosa McDonald

Anna Becker Park has been an essential part of the Belen community for nearly 70 years. Hundreds drive by it each day. Many stop to enjoy the park and its facilities each week. In fact, we refer to Anna Becker Park so often that the name seems to roll off the tongue as if it were a single word. But few know how the park got its name, much less who Anna Becker was in Belen history. As it turns out, Anna Becker Park was a generous gift to Belen by one of the community's greatest benefactors, John Becker.

Business and Community Contributions

As one of the most successful merchants in Belen history, John Becker contributed to his town's growth in many ways. Opened in 1877, Becker's mercantile store was the center of local trade for almost a century. His flour mill ground wheat for farming families up and down the Rio Grande Valley. His wool storage business purchased wool from local sheep ranchers and shipped it to distant markets by the trainload.

Becker's Town and Improvement Company opened large new sections of town, including the new railroad yards located eight blocks east of Belen's Main Street. And Becker's First National Bank of Belen was the dominant financial institution in town from its founding in 1903 until its sale in 1995.

There is no doubt that John Becker profited handsomely from these many enterprises, but so did the people of Belen and the town as a whole. Several generations of local farmers, ranchers, and store employees based their livelihood on John Becker's operations. Consumers bought goods, families purchased homes, and residents deposited savings and secured loans through one or another of Becker's businesses. It was difficult to find anyone in the Belen area whose economic life was not touched by this early business pioneer.

But John Becker contributed to Belen and its citizens in non-business ways as well. A list of his many civic activities and gifts to his community could literally fill pages. Providing more than half of the cost of construction of the Zion Lutheran Evangelical Church (later the Federated Church,

130

the Presbyterian Church, and now the Noblin's Funeral Home) was one of Becker's most generous contributions. Becker also donated land for the building of Valencia County High School, the first secondary school built in our community.

The Park's Beginnings

And John Becker donated the land for the creation of Belen's first town park, located on a 300-by-419-foot plot of land on the north side of Reinken Avenue. Becker had used this land as a *desagüa*, or pond to drain off excess water from his irrigated alfalfa fields, located just to the south. The pond, long known as the Belen Lake, was also used as a recreation area in both summer and winter seasons. The lake was deep enough for row-boating. And, demonstrating how cold winters could be in those days, the lake froze so often that residents of all ages used it for ice skating, a new sport for most members of the local community.

But the Belen Lake proved to be hazardous as well, especially in the summer months when swarms of mosquitos infested the still water, endangering the health of nearby residents. No one drowned in the lake, but the danger existed for unattended children at play. Bill Gore remembers the day he and his brother Bob fell off a makeshift raft and had to scramble ashore, gratefully unharmed.

Ice skating on Belen Lake

Well aware of these problems, town leaders ordered that the lake be filled in. Dirt was trucked in to fill most of the pond, but a highly unusual item was used as well. Clifford Keith, the legendary coach at Belen High School, owned an old Model T Ford, affectionately known as the "Silver Bullet." Coach Keith generously let his players and friends borrow the car whenever they needed transportation, be it to a game or on a hunting trip. After much use, the Silver Bullet was recognized to be beyond repair. Lacking a place to dispose of it, Coach Keith decided to use the old car to help fill in the Belen Lake. According to local legend, the Silver Bullet still sits buried somewhere below the surface of the park today.

Anna Becker

John Becker had platted the land for the park as early as 1904. His only request was that the new park be named in honor of his wife, Anna. Anna Becker was born Anna Vielstich in Lesum, Germany. Like John, Anna and her family were devout members of a Lutheran sect known as the Zion Lutheran Evangelical Church. One of the sect's strict rules required all members to marry within the church.

Like many German families of the nineteenth century, Anna's family migrated to Wisconsin, settling in Milwaukee, where a large Zion Lutheran Evangelical community thrived by the 1870s. When young John Becker searched for a suitable wife, he naturally thought of Wisconsin as a likely source of a German bride belonging to his sect of the Lutheran church. John met Anna on a social trip to Wisconsin. We know little about John Becker's courtship of Anna Vielstich, other than it must have been difficult, given the considerable distance between Wisconsin and New Mexico. The couple nevertheless married in Santa Fe on November 2, 1877. John was 27. Anna was 26.

Anna moved to Belen to live with her new husband in living quarters on the north side of the mercantile store he had built on South Main Street. Photos of the interior of their home do not exist, but we can imagine it was decorated with as much German furniture as the Beckers could find so far from their European homeland.

Although surrounded by Hispanic and Indian cultures, the Beckers never attempted to dominate or replace native ways directly. In fact, based on their strict religious beliefs, the Beckers and most other German immigrants in Valencia County were determined to preserve their own language, culture, and religion at home and as a separate ethnic group. We can nevertheless imagine that Anna Becker missed her family and friends in Germany and Wisconsin. Husband John helped fill this void by inviting several members of Anna's family to live and work in Belen.

Anna's Uncle Jacob thus came to Belen to serve as the floor supervisor in Becker's store. John's brother Fred married Anna's sister, Johanna, and lived in Belen, as did Anna's nephew, Paul Dalies, her niece, Hannah Dalies, her half-brother, Lueder, and her cousins, the Endersteins. Anna also satisfied her longings for home and German culture by accompanying her husband on trips to Wisconsin and on fairly regular trips to Germany.

Meanwhile, John and Anna Becker expanded their immediate family with the births of four sons (Hans, Louis, Gustav, and Bernhart) and two daughters (Anita and Lucie). A German nanny, Bertha Ruiz, helped Anna raise her growing family. Bertha arrived from the German community in Ripon, Wisconsin, in 1889 when she was only 16 years old.

The John Becker family

As the Becker children grew to maturity, several entered one phase or another of the family's extensive business interests. When Lucie grew to adulthood, her father built her a two-story house to the west of his store, within yards of the Becker family home. As the story goes, anyone in the store at lunchtime could expect an invitation to dine at Lucie's, along with the rest of the family and the store's large staff.

The Beckers' oldest son, Hans (or John Jr.), joined the store's staff at an early age, making the mercantile business his career until his death in 1939. The youngest son, Bernhart, better known as Bernard, also worked in the Becker store until he enlisted in the U.S. Army during World War I. Louis, known as L.C., worked in the First National Bank of Belen through most of his life, serving as the bank's distinguished president until his death in 1971.

Anna herself was an integral part of her husband's business, working in his store and serving local customers for many years. Anna learned to speak Spanish soon after her arrival in New Mexico. John insisted that all of his employees speak the local language, to better accommodate their predominately Hispanic customers.

Anna could be a shrewd, sometimes insistent salesperson. One customer recalled the day she went to the Beckers' store to buy new winter coats for her two daughters. Anna showed the customer the coats in stock, but each was several sizes too large for the woman's children. Anna nevertheless convinced the woman to buy the oversized garments, arguing that the girls would grow into them eventually!

Anna Becker's private life was filled with activity, including many German social events. Picnics, featuring good German food and music, were especially popular. Many danced to German songs on outdoor wooden dance floors. Photos show Anna surrounded by loving family and friends, clearly enjoying her life in the Rio Abajo.

But Anna's life was not without tragedy. Two of her children died early deaths, one living less than a month in 1879 and the other living less than a year, from September 26, 1891, to September 3, 1892. Eighteen-year-old Gustav, Anna's third oldest son, was killed in a football accident on October 7, 1903, while attending the Northwestern Military Academy in Lake Geneva, Wisconsin.

Anna Becker lived to be 71 years old, dying of natural causes on December 4, 1922. John survived his first wife by 10 years, taking a second wife, Ina Innebickler, in 1927, but joining Anna in death after suffering a short illness in the spring of 1932. John and Anna were buried side-by-side in Belen's Protestant cemetery. Their two children who died in infancy are buried nearby.

Building the Park

The park to be named in Anna's memory became a reality soon after John and Anna's deaths. A local park committee was organized to plan the important project in 1934. With no funding available from a debt-ridden town government during the Great Depression, several civic organizations took up the slack, providing time and whatever funding they could afford. Members of Belen's Eastern Star Lodge thus built a flower garden in the shape of a star at a cost of $25. The star is still visible in the park's northwest corner.

The Veterans' Council appropriated $45 to install a cannon in memory of U.S. foreign wars. The Knights of Columbus pitched in another $60 for a drinking fountain. The Tubercular Association installed a children's merry-go-round for $84. Belen's chapter of the Women's Christian Temperance Union, or WCTU, sponsored the construction of the most ambitious project in the new park: a gazebo or bandstand. WCTU members had raised $120 for a wooden bandstand but were persuaded to build a more lasting structure with a concrete base, indoor restrooms, and a storeroom below. Praised as "a credit to any large city," the more permanent structure cost the WCTU an additional $145. The Becker family contributed $50 of their own money to build a concrete marker in honor of their matriarch. A small bronze plate on the marker bears the simple engraving, "Anna Becker Park: Dedicated by John Becker in Memory of His Wife." Although sometimes obscured by large shrubbery, the marker still stands on the park's north side.

While local groups and the Becker family bore the cost of materials, federal public works programs provided the labor to build Anna Becker Park. New Deal agencies of the 1930s, including the Civil Works Administration (CWA) and the Federal Emergency Relief Administration (FERA), employed an average of 25 men daily, paying their wages and aiding many destitute families at the height of the depression.

Enjoying the Park

The residents of Belen made good use of their new park from the moment it was completed. Band concerts were held each Saturday evening for the balance of the summer in 1934. Over the years, children played; families enjoyed picnics; friends visited; youth groups held ice cream socials; and residents celebrated holidays, including the Fourth of July and Martin Luther King Jr. Day.

Appropriately for the town of Belen (Spanish for Bethlehem), the most impressive holiday celebrations were held during the Christmas season from 1963 to 1974. Led by the Belen Chamber of Commerce, organizations from the Knights of Columbus to the Pilot Club helped make the annual event a great success. As many as 27 displays filled the park, with children's displays on the north end and religious displays to the south, along Reinken Avenue.

Much has changed at the park over the years. The restrooms below the bandstand are long gone. The park's cannon was moved to Los Lunas when some objected that it was too militaristic and potentially dangerous for kids to climb on, although hundreds of local residents had done so as children. Recent changes have included the construction of additional parking spaces, the purchase of new playground equipment, and the addition of a large, covered pavilion. The pavilion was first used as part of the 2003 Christmas celebration, just days after it was installed.

Anna Becker Park is still the center of many events in Belen, just as the plaza is the center of community life in Tome and Daniel Fernandez Park is the center of many social activities in Los Lunas. Like public parks throughout the world, each park in Valencia County is the heart of its respective community and that community's proud cultural identity.

How fitting that John Becker gave Anna Becker Park to Belen in memory of the very heart of his life and his family. His was the perfect gift, culminating a lifetime of giving to the town he and Anna had loved so much in the Rio Abajo.

Going to the Movies in Valencia County

Richard Melzer

Like most Americans, the residents of Valencia County have always loved to go to the movies. At one time or another, Valencia County has had six movie theaters, including the Goebel, the Central (later renamed the Cortez), and the Oñate in Belen, the Zia Drive-In just north of Belen, the Zia Theater in Los Lunas, and now the Starlight Cinema 8, also in Los Lunas.

Early Theaters

Goebel's Opera House was the first Valencia County establishment to show moving pictures, dating back to before World War I. We know little about the Goebel Opera House beyond what is revealed through its ads in the *Belen News*. These ads tell us that for a nickel or a dime (probably depending on seating location) customers could see short silent movies at 7:45 and 8:45 p.m., five days a week, plus a 2:45 p.m. matinee on Sundays. Special presentations could last longer. On May 12, 1915, viewers saw "Across the Pacific," a "wonderfully interesting ... photo play" about "war, intrigue, and love" presented on no fewer than five reels of film.

World War I brought changes to the Goebel and all of Valencia County. As part of the war effort, local leaders made short speeches at the opera house, appealing to movie-goers to contribute to the war in many ways. Known as Four-Minute Men (they promised to speak for no more than four minutes), leaders like John Becker, Jr., urged his listeners to buy war bonds, conserve resources, and enlist if they were qualified and not already drafted. Becker addressed more than 4,000 local residents over several months, usually while the projectionist changed reels.

The terrible Spanish flu epidemic forced the Goebel and all other public places to close temporarily in the fall of 1918. The Goebel's permanent demise soon followed.

The new Central Theater, at 204 North Main Street, was Belen's only movie house in the 1920s. Located where Hub Furniture is today, there are

137

still many remnants of the old theater if you look closely with the help of current owner Bennie Sanchez. On the second level, for example, it's possible to see part of the old projector booth along the north wall. Old timers recall that the projector was so large and heavy that it had to be lowered into the theater with a crane before a new roof was completed. A March 1924 Central Theater ad proudly announced that "Our new ceiling will soon be yours for a warm theater."

Movie fans watched hundreds of films at the Central in its heyday of the 1920s and 1930s. Of course, only silent movies could be shown in the 1920s, but this seldom deterred local residents who appeared in large numbers to see such classic films as "The Birth of a Nation" and "The Courtship of Miles Standish." Tom Mix and other cowboy stars appeared in popular Westerns. Some films, like the "Jungle Goddess" (1924), were shown as serials in as many as nine weekly episodes. A local pianist provided background music to fit the exciting action on the screen. With many moveable seats, dances often followed feature presentations.

But the Central hardly monopolized dances or entertainment in Belen. Other dance halls drew large crowds, as did carnivals and Chautauquas that arrived by train from points across the map. Smarting from such competition, Gordon Hicks, the Central's manager, asked Belenites to "bear in mind that [his theater was] giving the people of Belen the very best in high class entertainment, at the same time having to compete with outside street shows which are actually invited by local people. Patronize the home show and keep the big picture coming."

The Talkies

The Central stood a better chance of competing with traveling shows as of April 20, 1930, with the showing of Valencia County's first "talkie." Although the first "talkie" in the country, starring Al Jolson as "The Jazz Singer," was released in October 1927, it took another two and a half years before movie-goers in Belen saw their first soundtrack film at the Central.

The arrival of the talkies drew front-page attention in the *Belen News*. "The Painted Angel," starring the "beautiful Billie Dove" and featuring "five big song hits," was the first 100 percent talking film shown in Valencia

County. "Redemption," starring the screen's greatest lover, John Gilbert, and "The Sophomore," "a peppy story of college life," followed within days. There is no record of how many movie fans attended these early shows, but we can imagine that the new films caused quite a stir in a small town like Belen.

As of the spring of 1930, the Central's newspaper ads boasted that the theater showed "ALL TALKING PICTURES." Will Rogers, "America's greatest wise cracking comedian," could now be heard, along with other comedians, as "a sure cure for the Blues." "Sally," a Ziegfield musical, had 32 "musical numbers" in July 1930. Adding to their appeal, an increasing number of movies were shown "entirely in color."

After many requests for a talking Western, the Central booked "The Long, Long Trail," with Hoot Gibson, that same summer of 1930. Hundreds of other action-packed talking Westerns followed, including "The Lone Rider," "Billy the Kid," and "The Indians Are Coming" in March 1931 alone.

The Central continued to draw large crowds even in the 1930s when the Great Depression hit Valencia County as hard, if not harder than the rest of the state or the nation. In fact, some argued that movies were excellent "gloom chasers" and "promoters of true happiness," regardless of economic conditions. In the words of Central's manager, "Defy family cares and troubles - make yourself and your children happy by seeing a good movie. Troubles and cares can't follow you to the theater. Good entertainment licks them every time."

Ticket prices were reasonable by Depression-era standards. Stars like Roy Rogers, Gene Autry, Edward G. Robinson, Mickey Rooney, Jeanette MacDonald, and Nelson Eddy distracted adult audiences for as little as 40 cents for regular showings and 25 cents for matinees. Kids got in for a dime, although kind-hearted ushers sometimes let poor kids in by conveniently looking the other way when they entered the theater.

Bennie Sanchez and his brother, Manuel, were two such children. One day the boys had only one dime, but wanted to go to the show. The boys arranged for Manuel to use the dime to buy a ticket and then pass it to Bennie so they could both get into the theater. Art Bustamante counted heads before the show began, but knew that something was wrong when he counted one too many customers. Bennie still remembers Art's flashlight shining in his face as he told the usher that he had somehow lost his ticket between the door and his seat. Art let Bennie and Manuel stay to enjoy the show.

Fond Memories at the Central

Many old-timers have fond memories of the old Central, either because they saw their first movie there or because they secured their first employment working for the theater's managers, Mr. and Mrs. Hicks. Lee Auge, for example, helped the projectionist change movie reels, watching for the small spot that showed on the corner of the screen when it was almost time to switch to the second projector where the next reel of film was ready to go.

Art Bustamante began working at the Central when he was only 13 years old. Before the theater doors opened, Art would sweep the floors and start a fire in the black wood stove during the winter months. Then he would change into a suit and tie and serve as an usher (and sometimes as the cashier, too). For certain movies, Art and his fellow ushers dressed in special clothing: cowboy outfits for Westerns and soldier uniforms for war movies. Art worked throughout his high school years, graduating in 1940.

Bill Gore also remembers his role as a member of the Central's staff, although his work was done outside the theater, not inside. As a good friend of the Hicks' son, Sam, Bill helped deliver handbills advertising upcoming movies. Bill enjoyed his house-to-house delivery route until one day when he refused to deliver a handbill to a house with a fierce-looking dog in its yard. Mrs. Hicks was not pleased.

Jack Aldrich never worked at the Central, but still remembered seeing his first movie there as a youngster. He could not remember the name of the movie, but he distinctly recalled the sound of movie-goers crunching peanut shells on the theater's hardwood floors as they made their way to their seats. Lee Auge remembers sitting with dozens of other local kids on the floor below the big screen to watch Saturday matinees.

The Oñate Invades Belen

A turning point in the history of movie theaters in Valencia County came in 1940 when a new, more modern theater was built by the R.E. Griffith Company, a national chain. The R.E. Griffith Company had recently purchased the old Central Theater and continued to show movies there until the mid-1950s. But it was the new 600-seat movie house, built at 710 Dalies Avenue, that drew the lion's share of attention from 1940 on.

The new theater's name was chosen in a local contest. Hundreds of names were suggested, but the Oñate was finally selected just prior to its grand opening on Friday, August 9, 1940, at 7:00 p.m. Several businesses, including the First National Bank of Belen, Becker-Dalies, Buckland Pharmacy, Safeway, and Juan's Beer Garden took out a full-page ad in the *Belen News* to welcome the R.E. Griffith Company to town. "Saturday's Children" was the first film shown at the Oñate. Opening just prior to the Belen fiesta helped guarantee large crowds of eager local residents and out-of-town visitors.

The Oñate had barely opened its doors when the United States entered World War II in late 1941. While the theater offered every kind of movie, from musicals to Westerns, it showed more and more war-related films as the fighting raged overseas. War films included "To the Shores of Iwo Jima,"

Interior of the Oñate Theater

141

"The Story of G.I. Joe," and "Back to Bataan," starring John Wayne. Everyone watched for news of the war on "March of Times" newsreels, a main source of world news prior to the age of television.

No one seemed to mind the new penny defense tax added to the price of children's tickets or the two-cent tax added to the price of adults' tickets. When copper and aluminum scrap drives were organized, kids were admitted free if they contributed copper items or aluminum utensils. Ken Gibson admits that such scraps were not always collected with their owners' consent, including his dad's. Later, anyone who bought a war bond was admitted to see a show free of charge.

Soldiers home on leave were given special attention in Belen. Lupe Fergusen remembered a visit by her future husband on leave while Lupe was still in high school. The coed was surprised when Belen High School's principal, Roy C. Stumph, told her she was free to go home early to be with her soldier. The young couple spent the afternoon at the Oñate. Lupe still cries over the movie they saw ("Sister Bernadette") not because she liked it so much, but because of the memories of young romance it still brings back.

Soldiers returned home to stay in 1945. Happy to have the troops home and eager to express its gratitude for their service, the Oñate admitted vets for free over a two-week period at the end of World War II.

As in their early history, movie theaters of the 1940s, 1950s, and 1960s continued to promote themselves as sources of good, clean fun. They certainly compared favorably with other forms of entertainment that came through Valencia County by rail and road. Traveling carnivals had particularly bad reputations. The *Belen News* reported that gambling, robbery, and the beating of several local men occurred when one such carnival came to town shortly after World War II. "Besides draining the town of funds," wrote the *Belen News*, "these carnivals carry with them some people who are a menace to the community and ... poison [for] the minds of our youngsters." The newspaper urged Belen's town council to either raise the license fee for carnivals so high it would "discourage carnivals from stopping [here]" or ban the shows entirely.

No such disruption was caused by movie theaters. Perhaps the worst trouble ever experienced near the Oñate Theater occurred when vandals fired BB guns, damaging the car windshields of several movie goers in 1961.

An Oñate Theater showbill from July 1951

With the exception of one failed robbery after hours, the Zia Theater offered a similarly safe environment in Los Lunas. Opened by Frank and Hattie Nieto in 1940 with a seating capacity of 320, the Zia's building was located where the Giant Convenience Store now stands on Main Street. Hattie herself made the theater's large curtain from velvet material. The family lived in a house behind the theater and the Mission Bar, a business the Nietos also operated for many years.

Movies and Promotions

Local theaters proudly presented such films as "The Harvey Girls" (with special relevance to the Belen Harvey House), "The Caine Mutiny," "On the Waterfront," "From Here to Eternity," and Humphrey Bogart's "The Treasure of the Sierra Madre." Westerns and comedies continued to be popular too. Individual stars drew particularly large crowds to the Oñate, the Central, and the Zia. Rock Hudson, Marilyn Monroe, Jimmy Stewart, Frank Sinatra, and Ronald Reagan were some of the biggest attractions.

And Valencia County boasted its hometown stars. Gloria Castillo, her brother Leo, and boxer Art Aragon received special billings when they appeared in movies like "The Ring" (1953), "Night of the Hunter" (1955), and "The Maverick" (1956). Gloria Castillo's movie debut was front-page news in the *News-Bulletin* in November 1955.

Belen's Gloria Castillo

144

When Elvis Presley gained superstar status in the mid-1950s, his movies, including "Loving You" (with seven "great songs!") attracted teenage girls in droves. In October 1956, the Oñate gave free Elvis patches to all teen fans. Recognizing a good business opportunity, Charles Seery opened the Elvis Presley Canteen at 305 South Main Street so that teen fans could have a place to gather before and after the movies. Seery announced that "we even plan to invite Elvis himself to visit our place." If invited, Elvis never came.

Beyond Elvis patches, the Oñate offered other special promotions to attract large crowds. Children were often targeted in these offers. At the end of the school year in 1954, for example, kids were admitted free to the theater to see the first installment of a Western serial, undoubtedly so that they would want to return to see the rest of the series at regular admission prices throughout the summer.

Vacation matinee books, good for 12 shows over 12 summer weeks, were available for only a dollar each. The Oñate advertised its air-conditioned interior, a real attraction in the summer months when few local residents had air conditioning at home and the temperature could soar to 105 degrees, as during the heat wave of July 1953. At summer's end, the Oñate allowed kids to see movies for free when they picked up their tickets at local stores (that happened to be selling school supplies) in 1957. Back in school, whole classes attended movies at discount rates on special occasions.

Other members of the family were catered to as well. On Mother's Day in 1956, mothers could enter the Oñate and eat a complete meal at Gil's Bakery free of charge, if accompanied by their entire family. Father's Day promotions were not as generous, although the Oñate offered to pay the premiums on a $1,000 life insurance policy for one year for the first baby born in Belen on Father's Day 1958. In perhaps the most unusual promotion of the post-war era, the Oñate gave free tickets to anyone who came to see the movie "Pillow Talk" (with Rock Hudson and Doris Day) while wearing pajamas and carrying a pillow to the theater.

The Zia, Central, and Oñate theaters appealed to Hispanic audiences with Spanish-language films on special nights of the week. Ellen June Place, who sold tickets at the Zia in Los Lunas, remembers that the line of customers often ran down the block on Spanish movie nights. Cantinflas, the famous Mexican comic, was a particular favorite.

The Zia Drive-In

A new theater gave indoor movie houses considerable competition by the early 1950s. Opened about a mile north of Belen on October 24, 1951, the Zia Drive-In was the first and only outdoor theater of its kind in Valencia County history. The Zia's season normally ran from about Easter to about Labor Day, although it was sometimes extended even in cold weather.

Admission to the Zia was usually 50 cents a person, with no charge for children. However, on special nights, whole cars were admitted for just a dollar, regardless of passenger load. Many Belenites still recall packing their cars with as many friends as possible on dollar nights. Others recall packing stowaways in their car trunks on nights when customers were charged by the number of riders in each vehicle.

Gilbert Tabet remembers driving into the Zia alone, but buying six bags of popcorn at the concession stand for his friends who joined him in the drive-in by jumping over a back fence. Suspicious that one boy would need six bags of popcorn, the management investigated, found several unpaid customers in Gilbert's car, and kicked the group off the premises.

Undoubtedly the most unusual vehicle to appear at the drive-in was a tractor (with plow attached). Art Fender remembers seeing a farmer drive his tractor into the theater, mount the speaker on his steering wheel, cover himself with a blanket, and enjoy the show eating a bag of popcorn.

A projectionist working at the Zia Drive-In recalls that the Catholic Legion of Decency gave instructions regarding profane language or "questionable morality" used in films. When a movie got to an objectionable place, indicated by a mark on the film, the projectionist would simply jump to the next mark, essentially "bleeping out" the "bad" words. We can only imagine how little of today's movies would be left if this practice was followed now.

Promotions abounded for paying customers at the Zia. Anyone driving a Chevy could get in free on Chevy Nights, while those who drove Fords got in free on Ford Nights. Prizes were also used to draw customers to the Zia. Reflecting an "if you can't beat them, join them" attitude, the drive-in gave a $5 prize for the car with the largest number of passengers on a dollar-a-car night in April 1957. A hundred-pound pig was given away at the show, as was a sewing machine, and an old jalopy on other occasions. Twenty-five chicken dinners were offered as prizes in August 1953. Live chickens were set free for the taking in a 1957 event. In an age when UFOs were increasingly popular, flying saucer nights were held throughout the mid-1950s. Prizes of up to $5 went to customers who caught the small round objects flung from the top of the Zia's concession stand.

Movies were always the main attraction at Valencia County theaters, but other events were also held as well. A beauty pageant was held on the stage at the Oñate within weeks of the movie theater's grand opening in 1940. The Belen fiesta queen was crowned on the same stage a year later. Fashion shows, dance recitals, children's plays, high school band performances, rock-and-roll concerts, and even a magician appeared on the Oñate's stage over the years. The latter, billed as "The Great Benson," claimed that he could make "a real live rabbit turn into a bird" and make "a rosebush grow and bloom in less than a minute."

A Zia Drive-In showbill from 1952

In another unusual event staged at the Oñate, the Rainbow Girls organized a celebration for the premiere of "A Remedy for Riches" (1941) by inviting local youths to appear at the theater dressed as movies stars. Among the dozens who participated, Eva Garcia came as Judy Garland, Ruth Esther Lindberg came as Mae West, and Frank Beyer came as Clark Gable. According to the press, the demand

147

for tickets was so great that the police "thought for a bit that the doors of the theater were going to be flattened by the crowd." Order was restored when the theater manager announced that the stage show cast had agreed to give two performances, rather than just one, as originally planned.

The "stars" arrived in fancy cars that drove them from outside Davis Floral on Dalies Avenue to the Oñate a few blocks away. Once in the theater, Ted Husing served as the master of ceremonies before a packed house. A nine-page script listed gags, songs, and dance routines performed by Belen's special "Hollywood" guests.

In 1949, the Becker-Dalies store sponsored weekly amateur nights, featuring "big acts of local talent." Thirteen-year-old Bertha Faye Garner won one amateur competition (judged by audience applause) by singing "You're Breaking My Heart." Bill Craig accompanied her on the piano.

But the prize for the most unusual event to take place on stage at a movie theater in Valencia County must go to a couple who agreed to be married on the Oñate's stage in June 1948. The bride, a practical nurse, and the groom, a local farmer, had seen the Oñate's offer to host a wedding advertised in the *News-Bulletin*. It sounded like a good idea, especially when wedding gifts from many local businesses were listed as enticements. Gifts ranged from a spare tire to a $100 wedding dress. Participating businesses included Becker-Dalies, Davis Floral, Trembly Jewelers, and the Fair Store.

Holidays were also celebrated with considerable fanfare at the movies. In 1957, Christmas was celebrated with as many as two hours of cartoons as well as with free popcorn for all kids under the age of 12. New Year's was rung in with "hats, horns, and favors for all." Easter promised eggs and prizes for children at the Oñate, while the Fourth of July was celebrated with fireworks at the Zia, unless it rained, as happened in 1957. April Fool's Day meant "anything can happen," according to the Oñate's management who warned that its shows "may be upside down or on the back wall - but you'll have the time of your life! It's gonna be crazy, man!"

Horror and Violence

The holiday that lent itself most to movie theaters and their surroundings was Halloween. In 1955, free hats and noise-makers were distributed for the Oñate's midnight show when "graveyard frolics, on stage and on the screen" were planned. Boris Karloff starred in "The Vanishing Body" on October 31, 1956. Of course, it didn't have to be Halloween for local theaters to feature horror shows. In fact, horror shows were among the most popular movies of the 1950s and 1960s. Most were Grade B films at best. Typical horror movie titles included "The Boy With the Green Hair" (1954), "I Was a Teenage Frankenstein" (1957), "The School Teacher and the Monsters" (1957), "The Thing That Couldn't Die" (1958), and "Teenagers From Outer Space" (1959).

"Macabre" (1958) was considered so terrifying that the Oñate advertised that "we have to insure your life for $1,000 in case of death by fright." The theater's management was quick to add that its offer was "not valid for people with known heart or nervous conditions." "Dr. Evil and His Terrors of the Unknown" (1960) was billed as "so scary" at the Oñate that women were advised to "bring an escort to protect you when the lights go out." Those who survived the horrors they witnessed were offered two-for-one free passes "to a near-future movie."

Horror films were not the only Grade B movies to appear on Valencia County movie screens. Many such films depicted questionable morals, especially for younger audiences. Long before Hollywood began rating its movies, theaters sometimes warned their audiences of "mature themes," although the warnings themselves were often worded to be intentionally enticing. In 1957, for example, the Oñate's management told customers that it "does not see fit to recommend 'The Bad Seed' for children. When you see it, you will understand why." In probably the strangest such warning to adults and their children, the Zia Drive-In warned that "The Shrike" (1956) dealt with "adult problems of life, which children will neither understand nor enjoy." "NO CHILDREN TICKETS SOLD" therefore appeared in large print, although the following words appeared in parentheses: "Children under 12 free with parents."

Violent themes received special notices. In 1956, the Oñate's manager, L.E. Rylant, told potential viewers that he had to "frankly admit" that James Dean's "Rebel Without a Cause" would "jolt every one of us with a frightening message" about juvenile violence. But Rylant hoped that such a jolt would somehow jar "mature citizens toward the guidance and understanding of youth." Rylant neglected to say what he hoped might be the message of "Rebel Without a Cause" for teenagers themselves. Perhaps predictably, a small riot broke out at Belen High School within a week of the movie's showing at the Oñate.

But violent, immoral films were the exception rather than the rule. As a result, most oldtimers have only fond memories of going to the movies in their youth. Others have fond memories of working at the Oñate and the Zia, just as many in their parents' generation had enjoyed working at the Central in the 1930s.

Helen Louise Ray worked as a cashier in the Oñate's ticket booth during most of her junior and senior years at Belen High School. She recalls that some ticket sellers and ticket takers did not always require tickets from friends or relatives who came to see a movie.

The Mathis family's twins, Joann and Betty Jo, recall working at the Oñate, with one of the girls selling tickets in the front and the other girl selling refreshments at the snack bar inside. A local man who was known to drink too much came to see a movie one night but couldn't believe his eyes when he thought he saw the same girl who had sold him his tickets also selling him his refreshments. He reportedly swore never to drink again.

Herb Ellermeyer's memories of his teenage job at the Oñate were good, with one exception. It seems that every payday Herb and his fellow employees were pressured to put most of their earnings in a pool to see who would win the entire sum. Herb remembers that he never won the pool and seldom had much money to show for all his hours of work at the theater.

Connie Luna remembers the good times she had while working as a ticket seller at the Zia Theater in Los Lunas. Her most memorable moment occurred when a driver ran a car onto the sidewalk outside her ticket booth. The out-of-control vehicle knocked over an exterior sign, but fortunately came to a halt before hitting Connie or the booth where she sat.

Ellen June Place also recalls that the Zia's owner sometimes asked unruly kids to leave her theater if they were disturbing other customers. Feeling sorry for these youngsters, Mrs. Nieto often brought them free bags of popcorn on the sidewalk outside. Ellen June remembers that she and other teenage workers hung their coats near the popcorn stand in the winter. As a

150

result, "we always went to school smelling of popcorn."

Closing Time

One by one, Valencia County's movie theaters closed down. The Zia in Los Lunas closed in 1954 when Frank Nieto died and home television began to seriously compete with the movies. The Zia's building was used as a feed store until it was eventually destroyed to make room for other businesses. The Cortez (formerly the Central) in Belen closed in the mid-1950s. Its 9,000-square-foot building was sold to Bennie Sanchez for $9,000 and a promise by Sanchez never to use the structure as a movie theater again. True to his word, Bennie remodeled the old building using money made from selling what was left behind in the theater, including its projectors, chairs, velvet curtain, and popcorn stand. Bennie's Hub Furniture still occupies the space with its original hardwood floors and thick adobe walls on South Main Street today.

The Zia Drive-In, like most drive-ins across the country, drew fewer and fewer customers in the 1960s. It closed for good in September 1968. The last two movies shown were John Wayne in "The Green Berets" and Dean Martin in "Five Card Stud." The drive-in's six acres were sold, with half the land sold to the Assembly of God Church, which built its church there on old Highway 85. The remaining land was sold to Ed Peter, who quickly sold all equipment, including the speakers and big screen. He couldn't recall who bought the screen, but did remember insisting on a written agreement that he was not liable if the new owner was injured or killed while removing it.

The Oñate's closing was not as simple or as conclusive. Commonwealth Theaters, its last corporate owners, closed the movie house in 1968. Gilbert Tabet bought it in early 1969 and went to great lengths to recarpet the lobby and aisles, reupholster the chairs, remodel the exterior, and install a new 14-foot-by-28-foot Cinemascope screen. The screen alone cost $600. The *News-Bulletin* editorialized that Tabet's venture was welcomed in Belen. "The fact that the theater is home-owned and home-operated should improve the chances of success." The newspaper's editor added that "The youth of our community have complained, and rightly so, for the lack of 'something to do.'" The remodeled Oñate was expected to help remedy this problem with "good clean" entertainment for the entire family.

Gilbert Tabet ran the Oñate for about a year, but, given his other business obligations, leased the theater to several different operators in the 1970s and 1980s. Abelino Sanchez and his daughter, Phyllis Hayes, leased the theater for the longest period, from 1976 to 1984. They enjoyed some success, especially when popular movies like "E.T." (1982) were shown. "E.T." drew such large crowds in Belen that it was brought back not just once, but three times.

But the Oñate was beginning to show signs of aging. Its old brick walls were broken into by vandals who damaged the movie screen and other parts of the interior. Phyllis Hayes also recalls that the building's ceiling had begun to leak. Competition from more modern, multi-screen theaters in Albuquerque hurt business as well.

Gilbert Tabet made one last stab at running the Oñate himself. In 1987, he and his wife reopened the theater with the hit movie "La Bamba." The crowds were so large that Gilbert's wife had trouble handling all the cash that flowed into the ticket box. But the Tabets' success did not last, and the demands of running their Circle T restaurant all day and the Oñate at night

The Oñate Theater converted to Harla May's Fat Boy Grill

proved too great. Gilbert recalls that his last movie was "Die Hard." He still thinks that it was an appropriate last movie because the Oñate had lasted so long and had "died hard." Later efforts to show boxing matches via closed circuit TV were never profitable.

Percy Yu of Albuquerque bought the theater, hoping to reopen it as a dinner theater or civic center. His plans did not work out. Anthony Baca, who used to own Belen's Tasty Freeze on North Main Street, bought the property next. After much labor, Baca converted the theater into Harla May's Fat Boy Grill, which opened in September 2004. Baca covered every square inch of the old theater walls with items of memorabilia, from hubcaps to album covers. The old screen is used to show old TV shows, classic movies, and modern sporting events. Harla May's overflows with nostalgia.

Mention the names of the Central, the Oñate, the Zia, and the Zia Drive-In to any oldtimer and you will see his or her face light up with fond memories of childhood matinees, first jobs, early romance, and just plain fun. We can only hope that the Starlight Cinema 8 in Los Lunas will be a source of similarly good memories for generations to come.

Edwin Berry and Tome Hill

Richard Melzer

It is difficult to imagine *El Cerro de Tomé* (Tome Hill) without the three crosses that crown its peak. It is just as difficult to see the hill's three crosses without thinking of Edwin Berry, the man most responsible for their planning, construction, and maintenance as a place of worship for nearly half a century.

Penitente Influence

Edwin Antonio Baca was born in Adelino on May 15, 1918, the oldest of seven children born to Manuel Atocha Baca y Vigil, of Adelino, and Leocadia Sanchez y Gallegos Baca, born in Jarales and largely raised in Adelino.

Having attended what is now New Mexico Highlands University in Las Vegas, Manuel Baca was a well-educated man for his day. Employed as a teacher, he taught in several communities, including Chilili, Jarales, Casa Colorada, Adelino, and Chapelle in San Miguel County. A devout Catholic, Manuel joined the lay Brotherhood of Our Father Jesus the Nazarene, better known as the Penitentes, while he lived in San Miguel County, a stronghold for the religious group.

The Penitentes in New Mexico date back to the eighteenth century when many men felt a religious void in their communities. With few Catholic priests to serve their religious needs, these men developed their own prayers, songs, and rituals, not to replace the Catholic Church, but to supplement it. Meeting in their *moradas* (chapels), the Penitentes worshipped throughout the year, but especially during Holy Week, Good Friday, and Easter. They provided many important services to their communities, including arranging for funerals and caring for destitute widows and orphans, as instructed in the Bible.

Unfortunately, the Penitentes were most known for their unorthodox religious practices, on Good Friday in particular. Members engaged in self-flagellation and symbolic crucifixions to express their sorrow and do penance for their sins. Knowing little more about the group, outsiders often

154

jumped to conclusions that its members were fanatical extremists. As Edwin Berry later explained, it was a secret society not because it had "malicious intent," but because "in those days it's the only way they could survive."

Moving home to Adelino to teach, farm, and raise his growing family, Manuel Baca soon joined the local Penitente organization. Manuel and his fellow Penitentes climbed Tome Hill each Ash Wednesday to erect a wooden cross that remained standing throughout the Lenten season. The Penitentes stayed by the cross, praying and singing from Good Friday to Easter Sunday morning. Local residents, including young Edwin, could hear their songs from far away. At sunrise on Easter Sunday they sang their final songs and removed the cross, symbolizing Christ's resurrection.

The Penitentes remained active throughout the year. As an expression of humility and penance, they often lay face down at the doorway to Tome's Immaculate Conception Church so that churchgoers could walk over them as they left Sunday Mass. Father Jean Baptiste Ralliere, the long-time pastor of Tome, did not disturb the Penitentes, but his successors discouraged their activities and many parishioners considered them to be foolish. As Edwin Berry recalled, some uttered hateful words like "*no seas tan pendejo*" ("don't be so stupid"). Someone went so far as to set the Penitentes' cross on fire while it stood atop Tome Hill during a Lenten season in the early 1920s.

Despite these attitudes, the Penitentes survived. Edwin in particular admired their perseverance and dedication. "They were all good men and all good citizens," Edwin insisted. According to Edwin, their main purpose was "to teach others morality and patriotism."

Work and War

As Manuel and Leocadia's family grew, there were more mouths to feed and more work to do. The oldest child, Edwin worked particularly hard and finally had to drop out of school during the Great Depression of the 1930s. Edwin worked on his father's farm, helping to grow alfalfa, wheat, corn, and chile. He helped grow tomatoes, onions, garlic, and other crops in his family's garden. He also spent several summers herding his grandfather's sheep in the Manzano Mountains. At other times he worked on railroad gangs and made *terrónes*, earning $3 for every thousand bricks he cut.

The United States entered World War II in late 1941. Edwin and three of his four brothers, Ramon, Doroteo, and Gladio ("Lalo"), soon entered the military and, after basic training, were shipped out to fight overseas. A member of the 5th Army, Edwin saw action in North Africa and Italy, mostly as a military policeman, an interpreter, and, later, as a baker. Although seldom on the front lines, Edwin witnessed great loss and suffering. His 19-year-old brother Ramon was killed by German small arms fire in Belgium on March

Edwin Berry

156

2, 1945, just 20 days after he arrived in Europe and 65 days before V-E (Victory in Europe) Day. Ramon posthumously received the Bronze Star for his heroic action.

In one of his most traumatic moments of the war, Edwin recognized the body of an old friend, Foch Romero, as it was transported in a Jeep driven by Foch's captain. Taken aback, Edwin forgot to salute the captain, who chided him for his neglect of protocol. Edwin apologized, saying that he had gone to school with Foch back in New Mexico. The officer responded, "Yes, Romero was one of my best soldiers. It is a shame to lose him."

Edwin suffered from both injury and disease while overseas. He contracted malaria while in Morocco and suffered a leg injury that threatened his life in Italy. The wound was so serious that his leg became gangrenous. Allergic to sulfa drugs and penicillin, he claimed that only salt water healed his leg and saved his life.

Despite the horrors he witnessed and experienced, Edwin found new friends and much happiness in Italy. The young solider met Enrico Pastore, a local Italian who worked on the American army base to help support his large family of ten children. Pastore graciously invited Edwin and two other American soldiers home to meet his family in September 1943. Edwin never forgot the family and its kindness to strangers.

Returning Home and Making Plans

Although still ill from malaria, Edwin reentered civilian life and became more and more active in his local church. Inheriting his music skills from his mother, he directed the Immaculate Conception church choir and became especially committed to the 5-act Passion Play that the parish performed from Wednesday to Sunday each Holy Week. Edwin played many roles in the Passion Play. He even helped sew many of the costumes needed for the large performances' many characters.

Grateful that he had survived the war, but saddened by the loss of so many men of his generation, Edwin helped build a memorial to the 16 soldiers from Tome and its neighboring communities who had died in World War II. The 16 men were Ramon Baca, Antonio Blea, Romulo Chavez, Paul Guerrera, Willy Lopez, Gregorio Lucero, Leandro Lucero, Feliciano Montaño, Luis Peralta, Clovis Perea, Arturo Saiz, Santiago Saiz, Jose Torres, Pedro Torres, Florenio Trujillo, and Juan Vallejos. The impressive structure, built in 1946, still stands near the entrance to the Immaculate Conception Church. The Belen High School band played "Onward, Christian Soldiers," while World War I veterans served as honor guards at its dedication. A smaller memorial for the veterans of the Korean conflict was added in the 1950s.

But Edwin hoped to do more to express his faith and assert his gratitude for those who had died in World War II. Remembering his father and the Penitentes' crosses at Easter, he began to plan the construction of a more permanent cross to stand at the peak of Tome Hill. It would be a major project, but he never doubted that he could complete it with the same strong faith that had helped him survive so much hardship in the war.

Tome Hill was an ideal place for Edwin to build a cross. The hill had had spiritual significance for every group that had populated the area, from Native Americans to Spanish colonists, over the years. Many of the hundreds of petroglyphs that covered the hill had spiritual meaning for those who had drawn them centuries ago.

Giving his ambitious undertaking much thought, Edwin developed a plan to begin work on his hilltop cross. His hand-written, well-illustrated plan included a statement of his three main purposes: to "build a true Christian monument atop this mount;" to "bring happiness, faith, hope, and peace to all people of Good Will;" and to "commemorate our fallen heroes, the boys who gave their lives in the war." He later added a fourth goal: It would be a monument to religious freedom and tolerance, according to the *News-Bulletin* of September 17, 1948.

Well aware of the great cost and labor his project would entail, Edwin wrote in his plans that while he would "bear all costs," he would "invite all good people to help me." Each volunteer was to bring a bucket "in which to carry ten pounds of cement up the mount" after the material was prepared in a cement mixer at the foot of the hill. Anticipating the need for food to fuel his brigade of workers, Edwin noted that each volunteer should bring enough lunch "for a good day's work."

Edwin declared that he was willing to do the work singlehandedly, anticipating that it would take about three years "if people leave me alone." If a small army of 500 people assisted, he was sure that "I can do the job

158

in one day." Having worked with volunteers in the Passion Play and in the building of the war memorial in Tome, Edwin promised to "listen to sound, constructive advice, or criticism." He clearly implied that he would decide what was "sound, constructive advice," and that he would be the project's final decision maker.

Edwin made a list of the "approximate cost" of the materials he would need, including $63 for the cross and cement, $20 for the "*Tablita* of the Law," $300 for a bronze plaque "plus a few dollars more for miscellaneous items." Edwin estimated that the altar he envisioned would measure 8' x 4', while a single cross, made of wooden railroad ties covered by scrap metal, would stand 16' above the altar and face southwest in the direction of the Immaculate Conception Church.

Edwin even made plans for the final dedication of his project. He declared that when all was ready, "I will invite Cardinal Francis Spellman of New York to deliver the sermon when we bless and dedicate our monument."

Building the Crosses

Work began on March 3, 1947. As with the best of plans, Edwin's helped clarify his vision, but little more. He did recruit volunteers, but few came and most were boys like Doroteo "Joty" Baca, Clemente Romero, Ladis Romero, and Jesus Sanchez who often had more energy than muscles for the hard work of hauling materials up the steep half-mile distance to the hill's top.

Seeing Edwin shouldering much of the work for days at a time, Lalo, Edwin's younger brother and fellow veteran, pitched in whenever he could. Years later, Lalo had fond memories of slipping along and laughing with Edwin as they made countless trips up the hill hauling water, lumber, scrap metal, sand, cement, and tools by hand and, sometimes, with the help of a mule.

Others helped in other ways. A.S. Torres, who owned a general store in Adelino, offered good advice and much of the needed supplies. But most people watched from a distance and while many admired Edwin's dedication, some thought that he was foolish, much like their parent's generation had thought that Edwin's father and his fellow Penitentes had been foolish when they erected a cross and worshipped at the top of Tome Hill.

Edwin Berry's original plans for Tome Hill

160

1947   Approximate total of cost

plaques 300.00
cross and cement 63.00
$ 363.00
20.00
$ 383.00

plus a few
dollars more of
miscellaneous c

The Tablets,
this Saw — wi
cost about $20
more or less —

Altar — 8 feet x 4 feet —
Monument shall face West

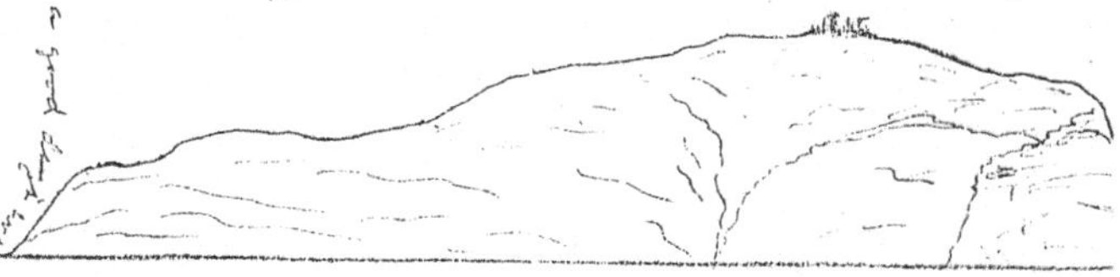

Cross 16 feet above
Altar —
Aluminum

This is my plan: — I will Build a true
Christian monument atop this mount — (Cerro de Torre)
— I will bear all cost — but I will invite
good people to help me with the work — and it will
bring happiness, faith, hope — and
— Peace — to all people of Good Will. —
An inscription will also commemorate the our fallen heroes — the
boys who gave their lives in the war —
I will invite Cardinal Francis J. Spellman of New York — to
deliver the sermon — when we bless and dedicate our monument —
If people leave me alone — it shall take me about 2
years to build it — if 500 persons will help me — I
can do the job in one year. 1947

By September 1947, Edwin had decided to alter his plans and build not one, but three crosses on the hill. The decision added much time, labor, and material to the project, but added greater spiritual meaning as well. Symbolically, Christ's cross would still face the church in the valley below, while the repentant "good" thief's cross would turn slightly toward Christ's and the unrepentant "bad" thief's cross would turn away. As Edwin later told his son Ricardo, it was as if the crosses were meant to be positioned as they were since the natural cracks in the rocks favored their placement and directions.

Edwin completed his great project in early 1948, about a year after he began. Cardinal Spellman did not attend the monument's dedication on March 25, 1948, as initially planned. In fact, given the lack of attention in the local newspaper, it must have been a humble ceremony, without fanfare or the blessing of high church officials. Now crosses stood high over the Rio Grande Valley, much as crosses have stood over other communities in New Mexico and throughout the world, including Tierra Santa in Buenos Aires, the Hill of Crosses in Lithuania, and Mount Soledad in San Diego.

Life Changes

Edwin suffered a major medical setback in 1948, shortly after his work on the crosses on Tome Hill was complete. Still suffering from malaria and perhaps exhausted by the intense labor of building the monument, Edwin fell so ill that he became, in his words, "black velvet blind." Hospitalized for a time, Edwin later said that he recovered by singing old *alabados* (hymns in praise of God, the Virgin Mary, and the saints). Regaining his strength and eyesight, he returned home to resume his activities, especially in the Passion Play, at the Immaculate Conception Church.

Learning hundreds of secular and religious songs with what some believed to be a phonographic memory, Edwin considered a career in music. He traveled to California and stayed with relatives, but could not land a job in the music business. Frustrated, Edwin went so far as to change his name from Baca to Berry in hopes of eliminating any unfair prejudice that might stand in his way. But nothing worked. Dejected, he returned to New Mexico only to find that interest in his beloved Passion Play had waned so much that it was no longer performed after 1956.

162

But Edwin filled this void in his life with new happiness. He had remained in contact with the Pastore family, traveling back to Italy in 1957 and exchanging frequent letters over the years. He became particularly fond of the Pastore's younger daughter, Assunta, and, despite their 10-year age difference, asked her to marry him. She initially refused, saying that she could not bear to live in distant New Mexico and leave her family behind in Italy.

But Edwin persisted, traveling to Italy again in 1959. With Assunta's father's support, Edwin was finally able to convince her to marry him and live in New Mexico. Edwin vowed to bring Assunta home to visit her family in Italy every ten years, at least. They were married in Assunta's home parish in Naples on June 7, 1959. Returning to the United States to make arrangements for Assunta's arrival, Edwin met his bride in New York City in September 1959. They celebrated their marriage with Edwin's family once they arrived in Adelino.

The couple had four sons in the ensuing years: Dante, born in 1961; Romano, born in 1962; Ricardo, born in 1963; and Eduardo, born in 1971. All were taught to speak fluent English, Spanish, and Italian. Assunta took them to visit her family in Italy numerous times. Meanwhile, she gradually grew to love New Mexico, often defending her adopted state as much, if not more than, its own natives.

Sharing His Culture

Although their numbers and activities had dwindled over time, Edwin joined Tome's Penitente brotherhood and studiously learned their songs, prayers, and rituals. Tome's last Penitentes, including Edwin's father, Placido Chavez, Reyes Chavez, and Guadalupe Rael, urged Edwin to do whatever he could to help preserve their culture and ways. Edwin's father, Manuel, died in 1974. Now, rather than keep the Penitente culture a secret to preserve it, Edwin felt compelled to share all he knew for the same preservation goal. He readily met with historians, anthropologists, journalists, reporters, photographers, and musicologists.

John Donald Robb, one of the most famous musicologists in New Mexico, visited Edwin's home quite often, starting in the early 1950s. The men became close friends, climbing Tome Hill together and discussing Edwin's vast knowledge of hundreds of religious and secular songs, many of which Edwin had inscribed in spiral-bound notebooks. Robb recorded at least 30 hours of Edwin's songs and included 14 of them in his book, *Hispanic Folk Songs of New Mexico*, first published in 1954. Edwin could recall each song's origin, its history, and how he came to learn it.

Edwin also became good friends with Father Thomas J. Steele, a Jesuit priest and historian who, with Fred Landavazo and Edwin's aid, studied Tome's Passion Play. Based on this valuable information, Father Steele's book, *Holy Week in Tome*, was published in 1976. The book's 17 hymns were largely based on Edwin's remarkable memory.

Reies Lopez Tijerina was Edwin's most controversial visitor in the 1960s. Lopez Tijerina led *La Alianza Federal de Mercedes*, the movement to reclaim old Spanish and Mexican land grants and to prevent the sale of those that still existed. Edwin did not agree with everything that Lopez Tijerina believed in or did, but Edwin joined *La Alianza* and the two men agreed that the Tome Land Grant should not be sold because it represented so much of Hispanic culture and heritage. After much acrimonious debate, the land grant was nevertheless sold to the Horizon Corporation in 1968.

Edwin and Lopez Tijerina remained in contact, with Edwin visiting his friend's Albuquerque office just days prior to its bombing by unknown assailants. Edwin dismissed those who considered Lopez Tijerina a malicious "loudmouth," predicting that the land grant leader might someday be respected and honored, much like Martin Luther King, Jr., was honored after years of criticism by his detractors.

In an effort to erase popular misconceptions about the Penitentes, Edwin donated blood as often as possible and insisted that modern Penitentes gave far more blood than they shed. A Good Samaritan, Edwin not only gave hitchhikers rides, but also brought them home to dinner before taking them to their destinations. As his son Dante remembers, being a Penitente was a state of mind for Edwin. "It meant loving Christ and doing good things for others."

Always opinionated, Edwin also wrote many impassioned letters to the editors of the *Albuquerque Journal*, the *Albuquerque Tribune*, and the local *News-Bulletin*. Edwin expressed his opinions on topics as varied as the Vietnam War, Richard Nixon, unsolved murders, land grants, and the plight of

164

Edwin Berry with drum

many of his fellow Hispanics. In 1977, for example, he wrote to the *Albuquerque Journal*, insisting that "the poor Indo-Hispanic is always under pressure from all sides and all elements. He is always in a rat race in the labyrinth of legal shenanigans" controlled by unscrupulous lawyers and judges.

Pilgrimages Begun

In yet another attempt to preserve his threatened culture, Edwin Berry began to climb Tome Hill each Good Friday morning. Others joined him, climbing as a group to the foot of the crosses he had erected so long ago. Some wore costumes (as in Tome's Passion Play) as they prayed at each of the 14 Stations of the Cross. A large statue of Christ was placed on the cross and then covered, symbolizing Christ's death.

In the ensuing years, the pilgrimage became a Good Friday tradition in the valley much like the pilgrimage of the faithful to the *santuario* in Chimayo in the north and the pilgrimage from Socorro to Polvadera in the south. Newspapers and television stations covered the event in Tome nearly every year. The pilgrimage was featured in the April 1994 edition of *New Mexico Magazine*.

Edwin led the procession up Tome Hill for many decades. He and Assunta baked bread for the part of the procession commemorating the Last Supper. Accompanied by increasingly large groups, Edwin climbed the hill, praying, beating a small Indian drum, and singing religious songs. Thousands still remember the short, stocky man in work trousers with his long, graying hair, and his deep, booming voice. You could not see or hear Edwin Berry without feeling his strong spiritual presence, no matter what your faith or professed religion.

Not Always Easy

Having created the crosses on Tome Hill, Edwin felt responsible for their maintenance and security. Residents along Hwy 47 often saw him driving slowly by in his green 1963 Dodge pickup, heading for the hill to add concrete steps on steep parts of the terrain, strengthening the crosses, or putting up barricades to discourage the use of 4-wheel drive trucks or ATVs. Edwin told people that he considered Tome Hill to be the perfect church: It was always open, was non-denominational, and never passed a collection plate.

Despite Edwin's efforts, vandals struck the monument and crosses at least twice. In one instance, someone tried to topple the unrepentant sinner's

166

cross. In another case, someone stole the memorial's heavy metal plaque. Edwin suspected who might have taken the plaque and let it be known that he would not press charges if the thief simply returned it. Edwin eventually received an anonymous phone call with information about where to find the stolen item. After retrieving the plaque, Edwin never returned it to the hill

Procession on El Cerro de Tomé

for fear that others might try to repeat the foolish crime. It is now located in the Tome Dominguez de Mendoza Community Center and Museum.

In a far greater tragedy, Edwin suffered a major stroke on November 11, 1996, while undergoing an angioplasty procedure to clear a blocked artery. Ironically, it was Veterans Day. Edwin struggled to regain his health, but he continued to decline, first at the VA hospital in Albuquerque, then at a nursing home, and finally at his home in Adelino, where he could be with his family and Assunta could serve him his favorite foods, at least in liquefied form. Reies Lopez Tijerina was among the many old friends who visited Edwin in those difficult times.

Over a hundred of his friends and relatives gathered at the Harvey House Museum in Belen on March 28, 1999, to give tribute to the man who had given so much of himself to his family, to his church, and to his community. The event was organized by the Valencia County Historical Society. Edwin sat among us to hear our words of admiration, but it seemed so strange that he was so silent and still. I fully expected him to jump up, beat a drum, begin to sing, and share all he knew of his beautiful culture, history, and folklore.

Edwin Berry died at the VA Hospital in Albuquerque on January 19, 2000, after suffering another major stroke the day before at his home, less than a mile from where he had been born 81 years before. Before his stroke, Edwin had told his son Ricardo that he had no regrets in life. In his words, "We have tried to be good to Tome Hill and Tome Hill has been very good to us and everybody in this valley."

While other issues like the land grant's sale, modern bridges, and widened roads have sometimes divided Tome, the hill and its crosses have served to unite the small community in ways no one could have imagined when a young veteran sat down to plan a fitting monument to his deep faith and fellow soldiers of World War II.

Health Care in the Valley: The Saga of the Belen Hospital

Richard Melzer

The residents of Belen—and all of Valencia County—have wanted a hospital for a long time.

As long ago as June 14, 1934, the *Belen News* reported that several local people had expressed the opinion that Belen "needs a hospital and needs it badly." A veterans' organization offered to raise money for a hospital with benefit dances and other fund-raising activities. One doctor even offered his services "for those not financially able to pay" their hospital bills. According to the local newspaper, all it would take to build a hospital in town was "just a little teamwork."

But a hospital for Belen would require more than teamwork in the 1930s, the decade of the country's worst depression, and in the early 1940s, when the world was consumed by World War II.

First a Clinic, Then a Hospital

Belen's first step toward creating a hospital of its own came at the end of World War II. Dr. Joseph Peterson, an osteopath, opened an osteopathic clinic in 1946. Built by Dr. Peterson's father-in-law, Sterling Barker, it was the first institution of its kind in the state. Dr. Arthur Llewellyn joined the clinic's small staff and, in so doing, began his 40-year medical career in the community.

Two years after its opening, the Belen Osteopathic Clinic was purchased by two other osteopaths, Dr. C. Richard Shelley and Dr. Leith Mitchell. Dr. Shelley would own part or all of the facility for the next decade.

Interest in a general hospital was rekindled just as Drs. Mitchell and Shelley purchased the local clinic in 1948. A Belen Community Hospital planning committee was organized and a hospital survey was conducted. The questionnaire asked residents various questions, including Is a hospital needed? Would you contribute money for the construction of a private hos-

169

pital? and Is your family covered by hospital insurance?

With favorable results from this survey, hard work by planning committee members, and required changes to upgrade the facility, Belen's clinic gained hospital status in 1950. Surgeries could now be conducted on site, and babies could now be delivered in a local hospital rather than at home or in distant Albuquerque. The long-awaited institution, located at 520 North Main Street, was called the Belen General Hospital. It had ten beds to serve a local population of 3,000 men, women, and children.

Luis Torres Arrives

Dr. Shelley added a valuable new employee to the Belen General Hospital's staff in 1950. A graduate of Albuquerque High School, Luis Torres had served in World War II from 1942 to 1946. While in the army, he was trained at the Walter Reed Medical School for Hospital Technicians. He worked at the Veterans Administration Hospital in Albuquerque for four years before being hired as a lab and x-ray technician in Belen. Assuming additional responsibilities over the years, Torres became the hospital's chief administrator in 1955.

Belen General Hospital

In 1958, Dr. Shelley announced plans to close his hospital. Eager to keep the facility open for the good of his adopted community, Torres organized a private corporation which purchased the hospital from Shelley and kept Torres on in his role as chief administrator.

Luis Torres was justifiably proud of the Belen General Hospital in the 1950s and 1960s. New equipment, a modern operating room, and a complete laboratory were added, as was a ten-bassinett nursery and ten more adult patient beds. Everything was financed by private funds.

Babies and Bills

Luis Torres was especially proud of the Belen General Hospital's delivery services where over 3,000 babies were born, including two of his own four children. In a typical family, Angie Chavez had given birth to her first two children (Roy and Sylvia) at home before 1950, but gave birth to her last two babies (Ruben and Rena) in the new hospital. Dr. Llewellyn delivered his thousandth baby, Judy Leona Espinosa, at the hospital on August 12, 1956. He sometimes delivered babies in his pajamas in nighttime emergencies.

Long before there were privacy regulations, the *News-Bulletin* reported the comings and goings of patients in a regular column called the "Hospital Record." Births were announced in a section aptly named the "Stork's Nest."

The hospital gave a certificate to the parents of the first baby born each year. Starting in 1947, local businesses contributed as many as 24 gifts for the first baby and its doting parents. In 1959, the gifts included a dozen roses for the mother from Davis Floral, a baby blanket from the Becker-Dalies Store, a baby bracelet from Trembly's Jewelry Store, a $3 gift certificate from Hub Furniture, ten free movie passes from the Oñate Theater, a $3 savings account at the First National Bank of Belen, $3 of baked goods from Gil's Bakery, a chicken dinner at the Whiteway Cafe, a one-year subscription to the *News-Bulletin*, and a jumbo hamburger, French fries, and a Coke from Circle T.

Most importantly, the community's infant mortality rate dropped with the use of modern hospital facilities and methods. Torres recalled that Belen's infant mortality rate was a dismal 27 percent in 1950, but soon dropped to one percent as more and more babies were delivered by doctors in the hos-

171

pital. Many more mothers survived childbirth as well. By 1958, the county was experiencing a baby boom, with 28.8 babies per thousand residents, a rate 17 percent higher than the U.S. as a whole.

When the "Remember in Belen When" Facebook page recently showed a photo of the hospital, 144 members of the "baby boom" generation responded, mostly noting that they had been born there in the 1950s and 1960s.

But hospital care costs money which many people could not afford to pay, at least in cash. Torres said that cash-poor farmers were often allowed to settle their bills with agricultural products like eggs and vegetables. One man paid for his child's birth by caring for the hospital's lawn until his bill was completely cleared. Another man's wife died at the hospital, despite the staff's great efforts to save her. Faced with a large bill, the widower paid a dollar each Monday, delivering the cash to Torres's office until his entire account was paid.

Luis Torres appreciated these efforts, but was said to be less interested in profits than in good care for his patients. He always told his staff that their first job was to care for their patients. "We can argue about the bill later."

Additional Improvements—and Problems

As the Belen General Hospital grew, so did its staff. Its 23-employee staff included a lab technician (Felix Sanchez from 1958 to at least 1976), three registered nurses (including Wilma Harper) and several nurses assistants, some of whom were trained in a vocational program at Belen High School.

All five of Belen's local doctors served on the hospital's staff. Legendary M.D.'s like Louis Levin, J.A. Rivas, and W. D. Radcliffe worked side-by-side with osteopathic doctors like Arthur Llewellyn, Ralph Brower, and Richard E. Brubaker. The doctors performed many surgeries, although patients requiring major surgeries were transported to Albuquerque's major hospitals, including Presbyterian, Lovelace, and St. Joseph.

Success stories with favorable outcomes abound. But there were tragic cases as well. In early 1972, for example, a student athlete from the New Mexico Boys Ranch entered the hospital for a routine tonsillectomy. Some-

172

thing went horribly wrong soon after the operation when he suffered a cardiac arrest and died. All of Belen mourned the popular young man's sudden death.

Torres and his staff worked hard to raise funds and make additional improvements over the years. For example, the hospital began blood-typing local residents so that people could learn their blood types and rare-blood type donors could be contacted in case of emergencies. By 1971, the emergency room was enlarged, a new delivery room was built, and more patient rooms were constructed.

But all these changes cost money and medical financing had begun to change dramatically with the introduction of government programs like Medicare and Medicaid in the late 1960s. Many modifications would have to be made if the hospital's patients were to qualify for these important new forms of coverage.

Belen General Hospital was able to face some of these newest challenges when it was purchased by Albuquerque's Presbyterian Hospital on September 1, 1971. With Torres retained as the hospital's chief administrator, improvements were made to meet Medicare and Medicaid's high standards.

But, as Torres had realized as early as 1965, the hospital's old building on Main Street was clearly too old and too small to meet many modern demands. Some local residents no longer trusted the outdated hospital, especially when they had easy access to larger hospitals in Albuquerque on the newly completed I-25. Personally, Torres spoke of retiring to spend more time working on his farm south of Belen, welding metal art objects (his hobby), or even running for mayor.

Planning a New Hospital

Local leaders began to seriously consider a new hospital by early 1975. While some residents and approving agencies expressed doubts about funding, future staffing, and competition with Albuquerque hospitals, many more people were optimistic about the project. By May 1975, Carter Waid's *News-Bulletin* spoke for a majority with an editorial that strongly supported the proposed hospital. By September 1975, the newspaper's headlines read, "New Belen Hospital Could Become a Reality in 1977."

But three issues had yet to be resolved. First, there was the tough issue of choosing a site. As many as five locations were offered by companies or private individuals. Four locations were west of the Rio Grande, while one was east of the river, in Rio Communities. All were offered free of charge. Strong opinions were expressed in public meetings and on the pages of the *News-Bulletin*. Some believed that the site should be as close to the center of Belen as possible. Others believed that the hospital should serve a larger region and could, therefore, be further away.

The proposed site in Rio Communities drew the most fire. Richard Aragon denounced the Horizon Community Improvement Association for lobbying for the hospital in a letter writing campaign when it was understood that no site owners would engage in lobbying efforts. Horizon also pledged as much as $250,000 for the hospital if it was built on Horizon land. "Just because they have the money," Aragon asked, "why should they have it [the hospital]? It's an unfair advantage." As Belen's city manager, Aragon was eager to "keep a business we already have in Belen."

A Belen businessman agreed with Aragon in a letter to the editor of the *News-Bulletin*. The businessman argued that the Horizon Corporation only wanted a hospital on the east side of the river so that the land development company could use it to help sell land. "The proposed hospital…will make an attractive addition to their advertising promotions."

Other site proposals could be accused of the same profit motive, with one exception. Lucille Lake, who lived on Mesa Road, offered ten acres of her family's land on Christopher Road, south of Belen High School. The land seemed ideal because it was close to I-25, meaning that patients could easily be transported to hospitals in Albuquerque in emergencies that could not otherwise be dealt with locally.

Lucille Lake said she donated the land in honor of her son, Phillip, who had fought in World War II, had returned home hoping to become a doctor, and had mentioned that he thought the ten acres would someday make an ideal location for a hospital. Phillip died in 1955. Mrs. Lake told Carter Waid that "Belen has been good to our family. I just wanted to leave something to our hometown."

The decision to accept Lucille Lake's generous offer was made in July 1975. A grateful Belen Chamber of Commerce gave her its distinguished

174

public service award that same month. Humbly receiving the award, Mrs. Lake expressed her hope that the hospital would be a blessing to everyone in Belen.

Naming and Funding the Hospital

The second main issue to be resolved had to do with the new hospital's name. Marvin Trembly, the chairman of the Belen General Hospital's board of directors, announced that the board had given the question "considerable thought" before making its decision in January 1976. The new facility would be named the Eastern Valencia Hospital. Trembly explained that the name was chosen because the hospital hoped to serve patients from throughout Eastern Valencia County, rather than Belen only, and volunteers had collected considerable funding from this larger region.

Funding represented the third major issue facing the proposed hospital. Planners estimated that half a million dollars would be needed to build a modern, 27-bed facility. A massive fund drive began on February 10, 1976, with a dinner held at the Horizon Country Club in Rio Communities. About 200 men and women attended, pledged to contribute, and listened to the keynote speaker, Tibo J. Chavez, Sr. An expert on herbal medicine, the local attorney's appropriate topic was "Folk Medicine and Modern Medicine of the Rio Abajo."

Co-chaired by Carter Waid and Herb Ellermeyer, the hospital's Development Committee made good progress from the start. The old hospital's 34 employees led the way with a pledge of $21,421, over double the staff's initial goal of $10,000. A photo of four staff members and Marvin Trembly, chairman of the hospital's board of directors, appeared on the front page of the *News-Bulletin's* February 12, 1976, edition.

Many businesses contributed generously as well. The First National Bank of Belen made the largest corporate contribution, giving $100,000. Belen Savings and Loan pledged another $30,000, while the Santa Fe Railway pledged money for new x-ray equipment. The Public Service Company pledged to match one percent of the total funds raised. Co-chairing a committee to solicit business contributions, Luz Chavez and Salo Garcia received large sums from several other companies in town.

175

Social organizations supported the new hospital, too. The Woodmen of the World contributed a flag and flag pole. The Tome-Adelino 4-H Club promised to plant plants on the new grounds. The Optimist Club in Rio Communities challenged civic leaders and political candidates to sit on a dunk board set up to raise funds in the Rio Communities shopping center.

Over 290 families and individuals gave as much as they could afford in large and small amounts. Richard Aragon, who served as the campaign's general chairman, told of a "very nice lady" who made it a habit to contribute a "varying amount" each month. Aragon urged others to follow her example.

With $335,258 contributed by April 1976, fundraisers erected a 15-ft. high "thermometer" to show the progress that had been made in relation to the $500,000 goal. Located at the intersection of Becker, Dalies, and Main streets, the thermometer's current totals were updated each Friday. Pledges eventually totaled $460,000, or 92 percent of the set goal.

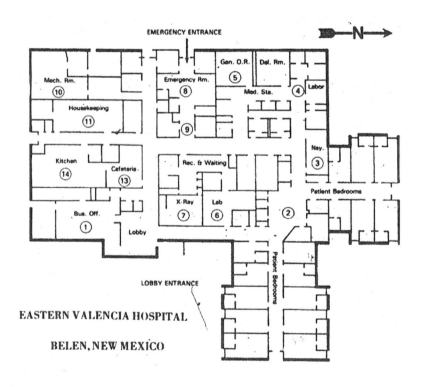

New hospital layout

Construction and Grand Opening

Although delayed by complications in the construction bidding process, groundbreaking for the new hospital occurred on Tuesday, June 28, 1977. Marvin Trembly and James W. Hall, chairman of the board of directors of Presbyterian Hospital, turned the first shovels of dirt to begin construction. Belen mayor Neal Alexander thanked the "literally hundreds of people who have made this possible."

The modern building was designed by the Flatow, Moore, Bryan and Associates architectural firm. Bradbury and Stamm of Albuquerque was the contractor. Construction took about a year. Costs equaled $2.6 million.

Local residents gathered to dedicate their new hospital on Sunday, July 30, 1978. A band played, speeches were made by Luis Torres and Marvin Trembly, and staff members led tours of the beautiful facility. One visitor spoke for many when she wrote to the *News-Bulletin* to express her "astonishment" at what she saw. Rita Karson said she felt like she was visiting "a hotel lobby rather than a hospital."

Unfortunately, Lucille Lake could not attend the grand opening because she had suffered a heart attack the previous Friday and was recovering at the Presbyterian Hospital in Albuquerque. Ironically, she probably would have been taken to the hospital on her contributed land if her attack had occurred even a few days later. She recovered well and, in fact, lived to be 101 years old.

Eastern Valencia Hospital opened for business on Tuesday, August 1, 1978. Natividad Garcia, a 75-year-old resident of South Main Street, had the distinction of being the hospital's first patient. She was admitted for treatment of a fractured hip on the hospital's first day of operation. A picture of her being wheeled in by a hospital nurse, accompanied by chief administrator Luis Torres, appeared on the *News-Bulletin's* front page.

Another patient appeared in a front page photo a few days later. Leonard Andrew Platteborze, the son of Mr. and Mrs. Leonard Platteborze of Los Lunas, became the first baby born in Eastern Valencia Hospital. Luis Torres kept his promise to provide free care for the first baby and its mother.

The new hospital remained busy from the start. On August 7, 1978, the *News-Bulletin* reported that 16 patients had been admitted from not only Belen, but also Los Lunas, Bosque Farms, Veguita, Peña Blanca, and Datil.

A month after it opened, the hospital reported that an average of thirteen patients were being treated per day. Thirteen surgeries (costing an average of $425 each) had been completed and 12 babies had followed Leonard Andrew Platteborze into the world (with bills averaging $250 each). Overall, patient costs remained the same as at the old hospital and equaled about 20 percent less than costs at Presbyterian Hospital in Albuquerque.

Many patients had been seen in the emergency room, often by a new young doctor named Roland Sanchez. Other physicians on staff included Ralph Brower, Richard Brubaker, Arthur Llewelyn, Jose Rivas, Larry Mason, and Edgar Romero. Eight registered nurses were joined by five licensed practical nurses and three nursing assistants. Led by Betty Jones, 40 volunteers helped with everything from working at the information desk and switchboard to escorting patients to and from their rooms.

Pleased Patients

Many patients expressed their satisfaction with the new hospital. Everyone liked the hospital's private and semi-private rooms, replacing the old wards and shared bathrooms. Some patients wrote letters to the editor of the *News-Bulletin*, reporting their pleasant experiences, despite initial doubts. Gloria Benavidez wrote that it was now safe to "go ahead and get sick and get admitted to our new hospital." Leslie Papier found the hospital to be "clean, well-equipped, staffed by competent, friendly people, and the food was good and plenty." Drs. Richard Brubaker, Ralph Brower, Larry Mason, and Roland Sanchez were given particularly high praise.

About the only problem that the new hospital reported was that some people kept going to the old hospital site on Main Street, despite a sign that directed them to the new facility on 609 South Christopher Road. A security guard was hired to guard the old property and direct patients to the new hospital in the evenings.

Updates

The new hospital was one of several new businesses, buildings, and institutions created in the 1970s to serve Valencia County's growing population.

178

Others included the new Catholic Church in 1973, the new country club and shopping center in Rio Communities in 1973, the Del Rio Plaza in 1975, and a new UNM satellite campus in 1978.

Unfortunately, like many small community hospitals, Belen's faced serious financial problems by the late 1980s; it lost $500,000 in 1988 alone. The Valencia Presbyterian Hospital turned to the citizens of Valencia County to seek financial assistance through the passage of a mil levy. After heated debates in the press and in public meetings, the mil levy was soundly defeated by a three-to-two margin in November 1989. Without adequate funding, the hospital closed in April 1990, 40 years after it had first opened. Dr. Rick Madden spoke for many when he told a reporter that the facility had been "a fine rural hospital." He called it a "sad day" when its doors finally shut. "We ought to play Taps."

While there was some talk about converting the hospital into a nursing home, the decision was made to convert it into a family health center operated by the Presbyterian Healthcare System. The facility was opened in mid-1990. It has served the community ably ever since.

Meanwhile, people had different ideas about what might become of the old hospital, long a landmark on South Main Street. Some thought it would make an ideal nursing home. Others thought that the city of Belen could use it for city offices. It was soon purchased by the Belen Public Schools and used as the schools' administration headquarters.

The old hospital was demolished in 2002 to make way for a new school administration building at the same location. Many mourned the old building, remembering loved ones who had been cared for there over the years. School board president Julian Luna and several members of the school administration staff were born there. Each family that had had a child born in the hospital could purchase a brick with the child's name on it to be placed in the new building's sidewalk. With mixed emotions, Luis Torres walked through the halls one last time. He concluded that he hated "to see this building go down, but we have to make room for progress."

After leaving the Eastern Valencia Hospital in 1984, Luis Torres served as the chief administrator at the Española Hospital for two years before retiring. He had been a member of the Belen city council, the Belen Rotary Club, the Belen Chamber of Commerce, the Valencia County Sheriff's Posse, and the Knights of Columbus. The Belen Chamber of Commerce chose him as its Citizen of the Year in 1976. He died on November 1, 2011, at the age of 89.

With a renewed interest in creating a hospital to meet the medical needs of their community, a large majority of the citizens of Valencia County voted in favor of financing the construction and operation of a new hospital in November 2006. Heated debates have been held to discuss the hospital's future location in Belen, Los Lunas, Rio Communities, or elsewhere. Other issues, including who would run the facility, have prevented progress on the proposed project.

As the *Belen News* suggested on June 14, 1934, all it took to build a hospital in Valencia County was "just a little teamwork." Teamwork gave the community hospital service for many of the eighty intervening years. The question is whether enough people are willing to cooperate as a team and work for a valuable common cause today.

180

Tragedy Begets Beauty:
Descansos *in Valencia County*

John Taylor

An instant of inattention or perhaps too much speed for the turn—a sudden realization that all is not right—an overcorrection—and then calamity strikes. With squealing of brakes and the awful crunch of bending metal, the car skids, tumbles, and rolls. People not wearing seat belts are thrown from the car and crushed as it rolls. When the dust finally settles, several individuals are dead or dying.

Family and friends of the victims are overwhelmed with sadness and grief. They go through the motions of living while they perform the necessary tasks—visits to the mortuary, arrangements with the church, rosaries, Masses, burials, and then just the emptiness where once a vibrant family existed. In their grief and sadness they want to memorialize their loved ones in a more public way and perhaps warn others of the dangers that lurk on the highway. From this desire, another *descanso* is born.

A Long Tradition

The Spanish word *descanso* means rest or resting place. The tradition of placing a small memorial at the place where someone breathed his last and where his or her soul left the body has its roots deep in Southwest Hispanic tradition. On long journeys such as those from Mexico to Nuevo Mexico during the Spanish and Mexican periods, the harsh conditions and lack of medical attention frequently led to deaths. There was no way to carry the bodies with the caravan, so they were simply buried along the trail with the graves marked with a cairn of stones or a simple cross.

Throughout New Mexico, it was common for pall bearers to carry the coffin of a deceased friend or relative on their shoulders from the church to the *camposanto* (cemetery). In some cases, particularly those in which the *camposanto* was some distance from the church, the men had to stop periodically to rest. These resting places were frequently marked with a simple cross.

In his book, *Descansos: An Interrupted Journey*, Rudolfo Anaya says:

The priest prayed; the wailing of the women filled the air; there was time to contemplate death. Perhaps someone would break a sprig of juniper and bury it in the ground to mark the spot, or place wild flowers in the ground. Perhaps someone would take two small branches of piñon and tie them together with a leather thong, then plant the cross in the ground. Rested, the men would shoulder the coffin again, lift the heavy load, and the procession would continue. With time, the *descansos* from the church to the cemetery would become resting spots.

In his book, *The Place Names of New Mexico*, Robert Julyan notes that the city of Las Cruces was named for a place where an Indian raid had killed three Spanish soldiers in the late seventeenth century. Their bodies had been buried at the location and crosses had been erected to note the graves. Essentially, Las Cruces began as a *descanso*!

Seal of the City of Las Cruces Chamber of Commerce

We are perhaps most familiar with the spontaneous *descansos* that appear following tragedies such as the Sandy Hook Elementary School shooting or the traffic accident in Paris that killed Princess Diana. These are typically collections of candles, photos, messages, or, when children are involved,

182

stuffed toy animals. The spontaneously donated material is eventually removed. Oftentimes, a permanent memorial is erected in the location.

Descansos *(temporary, top; permanent, bottom) at the site of the Sandy Hook School shooting*

Descansos have been memorialized in print and in film. There have been lawsuits filed and legislation passed. Some states (for example, Colorado and Florida) have banned them altogether, while others require a fee ($1,000 in California) for their erection. Some states have developed a standardized road sign to note the location of a fatal accident. Others restrict the amount of time a *descanso* or sign can be displayed (typically, no more than two years).

Here in New Mexico, arguably the U.S. birthplace of the *descanso* tradition, things are quite different. There are no state laws or Valencia County ordinances specifically governing the size, style, or placement of roadside memorials, so the standard rules about infringing on the right-of-way or providing a hazard to drivers prevail. In fact, state highway workers are directed to take extreme care when mowing or working around *descansos* along our streets and highways. If the work that is required actually necessitates the removal of the memorial, care is taken to replace it after the work is completed. A recent story in the *Albuquerque Journal* described just such an occurrence in connection with the Paseo del Norte interchange project.

Not everyone is so careful of *descansos*, however. Several years ago, a group of vandals, rumored to be members of a cult of some sort, ripped up several *descansos* along I-25 and I-40 and dumped them on Albuquerque's West Mesa. This did not deter the loved ones from replacing them as soon as the vandalism was discovered.

A survey of *descansos* in Valencia County (not including the Isleta and Laguna reservations to our north and west) yields some interesting information. The author was able to find, identify, and document more than 85 separate *descansos* representing at least 92 individuals. The "at least" caveat is needed because several of the memorials have no name and may represent an incident with more than one fatality. The earliest of the dated memorials is 1988, although many of them have no date noted. More recent dates include February 19, 2014, memorializing the murder of a 12-year-old boy by his supposed friend in Meadowlake, and February 26, 2014, memorializing a work-related fatality during a construction project on Chughole Lane in Peralta. The youngest victim recognized by a *descanso* was one-year old and the oldest was 74. Some of the descansos list only a first name, while others list full family names. Many have additional inscriptions such as, "Home boy—we miss you—see you on the other side" or "*Querida Madre y Amiga en Memoria de la Familia.*" One simply says, "*Mijo.*"

The memorials themselves range from simple crosses of wood or metal to elaborate multi-cross memorials set in concrete. Many are set up with solar-powered lights so that the memorials are visible at night. Some have been decorated with plastic flowers, rosaries, statues of the Virgin Mary, or crucifixes, while others are unadorned. Some are well-tended, with clear holiday remembrances from Christmas, Valentines, Easter, or the individual's birthday. Others are almost invisible behind trash and tumbleweeds. Many are weathered to the point that the names and dates are no longer decipherable; others are freshly painted. Many of the crosses reflect ornate metal work; others are simple painted pipes. Two are nailed to cottonwood trees.

184

Traditionally, *descansos* are set at the location where the individual breathed his or her last. In some cases, an initial memorial is set up very soon after the accident. One set of grieving parents was so intent on seeing where their son died that they got to the scene before his pool of blood had even been cleaned up. This particular family then went to the last place they had seen their son alive—his grandfather's ranch—and recovered some old, weathered wood. They used this wood to set up the first memorial. Later, they returned to install a more elaborate and permanent *descanso* at the site of the accident.

Some memorials have two or even three crosses—one small and older and the others newer and larger. Perhaps these are situations where an initial memorial has been "upgraded" more recently or a case where the first memorial was vandalized and then reinstalled with the more permanent display. Some of the memorials are set up like miniature gravesites, with a cross and a small "plot" delineated in stones or concrete arranged in front.

One of the memorials has an angel and five crosses, representing five family members from Albuquerque, ranging in age from 3 to 32. The family was traveling northbound in a van loaded with ceramic tile on I-25 just south of Belen at about 1:30 a.m. The 14-year-old driver drifted to one side of the road and attempted to reenter the highway. She overcorrected, the heavy tile load shifted, and the van slid, then rolled over. None of the passengers was wearing a seat belt and five were thrown from the car and died at the scene. The driver and one passenger escaped with minor injuries.

A memorial on the Manzano Expressway has two identical crosses that reflect an accident that claimed the lives of twin 20-year-old brothers. One brother died at the scene and the other passed away almost three months later, presumably as a result of injuries suffered in the accident.

Some of the families that erected memorials have gone to great pains to personalize the setting. A two-year old boy is remembered with stuffed animals, toy trucks, and cars. A motorcycle rider's *descanso* has a metal chopper sculpted on the top. Several have horse images carved or welded to the crosses. Hearts are a common motif—some permanent and some added, probably on Valentine's Day. Santa hats and Christmas stockings still flutter in the breeze.

There is at least one *descanso* in the county that memorializes a young

186

man murdered by one of his "friends." The boy's mother placed a small memorial (shown at the top below) in the open field at the location where his body was discovered hidden under a mattress. His family and friends have installed a larger cross (shown at the bottom) just north of the original site where they intend to have a park with recreational equipment and picnic areas dedicated to the young man's memory.

Ghost Bikes and Danger Zones

On Route 6, just southwest of the intersection of Route 47 and Main Street in Los Lunas and at the intersection of Camelot Avenue and Panada, also in Los Lunas, are two examples of a unique type of *descanso* called a white or ghost bike—a bicycle fixed in place and painted white. The ghost bike on Route 6 uses the crossbar to record the name of the 58-year-old cyclist who was killed at the site. The one on Camelot is a combination of a metal cross and the ghost bicycle. It memorializes the death of a 12-year-old boy and includes his photograph on the cross. The young man was apparently trying to catch a friend's dog when he veered into the street and was hit by a truck.

This tradition of memorializing cyclists who were killed is a relatively new one, probably starting in 2003 in St. Louis. It has spread across the country, and there are several such memorials in Albuquerque and elsewhere in the state.

If the number of *descansos* per mile is any indication, I-25 from the north Valencia County line to the south Belen exit seems to be a particularly dangerous stretch of highway. In fewer than 15 miles there are 17 *descansos* representing at least 22 individuals. In general, the long stretches of higher-speed roads (I-25, Route 47, Route 314, etc.) have the largest number of *descansos*, probably reflecting the strong influence that speed has on the incidence of fatal accidents.

So, the next time you are out and about, watch for these memorials. They represent lives cut short and families that still grieve for their loved ones. In addition, they are messages to each of us of the hazards represented by cars hurdling down the road at 60, 70, or even 80 miles an hour. Please be careful so that you do not become the subject of one of these tragic but beautiful reminders of lives lost.

WARS

The Pueblo Revolt in the Rio Abajo

John Taylor

Friar Juan Pio and his mounted escort, Pedro Hidalgo, left Santa Fe before first light. The trip to Tesuque would take two or three hours, giving Father Pio plenty of time to set up for Mass once they arrived. It was pleasant and cool as the sun peered over the Sangre de Cristo Mountains to the east. The friar thought about his homily and fingered his rosary as he trudged along the familiar trail.

As the two men crested the hill and entered the village, there was a disquieting silence. The pueblo appeared deserted—no dogs barking and not even any cattle in the nearby fields. Moving just beyond the village, near a deep ravine, the priest saw the men of the village, armed with bows, arrows, lances, and shields, and covered with war paint. Still intent on bringing the villagers to Mass, he strode toward the ravine, saying, "What is this, my children? Are you mad?"

Hidalgo recoiled in horror as the priest was pierced with several arrows by warriors leaping out of the ravine. Wheeling his horse, the terrified soldier raced back up the trail toward Santa Fe amid a flurry of arrows as the warriors turned their attention to him. It was Saturday, August 10, 1680. The Pueblo Revolt had begun.

Causes of the Revolt

The events that began on August 10 were not a spontaneous uprising. In fact, they had been decades in the making. The Pueblo Indians throughout the Spanish colony of Nuevo Mexico had chafed for 82 years under the Spanish yoke. They had watched as their children and kinfolk had suffered and died from dreadful new diseases, especially smallpox. They had endured virtual slavery in the fields and mines of the Spanish overseers. Many had

195

been beaten, tortured, or even killed outright for trying to maintain their cultural identity and ancient ways.

Perhaps worst of all were the tonsured Franciscan friars who had tried to take away their gods. The *kachina* (or *katsina*) religion had taken hold in the Puebloan culture sometime in the early 14th century, supplanting the previous religion. It had transformed religious practices and had become intimately involved with all aspects of Pueblo life. *Kachinas*, spirit beings that could intercede with the gods on behalf of the people, were invoked to bring rain, to provide a bountiful harvest, to cure disease, and to ward off attacks by nomadic raiders.

The Franciscans vehemently (and often violently) rejected the *kachinas* and all of their masks and symbols. They tried to persuade the Indians that belief in Jesus Christ would accomplish all that the *kachinas* were supposed to accomplish, and much, much more.

However, the decades of the 1660s and 1670s seemed to belie the friars' assurances. A terrible drought persisted and raids by the Apaches and Navajos, now mounted on captured Spanish horses, only intensified. Many Indians saw this not only as a demonstration of Christianity's failure, but also as a clear sign from the *kachina* spirits condemning the natives for turning away.

Some of the friars were gentle in their approach, relying more on persuasion; others were draconian and brutally punished any hint of a return to the religion practiced in the *kivas*. The Indians reacted differently—some became devout Christians; others tried to get along by going along; still others resisted passively. However, a small group of Indians had been gathering secretly in the *kivas* of the northern pueblos to discuss more direct resistance.

Leadership and Plans

Po'pay, a shaman at Ohkey Owingeh, a Tewa name meaning "Place of the Strong People" but called San Juan by the Spanish, proposed a scheme not just to resist but to overthrow the oppressors. This was not the first hint of Pueblo resistance or rebellion that the Spanish had encountered. Vicente de Zaldivar, a nephew of the first colonial governor, Juan de Oñate, had fought a bloody battle against the Acomas in 1599, less than a year after the colony was established. In the 1660s, war chief Esteban Clemente from

Abo in the Salinas district had fomented a plot to overthrow the Spanish and restore the *kachinas*. The plot was discovered. Clemente was hanged, and his body was left exposed as a reminder and threat to others who might be like-minded. And there had been other attempts to regain control and restore the religion. All had been put down with a heavy hand by the Spanish.

Po'pay also had a personal agenda to be settled. In 1675, he, along with 47 other native leaders, had been arrested and imprisoned for returning to their traditional practices. Three of the men were hanged, one committed suicide, and the rest, including Po'pay, were flogged, then released. From that point on, Po'pay's hatred passed the breaking point and he began to actively plan his revenge.

Statue of Po'pay in the National Statuary Gallery in Washington, D.C.

Po'pay and his co-conspirators had originally planned for a unified uprising to start on August 13. They had sent messengers to the other Pueblos with knotted cords—one knot to be untied each day. When the last knot was untied, the uprising would begin across the colony.

The Revolt Begins

However, the messengers were intercepted and revealed the secret plan under torture. In addition, some Indians who were sympathetic to the Spaniards reported the plot to Governor Antonio Otermin. When surprise was lost, Po'pay and the others told the people to rise against the Spanish on the 10th. The results were swift and bloody. *Hacienda* after *hacienda* was attacked and all occupants—men, women, and children—were slaughtered. Churches were burned and sacred artifacts and fixtures were smeared with excrement or otherwise desecrated. Priests were singled out for particularly horrendous torture and eventual death. Nearly 400 colonists were killed including almost 40 Catholic priests.

Survivors of the atrocities in the Rio Arriba district (north of Cochiti) fled to Santa Fe, while those in the Rio Abajo (south of Cochiti) retreated to Isleta.

Signature of Governor Antonio Otermin

Po'pay and his principal deputies were all from the northern Tewa-speaking pueblos. In addition, there were delegates from the Keres pueblos (Acoma, Zia, Cochiti, Santa Ana, and Santo Domingo) and from the Zuni and Hopi settlements further to the west. The southern pueblos from Isleta south to Socorro and Senecu were not directly involved because Po'pay worried about their loyalty. In addition, many of the once-thriving Piro-speaking communities, especially those east of the Manzanos, had been abandoned in the 1670s because of the drought and continued nomadic raids.

1680 Pueblo Revolt at Hopi

There were two main villages south of today's Albuquerque—Isleta, by far the larger of the two, on the north, and Socorro on the south. In between were a few scattered *haciendas* (self-contained family "villages") or *ranchos* (isolated ranches) which allowed residents to have a central fortified living area from which they could defend themselves from the marauding nomads. Many of the *haciendas* were built over the ruins of abandoned Indian settlements because of the availability of existing building materials. The settlers also realized that these locations had been chosen by their original occupants because they were less vulnerable to the periodic flooding of the Rio Grande.

The Sandoval y Manzanares home, near present-day Los Lunas, had been settled in the middle of the seventeenth century by Mateo Sandoval y Manzanares. The *estancia* (an estate) was located on or near an abandoned pueblo originally named Piguina-Quantengo by the first Spanish explorers. Across the river from this *hacienda* was the *estancia* established by Francisco de Valencia (near present-day Smith's Market) between 1630 and 1640. Further south, just southwest of *El Cerro de Tomé* was the *hacienda* of Tome Dominguez de Mendoza, granted to the family by the colonial governor in 1660. Continuing down the east bank of the river was the *ranchito* of Fe-

199

lipe Romero (near present-day Contreras) and the small village of La Joya, then known as Sevilleta. Further south, on the west bank was the village of Socorro, founded in the early seventeenth century as the headquarters for the Franciscan mission to the Piro Indians, and the nearby Piro pueblos of Senecu, Pilabo, and Alamillo. Both Sevilleta and Socorro were jumping-off points for the dangerous journey south across the *Jornada del Muerto* or Journey of the Dead Man.

Exile

Governor Otermin was the official in overall charge of the colony and had his headquarters in Santa Fe. His lieutenant governor, Alonso Garcia, was in charge of the Rio Abajo and had a *hacienda* and small troop garrison south of the location of modern-day Albuquerque. When Garcia was informed of the carnage to the north, he evacuated survivors in the Rio Abajo to Isleta as Otermin had previously ordered. The governor's original plan was to link up with Garcia at the pueblo, but when Garcia was informed that Otermin and everyone to the north had probably been murdered, he decided to evacuate Isleta and move south to the safety of El Paso. On or about August 17, Garcia, the refugees, and a few Christianized Isletans moved out.

Otermin and about 1,000 men, women, and children who had survived the slaughter in the northern settlements, held out in Santa Fe against an overwhelming force of Puebloans from August 15 to August 21. Finally, deciding that further resistance would only lead to disaster, Otermin and the refugees left Santa Fe on August 21, reportedly "without a crust of bread or a grain of wheat or maize."

Governor Otermin had hoped to meet Garcia at Isleta, but when the beleaguered colonists reached that pueblo, it was deserted. In fact, all of the Spanish settlements of the Rio Abajo were razed and many put to the torch. As the column of refugees had passed the *hacienda* of Captain Cristobal Anaya just north of Sandia, Otermin had noted "buildings looted, all the livestock run off, and the naked bodies of the Captain, his wife, six children, and servants scattered before the main door."

Most residents of the Rio Abajo escaped, some with but the shoes on their feet. However, some thirty-eight members of the Dominguez de Men-

200

doza family were killed. Two of Tome's daughters, Damiana and Francesca, who lived further north with their husbands and families, were among the dead.

Failing to link up with Garcia, Otermin continued south, ever conscious of the natives who shadowed the column from the nearby hilltops. Otermin finally caught up with Garcia south of Socorro in early September and the combined column reached El Paso in early October. It had been a costly retreat—of the 2,100 colonists who had escaped the Revolt, only 1,946 made it to the safety of El Paso.

Once his charges had been settled in camps along the river, Otermin was determined to return to the north and recapture his lost colony. In November 1681, he marched north with a force of 358 soldiers and Indian allies. Passing through Sevilleta (later called La Joya), they found the village deserted and a *kiva* newly constructed from the ruins of the Catholic church. Reaching Isleta, they were disappointed by the sullen reception. Father Ayeta, who had accompanied the expedition, said that the natives had "been found to be so pleased with liberty of conscience and so attached to the worship of Satan that up to the present not a sign has been visible of their ever having been Christian."

Juan Dominguez de Mendoza, the son of Tome and one of Otermin's lieutenants, continued north to Cochiti but found nothing but destruction, desecration, and continued defiance. So, on January 2, 1682, in the face of terrible cold and decreasing supplies, Otermin decided to return to El Paso, taking with him 385 Isletans. (It is not clear whether these Indians went voluntarily or as prisoners.) As the column moved south, they noted the destruction of villages and churches. Where possible, the friars that had accompanied the expedition retrieved and burned damaged or desecrated church fixtures.

In 1687, Otermin's successor, Don Pedro Reneros, attempted to reconquer the north. He captured and burned Tamaya (modern-day Santa Ana Pueblo) but was defeated in a pitched battle at Zia. Again, in 1688, Reneros's successor, Domingo Jironza Petriz de Cruzate, mounted another reconquest. This time, Zia was successfully besieged, but the Spaniards realized that their expedition did not have the wherewithal to conquer the rest of the area, so they, too, returned to El Paso.

201

In 1688, Po'pay died. His bold concept of a unified Pueblo empire with a resurgent *kachina* underpinning had proved unsuccessful. While a great organizer and charismatic individual, Po'pay had proved to be a draconian and ineffective leader. Perhaps more important, however, the restoration of the *kachinas* had not broken the drought, nor had it stopped the raiding Apaches and Navajos.

In 1690, the Viceroy appointed 49-year-old Don Diego Jose de Vargas Zapata Lujan Ponce de Leon y Contreras as Cruzate's successor. On August 21, 1692, after sorting out some administrative issues, de Vargas moved north with a force of just under 200 men. He moved quickly, passing the abandoned Piro settlements of Socorro, Senecu, Alamillo, and Sevilleta. He found the *hacienda* of Tome Dominguez de Mendoza in ruins and remarked that the "sandy roads were almost impassable." De Vargas camped near the burned out Valencia *hacienda* on September 8, the Feast of the Nativity of the Blessed Virgin Mary, and the priests heard confessions and celebrated Mass.

The *re-entrada* reached Santa Fe on September 13, 1692, and entered the city in triumph the next day. The natives, worn down by the drought, sick of Po'pay's successors, and fighting amongst themselves, did not resist. In fact, not a single drop of blood had been shed on either side. This apparent end to the violence of the previous decade was short-lived, however, and Governor de Vargas was forced to lead several punitive expeditions against the Pueblos between 1693 and 1696. However, for better or for worse, Spanish control had been reestablished in Nuevo Mexico.

The Rio Abajo, although minimally involved in direct fighting, had been severely traumatized during the Revolt. Virtually all of the Spanish infrastructure had been destroyed, and many of the native settlements had been abandoned. No one from the Dominguez de Mendoza family ever returned to their homestead and it was re-granted to a group of *genizaros* (mixed-race citizens) in 1739. Ana Sandoval y Manzanares, daughter of Mateo, petitioned the Viceroy in Mexico City for a return of her father's land. When the petition was granted in 1716, she and her family reoccupied the land, renaming it Merced de San Clemente.

The Piro Indians from Sevilleta south to Socorro had not participated in the Revolt and had fled with Otermin to avoid confrontations with

Don Diego Jose de Vargas Zapata Lujan Ponce de Leon y Contreras

Po'pay and the rebels. When they reached the El Paso area, they settled in a village that they named Socorro del Sur. With a few exceptions, they never returned to their ancestral homes. Because there was no longer a population to minister to, Socorro was not reoccupied for about a hundred years. La Joya (Sevilleta) was not resettled for 120 years for similar reasons.

Although a number of former Isletans elected to remain in the new village of Ysleta del Sur, southeast of El Paso, where they had settled after leaving the pueblo with Garcia and Otermin, Isleta was gradually reoccupied by a combination of returning refugees from Ysleta del Sur and Socorro del Sur and some individuals from Sandia. The desecrated Isleta church, formerly dedicated to San Antonio, was rebuilt in 1720 and dedicated to San Agustin.

Over time, peace and prosperity returned to the Rio Abajo. Villages were resettled or established, Indian raiding continued but slowly diminished, and the Catholic Church reestablished its influence, although in a much less draconian fashion. The only truly successful Native American revolt in North America was over—gone but not forgotten—ending another bloody chapter in the ongoing history of the European occupation of the Americas.

The U.S.-Mexican War Comes to the Rio Abajo, 1846

Richard Melzer

The time is early September 1846. The scene is a dusty road in northern Valencia County. Seven hundred American soldiers are marching down the Rio Grande Valley. Some are on foot, but most ride horseback. Although well-armed and vigilant, they are not in battle formation. All is peaceful— thus far. The residents of Valencia County have never seen such a formidable military force, no less so many Anglos at one time, in one place. Anglos had come amongst them before, but usually as merchants or travelers and always in small numbers.

Left: Kearny proclaims New Mexico a part of the U.S. from and 1846 engraving (wikipedia) Right: General Manuel Armijo

Local residents know that these American troops are part of an even larger force known as the U.S. Army of the West. Led by Brigadier General

Stephen Watts Kearny, the 1,648-man Army of the West has just recently invaded New Mexico and captured Santa Fe, without firing a shot. New Mexico's last Mexican governor, Manuel Armijo, has fled south along the same road that the Americans now travel. New Mexico has thus fallen to the United States in a major campaign of the U.S.-Mexican War of 1846 to 1848. As of August 18, 1846, the American flag now flies over the Palace of the Governors where the Spanish flag and, most recently, the Mexican flag, once flew.

Rumors of Resistance

Despite his initial bloodless conquest of New Mexico, General Kearny has heard rumors of possible resistance to American rule in the Rio Abajo. It is reported that a number of proud New Mexicans harbor resentment because Governor Armijo did nothing to resist the U.S. invasion. Leaving Santa Fe on September 2, Kearny has headed south at the head of his 700-man force to investigate and, if necessary, suppress this rumored source of trouble.

We have no way to know what the residents of Valencia County thought of General Kearny and his army of strangers as they traveled through the Rio Abajo. *Valencianos* left no diaries, journals, letters, or autobiographies to document what they saw or how they felt at this critical juncture of New Mexico history. But while we lack written documentation of how *Valencianos* viewed the large military force that suddenly appeared on their horizon in 1846, we have considerable evidence about what American soldiers saw and felt as they entered the region. At least seven American soldiers and officers kept journals or wrote memoirs about their experiences during Kearny's march of mid-1846 and during later campaigns of that same year. American writers included James Abert, Philip St. George Cooke, Frank S. Edwards, Marcellus Edwards, George Rutledge Gibson, John T. Hughes, and Frederick A. Wislizenus.

Before looking at Anglo descriptions of Valencia County and its residents during the U.S.-Mexican War, it is essential to remember that the U.S. soldiers who recorded their impressions were first and foremost ethnocentric American citizens. They interpreted what they saw and heard through their own perceptions as Anglos who had spent their entire lives in the United

206

States. As a result, their words sometimes seem crass and unkind in retrospect. But they could no more view what they saw from another point of view than if a New Mexican had been asked to describe what he saw and heard on a trip back East with other than a New Mexican perception.

Our Anglo writers were also filled with a patriotic fervor that had motivated them to volunteer for the Army and serve on foreign soil. By and large, the New Mexicans they met were viewed as Mexicans who were the enemy during the U.S.-Mexican War. Americans minced few words in criticizing their enemy and usually focusing on faults, rather than on virtues.

Anglo Observations

So what did these admittedly biased Anglo writers of 1846 say about Valencia County and its residents? Most Anglo writers first commented on the terrain they passed through, especially the "magnificent" mountains to the east and the Rio Grande to their west much of the time. The Rio Grande was admired as a steady source of water for irrigation, although it was sandy, shallow, "and nowhere navigable, not even for canoes." At least one soldier appreciated the abundant catfish and turtles he found in the river. Others noted the diversity of birds, including hawks, cranes, wild geese, ducks, swans, and even pelicans.

Most writers also reported on road conditions, an understandable concern for an army on the move. The *Camino Real,* or main north-south road connecting Santa Fe to Mexico, was little more than a wide dirt path subject to blowing sand in dry months and deep mud in wet ones. Teams of livestock often had to be doubled up to pull military supply wagons through the most difficult terrain. As many as twenty men were sometimes needed to assist the animals in moving stuck wagons. This "very severe work" made travel slow and "discouraging."

Weather conditions were also important. Summer temperatures were reportedly as high as 95 degrees in the shade. Winter months were plagued by freezing temperatures that nearly froze the Rio Grande and left such a thick frost on Army tents that officers sometimes had to delay breaking camp until mid-morning. Many soldiers suffered from colds and similarly unpleasant ailments.

American soldiers had surprisingly little to say about the physical characteristics of the communities they passed. They did nevertheless admire some villages for one reason or another. Isleta, "with its church, green fields, and cluster of cotton and orchard trees," was called "picturesque in the desert around us." Valencia was said to be a "large and handsome town" with many vineyards, melon patches, and fruit trees. Tome was described as "extensive" with good irrigation and "remarkably fine" corn and wheat fields. Predictably, Anglo soldiers admired what they had been taught to admire in their culture, especially production and efficiency.

Local Response

With dwindling livestock and supplies, American soldiers were particularly interested in trade for the food and animals they needed to continue their march. Some *Valencianos* were cooperative and helpful in this regard. Many soldiers appreciated the fruit that Isleta Indians brought to their army camps to sell. But other *Valencianos* were far less cooperative. American soldiers complained that some Hispanics charged "extravagant" prices or simply refused to do business with the foreigners, treating their offers "with contempt." Irregularly paid and low on cash, soldiers went so far as to tear off the buttons from their uniforms to use as items to trade. Army buttons were typically valued at twelve and a half cents each.

There are at least three explanations for this general unwillingness to trade food or livestock with the U.S. Army. First, many *Valencianos* refused to trade with American troops because, just as most soldiers considered New Mexicans to be their enemy, most New Mexicans considered Anglos to be theirs. According to one Anglo author, "The [local] people generally have hostile feelings [toward us] and would be able to render efficient aid to any force sent against us." For many Hispanics, trading with Americans was tantamount to aiding and abetting the enemy.

Next, and more tragically, local residents hesitated or refused to trade livestock because their farms and ranches had recently been victimized by a series of raids carried out by Navajo warriors. Several local men had been killed and thousands of sheep had been driven off in the raids. While some livestock had been returned and some Indian raiders had been killed, the problem and the

208

shortages persisted, especially as the winter of 1846 drew near.

Finally, local residents were disinclined to trade crops because they had little extra to spare. The valley was experiencing a prolonged drought and its citizens were recovering from one of its periodic smallpox epidemics, as Dr. Oswald G. Baca has documented in his extensive research.

Soldiers often mentioned that grass for grazing and wood for fuel were scarce. What Lieutenant Richard Smith Elliott said of New Mexico in general was equally true of Valencia County: "This is a barren country, affording but scanty substance for man or beast. We are consuming everything in it—flour, grain, and corn. What the inhabitants are to do next season is more than anyone…can tell. The truth is, the presence of our army here is a great curse to the people."

Faced with problems in replenishing their supplies and in replacing their livestock, U.S. officers and soldiers sometimes resorted to confiscating what they could not purchase. When unable to procure forage for his horses in Los Lunas, an American officer ordered twenty of his men to a house where "the lock was broken, and we entered, filling our sacks [with corn], and packed them down to [our] camp." Other soldiers were known to take wood for fuel and such things as cattle and grapes for food.

Such blatant thievery "created considerable excitement amongst the population" in Los Lunas and similarly afflicted communities. This was especially true because General Kearny had specifically promised that his troops would never take property in New Mexico without compensation. In Kearny's famous words, his army would take neither "a pepper [chile] nor an onion" without fair pay. The general had clearly made this vow in both Las Vegas and Santa Fe.

Understandably concerned about the fate of their community, some thirty "well-dressed, intelligent looking" citizens of Peralta had gone so far as to travel to Kearny's camp south of Albuquerque before the American troops had even entered Valencia County. John Hughes recalled that these gentlemen saluted Kearny as their new leader and assured him that "all was tranquil and orderly in the Rio Abajo, and that the people there desired to be his [friends]." The residents of Valencia County simply asked that "their lives, families, and property might be protected." Assured of such protection by General Kearny, the delegation seemed satisfied and departed.

Highly Critical

But Kearny's men did not keep their commander's promise. Instead, the Americans gave little thought to local conditions and simply criticized most local residents for their unwillingness to trade. Few kind words were used to describe even those who were ready to do business with the invading army. Priests received the brunt of such criticism. Although acknowledged as the leaders of their respective communities, priests were variously described as "low," "vulgar," "immoral," and generally "disappointing." Several were said to shamelessly "live openly with...more than one woman," having any number of children from these illicit relationships. Priests were also criticized for owning and operating stores. To make matters worse, their stores were reportedly open on Sundays and were often stocked with "native whisky." Some priests were even accused of cheating in their business dealings.

Frank Edwards thus recalled a "jolly looking old monk" at Isleta who did not run a store, but was happy to accommodate Edwards's search for corn to feed his troops. The priest first shared a "bottle of good wine," perhaps to impair the American's business sense and powers of observation. Finishing their wine, the priest took Edwards to a storage room filled with Indian corn. After agreeing to purchase much of the corn, Edwards discovered that "the padre was trying to cheat me, both in measure and count." Not to be outdone, the officer "accidentally" put out the light in the room and ordered his men to fill up their sacks and even their pockets with the precious corn. When light was restored, "the old fellow...noticed the fullness of the sacks," but decided not to argue since he had simply been outdone at his own game.

Edwards encountered a more cooperative priest who ran a store in Sabinal. The priest willingly sold Edwards two black sheep for a dollar each. The officer was nevertheless amused as the priest in his "long silk gown" tried to round up the purchased sheep. One animal bolted between the cleric's legs, "knocking him down, while the other jumped over his head." Not discouraged, the priest finally corralled the sheep and delivered the pair to Edwards. Edwards declared that he had never seen "a more ridiculous figure" than the priest with his two errant black sheep.

If American soldiers thought so little of Hispanic priests, what was their opinion of the other local citizens they encountered? As young soldiers, sev-

210

eral Anglo authors offered observations regarding the female population they met in their travels through Valencia County. Their opinions of the fairer sex were decidedly mixed. On the one hand, Frank Edwards admired the "pretty appearance" of the dresses worn by the Indian women he met at Isleta. In sharp contrast, a group of soldiers found the women at a *fandango* (dance) in Peralta to be so "homely" that "we cared not to dance" with them. The soldiers expressed their regret that the "young and fair *señoritas*" of Peralta chose to stay home, "being shy of men who wore sidearms." Marcellus Edwards was far more complimentary in his evaluation of a wealthy young woman of the Chavez family. The American officer went so far as to describe this woman as "the most beautiful creature on earth" with charms "beyond description." Philip St. George Cooke had similar praise for a thirteen-year-old girl with alluringly "large liquid eyes" and her equally "fine looking" mother. Cooke noted that the thirteen-year-old he so admired was already married, "as usual here, at that age."

Most members of Valencia County's upper class received more favorable comments than the average citizens of the valley. The Chavez, Otero, and Luna families were especially praised for having sent some of their sons to schools in the United States and for having large, productive estates. Frederick A. Wislizenus even compared the Chavez hacienda in Los Pinos (now Bosque Farms), with its cornfields, "extensive" pasture, efficient irrigation system, and "comfortable" big house, to a prosperous Southern plantation. Ironically, this same *hacienda* would be occupied by Confederate troops during the Civil War Battle of Peralta some sixteen years later.

Arrival in Tome

The Army of the West ended its journey in Tome. Located in the heart of the Rio Abajo, Tome had been where Manuel Armijo had previously launched a successful military movement in 1837. General Kearny may have suspected that the village was the hotbed of the rumored trouble that had drawn him on this hundred mile march down the valley.

Kearny and his troops arrived just in time for Tome's annual fiesta. As the U.S. soldiers approached the village and encamped on its outskirts, they noted that making war seemed the last thing on the villagers' minds. Ac-

211

Kearny encampment near Tome Hill, 1846

cording to one estimate, as many as three thousand *Valencianos*, or more than three times the village's normal population, had come from far and near to participate in the colorful events scheduled on the Tome plaza.

On the evening of September 7, 1846, those in attendance on the plaza were treated to four hours of an "incessant discharge" of "very tolerable" fireworks. According to John Hughes, the sky was filled with "long, zigzag streams of fire" as high as 300 feet in the air. The fireworks either exploded in the night sky or "among the throng..., producing great confusion and tremendous shouts of laughter."

In another part of the plaza, hundreds of spectators had gathered to watch a play performed by several male and female actors on a raised stage. Not knowing the Spanish language, most soldiers were "unable to appreciate the merits of the play." It was a wonder how anyone heard the actors' lines with the accompanying "music of instruments,... discharge of rockets,... shouts of the throng," and almost constant ringing of church bells. Lieutenant Hughes disapprovingly noted that "the women were promiscuously intermingled with the men." As always, American values crept into the soldiers' observations about all they saw and heard.

"Induced by curiosity," many American soldiers left their camp and went to the plaza without securing the permission of their commanding officer. As many as eighty of the wandering men were rounded up by the unpopular officer. As punishment, they were assigned to extra guard duty the following day. After considering various forms of retaliation against their superior, several soldiers settled on a plan. The disgruntled troops tossed the entrails of a butchered sheep into the officer's tent, causing the man's bedding to be "blooded and his tent filled with the stench." As volunteer soldiers from a democratic nation, these American soldiers perceived limits to the powers of the officers who had been sent to lead them. Forcing them to stay in camp a short distance from the scene of welcome reverie was clearly asking too much, in the soldiers' opinions.

The celebration in Tome continued the next day with additional excitement and events. A religious ceremony was held at the Catholic Church, followed by a colorful procession around the plaza. The church was filled to overflowing, with six priests, led by Tome's parish priest, Father Jose de Jesus Cabeza de Baca, in attendance. Perhaps to show his respect for the Catholic faith and to demonstrate the peaceful purpose of his mission, General Kearny and members of his staff participated in the ceremonies, holding "long, greasy tallow candles." The priests walked in the procession under a "gilded canopy" with men firing rifles and altar boys "throwing rockets…, making the heavens dizzy with streams of fire." Singing and instrumental music were "strangely commingled" with the sounds of guns, church bells, and fireworks.

Later events included dancing, horse racing, and gambling, of which the locals were "remarkably fond." Although the soldiers had had difficulty in trading for food, "great quantities" of fruit, sweet cakes, "and various other commodities" were sold by "market women" gathered on the plaza. Booths for the sale of liquor were also found in adjoining rooms at *fandangos*. Brandy and wine were served by the glass, but no mention was made of excessive drinking or of public intoxication. The day ended without fights or violent incidents of any kind.

Leaving Tome

Satisfied that all was calm, General Kearny and his troops left Tome shortly thereafter. Kearny thus ended his twelve-day campaign in the Rio

Abajo. Happily, his army had not encountered violent resistance even in Tome, where they could have easily been ambushed by rebels disguised as merrymakers and armed with rifles and explosives.

Valencianos chose to resist the U.S. Army in more subtle ways, especially through their general refusal to trade with and supply the invaders. Under Indian attack and in the throes of a prolonged drought, it would have been impossible to do more at that time. Ironically, the only real trouble the U.S. army faced was not with the local population, but within its own ranks, between those who went AWOL and a strict officer who had had them punished for attending the fiesta in Tome.

Kearny thus returned to Santa Fe, convinced that "the people of New Mexico are perfectly quiet and can easily be kept so." He was, in fact, so confident that all was now quiet that on September 25 he marched on to California with the majority of his army, leaving a small force to occupy New Mexico.

But Kearny was wrong about conditions in New Mexico. While things were overtly calm in the Rio Abajo, they were far from tranquil in the north. By the end of 1846 a plot against the Americans had been revealed and, in early 1847, a terribly violent revolt had taken place in Taos and Mora in the Rio Arriba. As many as twenty-three Americans and American sympathizers were killed. Charles Bent, whom Kearny had appointed as New Mexico's first civilian governor under U.S. rule, was among the first killed in the uprising in Taos. It would take a large military campaign and much bloodshed before this rebellion was finally suppressed and before true peace was restored to New Mexico.

Meanwhile, life went on in the Rio Abajo, much as it had for decades before. It would take time and many powerful forces, including the Civil War and the coming of the railroad, to truly alter Valencia County, for better or worse, under American rule.

214

The Battle of Peralta
in the Civil War, 1862

John Taylor

It certainly wasn't the way he had hoped to awaken on this cool April morning. The governor's *hacienda* had provided all the comforts for him and his men—warm beds, a well-stocked wine cellar, and a bevy of young *señoritas* who were anxious to *fandango* with the young Confederate soldiers. But the unmistakable sound of exploding cannon balls, shouted orders, and scattered musket fire, plus the pounding on his door and the shouts of "Colonel Green! Colonel Green!" suggested that his rest was over.

Colonel Tom Green, 5th Texas Mounted Volunteers

215

Cursing under his breath and trying to ignore the pounding in his head (wine hangovers always seemed to hit him hard), Tom Green, colonel of the 5th Texas Mounted Volunteers, sat up and pulled on his boots. Another day on the battlefield loomed.

A Confederate Army led by Brigadier General Henry Hopkins Sibley had come into the Territory of New Mexico in the winter of 1862. After setbacks at Valverde and Glorieta Pass, they began a retreat from Santa Fe on April 7, 1862. The vanguard reached Albuquerque at about 10:00 p.m. on the evening of April 8.

On April 13th, half of the army under command of Brigadier General Sibley crossed the river by ferry and moved south along the west bank. The other half, about 900 men under the command of Colonel Green, proceeded south along the east bank, stopping at the home of Confederate sympathizer Judge Spruce Baird on what is now South Second Street in Albuquerque.

Confederates crossing the Rio Grande at Albuquerque on April 13, 1862

Arrival at Los Pinos

Early on the morning of April 14, the eastern contingent straggled south along the trail through Isleta Pueblo. The going was tough—wagons and cannons mired down in the heavy sand and some were abandoned. Teamsters swore and horses struggled through the deep sand. Eventually, Green and his men reached Los Pinos (now Bosque Farms), home of the territorial governor, Henry Connelly and his family. The governor had moved his fam-

216

ily out of the *hacienda* in late February when the Confederates moved north after the Battle of Valverde. He had relocated the territorial government to Las Vegas and had left his foreman and workers in charge of the estate in Los Pinos.

The Connelly's Los Pinos *hacienda* (located just west of State Route 47 near today's Los Pinos Drive in Bosque Farms) must have seemed like a palace to the tired Confederate soldiers. Not only was it a beautiful home, but it had a well-stocked wine cellar, warm beds, and fodder for the livestock. In addition, the girls from Los Pinos and nearby Peralta were excited to see a new crop of young men. Soon a fiddler and guitarist appeared and a *fandango* was in full swing. There was dancing, and drinking, and singing, and more drinking into the wee hours of the morning—a welcome respite from days of marching and fighting and meager rations.

Canby and the Union Army

Unbeknownst to the partying Texans, Colonel Edward Canby, commander of the Military District of New Mexico, and about 2,500 men were quietly moving south along the foothills of the Manzano mountains. Canby had moved north from Fort Craig, Colonel Gabriel Paul had moved south from Fort Union, and the two armies linked up in Tijeras Canyon. On April 8, their combined force had conducted a brief artillery bombardment of the small Confederate force defending the supply depot in Albuquerque. Canby and Paul withdrew on the night of the 8th without attempting to capture the depot.

Canby's overall strategy was to harass the Confederates and drive them out of the Territory, not to bring on another pitched battle or to capture their army. This strategy was not popular with the men who thought that Canby was either excessively cautious, cowardly, or overly friendly with Sibley, the Confederate general who had previously served with Canby before the war began. Many Union officers and men were itching to exact revenge on the Confederates after Union defeats at Valverde and Glorieta Pass. However, Canby realized that he did not have the supplies or forces to feed, hospitalize, and imprison a large number of soldiers. He just wanted them gone!

When Canby and Paul reached Hell Canyon, a large arroyo running

Colonel Edward R. S. Canby

west from the Manzanos to the Rio Grande near Isleta, they turned west and set up camp at Chical, a small settlement near Isleta and just below the escarpment that dropped from the mesa into the valley. It was early in the morning of April 15 and the strains of music could be heard from the party underway at the Los Pinos *hacienda*. The Union soldiers settled down for a few hours of rest. The stage was set for the last confrontation between the Union and Confederate forces in New Mexico.

The Fight

At about 6:00 a.m., Canby roused his troops and deployed his artillery. They began shelling the Connelly *hacienda*. Also at daybreak, Gabriel Paul led a troop of cavalry against the abandoned wagons on the trail north of the village. Although the pickets guarding the wagons put up a spirited defense, several were killed and the rest retreated to the safety of the *hacienda*. Colo-

218

Colonel Gabriel Paul after promotion to brigadier general

nel Paul then deployed his troops in the woods to the north of the *hacienda*.

Colonel Green wasted no time deploying his defense. Major Charles Pyron was sent to defend the left flank, the area between the *hacienda* and the river. Captain Bethel Coopwood and his men took positions in the center and right, crouching behind the adobe walls and fences to the front and east of the *hacienda*. Green sent his own regiment, the 5th Texas Mounted Volunteers, to the far right, beyond Coopwood's men. Finally, he placed lookouts, including Sergeant Ben Davidson, in the cupola of San Jose de Los Pinos, the Catholic mission chapel on the Connelly property.

What Davidson saw from his elevated position was disconcerting. He estimated that a Federal force of about 3,000 men was massing across their front from the riverbank on the west to the escarpment on the east. Green, with only 900 men, was equally concerned. He told his men to dig in and prepare for the inevitable assault.

Canby decided to probe the Rebel defensive position, first moving to-

Major Charles Pyron, Captain Bethel Coopwood, and Sergeant Ben Davidson

ward Pyron's position. When that move was reported to Green by the outlooks in the church steeple, he quickly deployed Lieutenant Phil Fulcrod and a battery of six six-pounder howitzers to the left to bolster the defense. The Union forces backed off, and Canby shifted his attention to Coopwood and the Confederate right. Once again, Green was apprised of the movement by Davidson and the others in the church cupola, so he directed Fulcrod to move his cannons to the right flank. He also had about 200 of his troopers move to a forward position about 200 yards in front of the *hacienda* to make it more difficult for the Union forces to maneuver.

It did not take long for the Federal forces to realize that their movements were being monitored from the elevated position in the church steeple, so they redirected some of their cannon fire toward the church. Their third shot hit the steeple and Davidson and his colleagues quickly skedaddled down the ladder.

While Canby was maneuvering north of the *hacienda*, his chief reconnaissance officer, Captain Paddy Graydon, led a contingent from his Spy Company around the east end of the Confederate lines. Following what is now Peralta Boulevard, they galloped into the center of the sleepy village about a mile south of Los Pinos. There were no rebel troops to be found, so Graydon and his men fired a few desultory shots into the air and against

220

the adobe walls and rode back to the Union lines. This was, in fact, the only "Peralta" part of the Battle of Peralta!

San José de Los Pinos *(top–photograph from 1867; bottom—drawing by Alfred Peticolas)*

Despite all of the probing and maneuvering, Canby had no real intention of a massed frontal assault. For one thing, the estate with its adobe walls, fences, and *acequias* provided a strong defensive position. For the same reasons, the terrain would slow and disrupt any frontal assault, resulting in many more Union casualties. In addition, Canby's overall strategy to rid the territory of the rebel army without another pitched battle argued against an attack on the *hacienda*.

On the west side of the river, General Sibley and the remainder of the Rebel army heard the sounds of battle. The general quickly sent elements of the 4th and 7th Texas Mounted Volunteers across the river at the Peralta ford. The fresh troops who reinforced both the right and left flanks of the Confederate deployment were a welcome sight to the beleaguered men of Green's battalion. Sometime later, Sibley himself, along with his chief of artillery, Major Trevanion Teel, attempted to cross the river with more artillery to reinforce Green's position. However, by this time, the Federal troops were well-positioned near the ford and Sibley and Teel were prevented from crossing.

Brigadier General Henry Sibley (left) and Major Trevanion Teel (right)

The battle, now confined to a spirited artillery exchange, continued until early afternoon. The Federal artillery managed to drive the lookouts from the church steeple, disrupt the Texan hospital, and scatter the rebel beef herd, but no major casualties resulted. The Confederate artillery, along with the terrain impediments and lack of enthusiasm for a frontal assault, kept the Union troops at bay.

It is said that Father Jean Baptiste Ralliere and some of his parishioners from the Church of the Immaculate Conception in Tome climbed to the top of *El Cerro de Tomé* and watched the battle unfold while singing hymns and praying. Given the distance (about ten miles) between Tome and Los Pinos, it is doubtful that they saw anything but smoke and dust, but the sounds of battle could very well have been audible at their location.

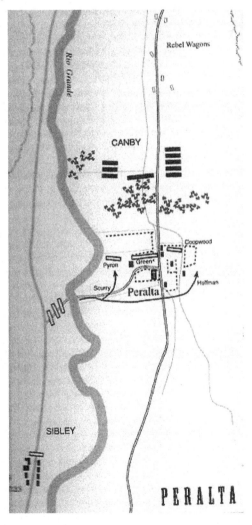

Overview map of the Peralta skirmish

In the middle of the afternoon, a typical New Mexico spring windstorm blew in, raising dust and restricting visibility. This effectively ended the artillery duel. Green took advantage of the poor visibility to break off a fight he knew he could not win and to evacuate his troops across the river using the Peralta ford. By 4:00 a.m. on April 16, the wet, tired, discouraged Rebel army was reunited in Los Lunas.

From Los Lunas, the rebels moved south along the west bank of the river with the Union army shadowing them down the east bank. When they reached the junction of the Rio Puerco and the Rio Grande on the night of the sixteenth, the leadership decided to veer west between the Magdalena Mountains and the San Mateos to avoid having to pass Fort Craig where they might have to fight another substantial Union army. This 5-day, 80-mile trek through the nearly waterless sands of the New Mexico desert further weakened the Rebel army. By the time they reached Mesilla near the end of April, they were no longer an effective fighting force. The 1,800-man Sibley Brigade stayed in Mesilla and El Paso for several weeks, regaining their strength, but they had no more taste for New Mexico. Sibley and some of his men left for Texas on June 1. By early July all of the Confederate forces had left the Territory.

The Battle of Peralta was not much of a battle and was not fought in Peralta. It would probably be more appropriate to refer to this small engagement as the Skirmish at Los Pinos. However, historians have named it and so it shall remain. No traces remain of the Connelly *hacienda* or the old church where cannonballs rained down on April 15, 1862. All that marks the site of this last Civil War engagement in New Mexico is an official state historical marker, located across from the Catholic Church in "downtown" Peralta.

How a Coin Toss Determined Captain Maximiliano Luna's Heroic Role in the Spanish-American War, 1898

Richard Melzer

The United States declared war on Spain on April 25, 1898. Traveling by horseback and by train, hundreds of New Mexicans rushed to the colors from towns across the territory. One of the first to volunteer was 27-year-old Maximiliano Luna of Los Lunas. Luna's telegram to Governor Miguel Otero arrived on the chief executive's desk within hours of the nation's declaration of war.

Why He Fought

Young Maximiliano volunteered to serve his country for several reasons. First, he volunteered in response to the sinking of the *USS Maine* in Havana Harbor on February 15, 1898; 266 American sailors had perished in that tragedy. Stunned Americans assumed (incorrectly) that the Spanish were responsible for this outrage. Like thousands of Americans, Luna charged off to war with the war cry, "Remember the *Maine*," on his lips.

Luna also volunteered to fight because he sympathized with the Cuban people. For months, Americans had read gruesome newspaper reports regarding the ill-treatment of Cuban men, women, and children at the hands of their Spanish oppressors. Responding to these reports, Luna's wife, Berenice, had been chosen to lead a Cuban Relief Committee in early 1898. Maximiliano was at her side as she worked to collect money and supplies to assist the victims of the alleged atrocities.

A poem written when the war began expressed the feelings of Luna and hundreds of his fellow volunteers:

We are coming, Governor Otero.
Yes, we're coming on the run.
For we've heard the proclamation,
That hostilities have begun

225

Between this glorious nation
And the monarchy of Spain.
On behalf of bleeding Cuba,
And our battleship, the *Maine*,
Likewise our noble seamen,
Who perished in the waves....

So we're coming, Governor Otero,
10,000 men, or more....
To help chastise a nation
Of murderers serene,
Of women and of children,
Though governed by a queen....

And then there was the issue of Hispanic loyalty to the United States. Many outside of New Mexico had the audacity to question if Hispanic New Mexicans would remain loyal to the U.S. if the country went to war with Spain, the territory's mother country from 1598 to 1821. Luna and other Hispanic men volunteered to fight in order to prove their strong allegiance to the U.S. over Spain in the current conflict.

Hispanics were especially eager to prove their loyalty to the U.S. because their territorial leaders had fruitlessly striven to achieve statehood for nearly half a century. Many factors had caused the delay, including questions about Hispanic language, education, and fitness for American citizenship. The Spanish-American War might serve to dispel these lingering doubts once and for all. Clearing this major hurdle, New Mexicans might finally finish their marathon race for statehood.

An Ideal Hispanic Soldier

Maximiliano Luna was the ideal person to help change the minds of those who doubted New Mexico's loyalty and worthiness for statehood. Born into the rich and powerful Luna family of Los Lunas in 1870, he had been educated by Jesuits in Las Vegas, New Mexico, and at Georgetown University in Washington, D.C. Bilingual, he felt comfortable in both the traditional Hispanic culture of Los Lunas and the so-called modern Anglo culture of Washington, D.C.

Captain Maximiliano Luna

Following his father, Tranquilino, and his Uncle Solomon's example, Luna had entered politics at an early age. By the time of the Spanish-American War, he had served as Valencia County's probate judge and sheriff. In 1896, he had been elected to represent Valencia County in the territorial House of Representatives, winning his election by a vote of 1,610 to 202. Few doubted that he was destined for even higher offices, especially if New Mexico became a state in the Union.

Luna was also an ideal candidate to serve in the U.S. Army because he had previous military experience. Despite his mother's opposition to his ever joining the military, he had helped to organize a territorial militia company in Valencia County and had been chosen to be its captain in 1893. In marrying Berenice Keyes in mid-1895, he was marrying into an old military family dating back to the American Revolution. His new father-in-law had fought in the Civil War and in the Indian wars thereafter. Colonel Alexander Keyes no doubt encouraged Maximiliano to volunteer, just as he encouraged his own sons to do the same in the course of their lifetimes.

Governor Miguel Otero was pleased that Maximiliano Luna was willing to volunteer. Knowing Luna for years, the governor realized that he could trust his friend with the responsibility of proving Hispanic New Mexico's loyalty to the U.S. Otero did not hesitate to appoint Luna as the only Hispanic captain in an elite new cavalry regiment reporting for duty in the Spanish-American War.

Roosevelt's Rough Riders

Theodore Roosevelt had helped organize the First Volunteer Cavalry Regiment at the outbreak of the war. The 1,250-man unit was recruited from across the country to include both upper class graduates of Ivy League schools back East and rugged cowhands of the far Southwest. Known for their riding skills and determination to fight, the press soon dubbed the unique regiment the "Rough Riders."

Few people realize that 352 Rough Riders, or roughly 30 percent of the total, came from New Mexico. Gathering in Santa Fe, the New Mexicans were divided into four companies, led by captains Frederick Muller of Troop E, Maximiliano Luna of Troop F, W.H.H. Llewellyn of Troop G, and George Curry of Troop H.

New Mexico's officers and their men were sworn into the army in a formal ceremony held outside the Palace of the Governors on May 6, 1898. Five thousand Santa Fe residents witnessed the ceremony and enthusiastically accompanied the soldiers to an awaiting train at the depot.

The New Mexico volunteers proceeded to San Antonio, Texas, where they met their fellow Rough Riders and trained for three grueling weeks. From there, they traveled by train to Tampa, Florida, where they joined thousands of other soldiers from across the country. The New Mexicans anx-

228

iously awaited orders to depart for Cuba and see combat on the front. They could only prove their loyalty and bravery in combat conditions, not on the back lines far from the action they craved.

Disappointing News

But just as Maximiliano Luna and his fellow New Mexicans prepared to board transport ships and face their baptism by fire in combat, the army dropped some bombshell news. So many men, horses and supplies had arrived in Tampa that there was only enough room on the military's transport ships to carry 16,085 soldiers and a few horses.

The army also realized that its invasion might well proceed through dense Cuban jungles where cavalry units would be useless. The already-famous Rough Riders would have to serve as a dismounted cavalry with several troops left behind to care for their horses until more ships could be spared for transport duty.

Of the New Mexico troops, either Luna's Troop F or George Curry's Troop H would remain in Tampa and be denied the golden opportunity to fight overseas in their territory and the country's behalf. The Rough Riders' command had thirty-six hours to decide who would go and who would stay behind.

Luna strenuously objected to being left in Tampa, reminding his superiors of the importance of his going to Cuba not only for himself, but also to represent the Hispanic population of New Mexico. According to one Rough Rider, Luna "put up a talk to the regimental and squadron commanders out in the open under a large pine tree." He fervently insisted that he needed to proceed to Cuba because "if he were not given this opportunity it would be a direct slap to the integrity of all loyal Spanish-Americans."

The Fateful Coin Toss

Witnessing the discussion, a fellow officer suggested that the only fair way to determine who should go and who should stay behind would be to flip a coin. As true gentlemen, Luna and Curry agreed.

Coin tosses have been used to decide critical issues many times in history. Coins were sometimes tossed prior to duels to determine which dueler would fight with the sun to his back, a major advantage. In 1903, the Wright brothers tossed a coin to see which sibling would attempt to fly the first flight in history. And in 1898, a coin would determine if Maximiliano Luna would fight in Cuba or sit in Tampa for most, if not all of the war.

A coin was selected and tossed in the air. All held their collective breaths. In one of the most dramatic moments in New Mexico history, Luna won. It was said that Luna rushed to embark on a waiting transport for fear that his victory might be reversed or the limited space on the waiting transport ships might be gone before he arrived with his men. Luna and his Troop F scrambled on board Transport No. 8, known as the *Yucatan*, ready to ship out to Cuba. It took six additional days before the *Yucatan* finally received orders to sail.

On June 22, the Rough Riders landed outside Santiago, Cuba. With Captain Luna and his men in the thick of the fighting, they helped win the three major land battles of the ensuing six-week campaign. In fact, in the famous Battle of San Juan Hill, the men of Luna's Troop F contended that they had reached the top of San Juan Hill before any other American unit. In the most famous photo of the war Lieutenant Colonel Theodore Roosevelt was shown surrounded by Rough Riders, including Max Luna, atop San Juan Hill.

Legacy

Captain Luna faced many challenges in Cuba, including a report that he had been killed in combat, but he returned safely to Los Lunas on September 2, 1898. His adventures in Cuba and in the Philippine Islands the following year made for other great stories, contributing to both Luna's legacy and New Mexico's struggle to prove its loyalty and worthiness for statehood.

Luna was always grateful and his commanders were always glad that he had had the opportunity to fight in Cuba. Shortly after the war, Teddy Roosevelt wrote *The Rough Riders*, his famous account of his regiment's short but glorious service in the conflict. According to Roosevelt, Luna's relatives

had been on the banks of the Rio Grande [since] before my forefathers came to the mouth of the Hudson...and [Luna] made the

230

plea that it was his right to go as a representative of his race, for he was the only man of pure Spanish blood who bore a commission in the army, and he demanded the privilege of proving that his people were precisely as loyal Americans as any others. I was glad it was decided to take him.

New Mexico finally won its statehood on January 6, 1912. Unfortunately, Max Luna had drowned in the Philippines 13 years earlier and could not witness that landmark event. But hopefully others, including Governor Otero, Luna's widow, Berenice, and his fellow Rough Riders from New Mexico, remembered Captain Luna as they celebrated an accomplishment he fought to help win—thanks largely to a simple coin toss made and won in Tampa.

Colonel Theodore Roosevelt, Captain Maximiliano Luna, and their fellow Rough Riders atop San Juan Hill, Cuba, 1898

World War I and the Gallup Deportation to Belen, 1917

Richard Melzer

The citizens of Belen contributed to the American victory in World War I in many ways. Young men volunteered for service in the U.S. Army, Navy, or Marines. Residents bought Victory Bonds to help finance the war. Many gave to the Red Cross. Families conserved food by growing Victory Gardens and observing Meatless Mondays and Wheatless Wednesdays. Hundreds attended patriotic rallies to hear stirring speeches and inspiring music. Everyone read the *Belen News* for the latest reports from the front.

Belen's war role was much like many other communities across the United States. But one event made Belen far different than most any town in the war years, 1917 to 1918. For two days in mid-1917 Belen "hosted" 34 suspected radicals deported from the coal fields near Gallup in McKinley County.

Coal Strike in Gallup

Belen's deportation incident began in early July 1917 when over 300 coal miners went out on strike against Gallup's main coal mining producers: the Diamond Coal Company, the Gallup Southwestern Coal Company, and the Gallup American Coal Company. Led by the United Mine Workers (UMW), the miners struck to gain union recognition and better pay, among other demands. Tensions ran high, especially because coal was an essential source of energy for railroads, factories, and homes during the war. According to the *Gallup Herald*, "Every pound of coal that comes out of the mines is as good in this war as a pound of gunpowder ... Every hour put in mining by a miner is as valuable ... as the same time put in the trenches."

Meanwhile, Governor Washington E. Lindsey had appointed a Council of Defense in each of New Mexico's 28 counties. The councils were created to help coordinate local war activities. Influenced by coal company officials, the McKinley County council charged that the Gallup coal miners' strike had been taken over by radicals who planned to call a general strike and instigate violence in Gallup. In fact, some believed that the strike was an act of treason, financed by German money. The council ordered McKinley County Sheriff R.L. Roberts to roundup the alleged agitators and deport them by train on July 31, 1917.

Gallup's alleged agitators were accused of being members of the most extreme labor organization of the early twentieth century. Founded in 1905, the Industrial Workers of the World (IWW) was an anarchist union reportedly bent on overthrowing capitalism with labor strikes and widespread bloodshed. An outspoken IWW leader, Frank Little, was about to be lynched by an angry mob in Butte, Montana, just as the events in Gallup began to unfold.

The idea of deporting suspected members of the IWW (also known as Wobblies) was not new. Seventeen days before the roundup in Gallup, over a thousand men had been rounded up and forced to leave the copper mining town of Bisbee, Arizona. Loaded onto freight cars with little food or water, the accused IWW members had been transported to New Mexico where they were dumped in the summer heat at an isolated location north of Columbus. The U.S. Army had assisted the Bisbee refugees by building a small camp and by providing food and essential supplies. Although few of the deported men were members of the IWW, the events in Bisbee undoubtedly inspired the Council of Defense's copycat acts in Gallup.

Roundup in Gallup

Sheriff Roberts carried out his orders to round up Gallup's suspected IWW leaders on the warm summer evening of Tuesday, July 31. Two armed deputies found most of the unwary suspects in their homes and boarding houses scattered throughout town. None of the accused resisted and no violence ensued. In all, 34 men were gathered up and confined in a makeshift "bullpen" between the McKinley County courthouse and jail. A 35th suspect could not be found, so the deputies arrested his pregnant wife and questioned her at her home and at the courthouse where she was kept in jail for several hours. Threatened with a gun and given the "third degree," the woman could not—or would not—reveal her husband's whereabouts.

Despite her ordeal, she delivered a healthy baby in early August.

At 7:00 p.m., the "Gallup 34" were marched in pairs from the courthouse to the local train depot between two rows of deputies armed with pistols and Winchester rifles. Fearing that the accused radicals might attempt to escape, Horace Moses, the Gallup American Coal Company's superintendent, followed in a truck driven by a company employee. With a machine gun mounted on the truck, Moses kept his weapon trained on the small procession moving slowly before him. Efforts had been made to clear the route of onlookers. But several hundred local residents had heard of the roundup and had gathered at the depot to witness the unusual event.

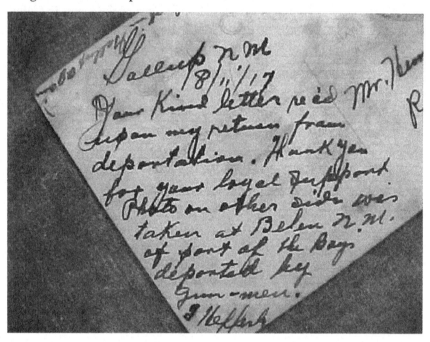

An August 1917 postcard from Frank Hefferly, thanking a supporter in the aftermath of the Gallup deportation. Hefferly may well have sent many such postcards, featuring a picture of the deportees, to thank those who helped the group in their hour of need.

The Santa Fe Railway's eastbound Train No. 22 (ironically named *The Missionary*) was scheduled to leave Gallup at 7:15 that evening. Just prior to its departure railroad workers attached an extra passenger car. The deportees were hustled on board the extra car and informed that they would be killed if they attempted to return to Gallup. Ten armed guards, five at each end of the car, accompanied the exiles. Moments later the train lurched into motion and slowly gained speed toward an unknown destination. Critics say that deputies in Gallup celebrated the men's departure with shouts, gunshots, and, later, drunken disorder. The exiles on board No. 22 claimed that their ten guards got "gloriously drunk," causing the men to fear for their lives.

Who Were the Deportees?

Who were the 34 men who were considered so dangerous that they were forced into exile to preserve law and order in their community? We know the names and backgrounds of only a few in the diverse group. The best known deportee was W.H. Hanns, the editor of the *Gallup Independent* and the *Carbon City News*, two of Gallup's three newspapers. Hardly a member of the IWW, Hanns had nevertheless supported the miners' strike in his newspapers' columns and editorials. He was, in fact, accused of planning the feared general strike at meetings held in his newspapers' offices. Deporting him was seen as an effective way to defuse the strike and lessen his considerable influence.

Frank Hefferly was only slightly less well known. Hefferly was a UMW organizer who had been instrumental in starting and leading the miners' strike. Clearly not a member of the IWW, Hefferly was nevertheless on the companies' short list of hated enemies, as were two other UMW leaders, including Hefferly's brother.

A fifth member of the exiled group was an Austrian immigrant. Frank Bauer's offense had had nothing to do with the strike. Bauer was included because he had failed to register for the draft and was probably suspected of allegiance to the enemy. (Austria-Hungary was a German ally in World War I.) There was nothing in Bauer's background to suggest that he was ever a member of the IWW. A sixth innocuous suspect was arrested in a mine. In fact, Steve Katzman was digging coal when he was apprehended and escorted to the bullpen beside the local courthouse.

An unnamed farmer was probably the least dangerous of the Gallup 34. Living six miles south of Gallup, the farmer had come to town simply to buy a new pump. Surprised to see armed men in town, the farmer had inquired about what was happening. His seemingly innocent question somehow aroused suspicion; he was apprehended and placed with the other detained men. His team of horses remained tied behind the hardware store where he had gone to purchase his pump.

The remaining deportees included Italians, Frenchmen, Mexicans, Austrians, and American-born residents, at least one of whom was a native of Gallup. Most were reputable, law-abiding citizens who had lived in Gallup for 20 years or more. Established members of their community, many had families and several had savings accounts in Gallup's banks. One was a railroad worker and another worked at the power plant in town.

A third of the deported men were members of the UMW, but none were card-carrying members of the IWW. As members of the UMW they were as opposed to the IWW and its radical goals as were the coal companies themselves. The IWW only hurt the UMW's mainstream goals and reputation, especially when labor's opponents lumped all labor unions together to adversely influence public opinion.

Some of the Gallup deportees in Belen

Exiled in Belen

Santa Fe's Train No. 22 pulled into Belen in the dark of night at 11:45 p.m. A railroad night watchman stood guard over the men as they debarked from the train and took shelter under a large tree near the depot. With pleasant summer weather, the night passed peacefully and without incident. On the following morning, residents of Belen awoke to the unexpected sight of nearly three dozen strangers left destitute near First Street.

News of the Gallup men's arrival in Belen drew national attention. Most newspapers assumed that the coal companies' accusations were true and that Gallup had freed itself of IWW troublemakers who had schemed to disrupt desperately needed wartime coal production. No one questioned how Gallup's purge of so-called troublemakers could be considered beneficial for tranquil Belen where the men had been unceremoniously dumped.

The "Gallup 34" were not destitute for long. Word of their plight reached national UMW leaders, who wired money to them via Western Union. Using these funds, the men ate at nearby restaurants, including, we presume, the Harvey House, located just north of the deportees' encampment on First Street. The refugees also looked for a building they might rent for shelter for however long they might stay in Belen. Required to remain in a group, renting separate rooms at local establishments like the Belen Hotel was not an option.

A photo of the men showed that they were "not an unhappy bunch," in the words of one observer. They were nonetheless outraged by the treatment they had received in Gallup. In a telegram to Governor Lindsey they declared:

> We most emphatically protest against the brutal, outrageous action of Sheriff Roberts and imported professional gunmen who in contravention of law and constitution deported us from Gallup, July 31. We were always peaceful and law abiding and no cause for such outrage...

Concern for the Exiles

Rumors regarding the deportees' destiny spread in Gallup, Belen, and beyond. Albuquerque prepared in case the deportees were sent there next. Expecting the worse, Albuquerque's police chief announced, "We've got work for them," by which he implied work on a chain gang. Some observers believed that the deportees' destination would be in far-off Raton. Some exiles spoke of going to Trinidad, Colorado, once they heard rumors that they would be arrested if they stayed in New Mexico. A few left, but most remained in Belen.

A second night passed with no decision made or announced. John Becker, Jr., the son of Belen's richest merchant, visited the refugees' make-shift encampment and telegraphed an Albuquerque newspaper that he was unable to find a single member of the IWW in the bunch.

Fellow UMW members did not sit by idly. In Gallup many signed a petition vehemently protesting the deportation. In the small mining camp in Madrid, New Mexico, 400 UMW members employed by the Albuquerque and Cerrillos Coal Company voted to walk off work in a sympathy strike until the Gallup men were returned home safely.

Some newspapers began to change their earlier favorable views of the deportation. Many now called it an outrage and a clear abuse of American freedom. The *Santa Fe New Mexican*, for example, criticized the "hasty" deportation as "high-handed" behavior that could easily become an abusive "popular fad" if allowed to occur in one town after another.

Governor Lindsey also shared a concern for the refugees, less because he was sympathetic to labor unions than because he believed that the McKinley County Council of Defense had overstepped its authority in ordering the roundup and deportation of American citizens. A prudent leader, Lindsey had dispatched special investigator Fred Fornoff to report on the situation in Gallup. Soon after his arrival in McKinley County, Fornoff, a former commander of the New Mexico Mounted Police, told Lindsey that the refugees' return to Gallup was essential if the coal strike was to be resolved anytime soon. New Mexico's status as an important source of wartime fuel would be in jeopardy if the conflict in Gallup lingered much longer.

Given Fornoff's findings and suggestions, Lindsey ordered that the "Gallup 34" be returned home immediately. The governor instructed Sheriff Roberts to protect the men's rights and, rather than taking matters into his own hands, request assistance from the state if any future concern for safety arose. Most importantly, Lindsey ordered a halt to all future deportations either into New Mexico or within the state. The chief executive knew that if he stood by and did nothing, overzealous leaders in towns like Gallup could use deportations as a convenient means to rid themselves of "undesirables" of all kinds in the name of patriotic duty during the war. Who knew where such vigilante activity might lead just when all attention was needed to defeat Germany and its allies in Europe? How could the United States and its allies claim to fight a war to make the world safe for freedom and democracy if American rights could not be protected at home?

End of a Crisis

And so the Gallup men returned home on August 4, having caused no disturbance during their 3-day stay in Belen. Traveling westward on the Santa Fe's Train No. 21, a quiet crowd of at least 200 local residents greeted the first group of ten exiles.

Conditions in Gallup soon changed for the best. Perhaps pressured by Governor Lindsey or embarrassed by the course of events that culminated in Belen, mining company officials agreed to negotiate with UMW leaders and the coal strike soon ended.

Five weeks after the deportation fiasco many people of Gallup were said to "rejoice" by staging the first "Labor March" in town history. Hundreds of UMW members marched from their union headquarters to the local opera house to celebrate both their colleagues' return and the end of the recent labor dispute. In a colorful display, a miner carried a large American flag to lead the procession, while other marchers carried small flags donated by a local store owner. Half of the miners wore carbon-lighted lamps on their hats, creating "one of the prettiest sights that anyone could wish to see," according to the *Carbon City News*. A labor rally at the opera house followed. A capacity crowd heard speeches by UMW leaders and by Gallup's mayor (and future governor of New Mexico) Arthur Hannett. Editor W.H. Hanns and his wife were guests of honor. American flags, red, white, and blue bunting, and a photo of President Woodrow Wilson decorated the hall, to confirm the miners' strong loyalty to the United States and its conflict overseas.

Not everyone in Gallup was pleased with the outcome of the deportation crisis. The *Gallup Herald* observed that there were still plenty of IWW members in Gallup "hanging around the street corners and the saloons at all times of the day," refusing to work, and discouraging others to work in the best interest of their community and the nation as a whole. In the *Herald's* conservative opinion, IWW really stood for "I Won't Work." Others continued to believe that a sinister alliance existed between the IWW and the enemy, led by Germany's Kaiser Wilhelm II. To these cynics, IWW also stood for "I Work for Wilhelm." If there was a lesson to be learned about assuming the identity and beliefs of strangers, some in Gallup had yet to grasp it during World War I.

Back in Belen, conditions soon returned to normal, or as normal as things could be in wartime. It does not seem that the bustling little town was intentionally targeted as the destination for the "Gallup 34." The unassuming railroad community had simply been a convenient destination decided on in the midst of a hurried series of events. The out-of-towners from Gallup had been a curiosity—and a small source of "tourist" dollars—while they remained in the Hub City. As in everything they did in this era, the citizens of Belen dealt with a potentially volatile situation as admirably as possible while helping their nation finally win the Great War by November 1918.

Joe Tondre, Jr.'s Letters Home
in World War II

Richard Melzer

We can support our wartime troops in many ways. One of the best ways is by writing letters to soldiers stationed far from the comfort and serenity of home. Letters are helpful because they remind soldiers, sailors, and Marines that they have not been forgotten and that their service is truly appreciated by those they left behind. Letters also confirm that the troops are loved and respected, necessary emotions all humans need to sustain them through difficult times.

As important as it is for troops to receive letters, it is equally important for them to send them. Writing letters can be cathartic in times of high stress and anxiety. Letters home allow writers to express their true thoughts and emotions at a time when emotions are often suppressed for the greater good. The value of letters to and from our troops has been vital in all wars in all periods of history. This was as true in World War II as it is today.

Off to War

Joe Tondre, Jr., was a nineteen-year-old college student at the University of New Mexico when he was drafted into the U.S. Army on July 9, 1943. Joe was the oldest child and only son of Ruth and Joe Tondre, Sr. Joe Tondre, Sr., was a powerful, highly respected Republican leader in New Mexico, but Joe, Jr., never thought of attempting to shun his duty based on his father's influence in Valencia County or state politics. Joe was eager to serve his country and to see parts of the world he might not otherwise hope to experience in his lifetime. Joe left Los Lunas to help fight the war in mid-1943.

Joe's first letter home, dated July 24, 1943, told of his six-and-a-half hour railroad trip from the depot in Belen to Fort Bliss, Texas, where he was to report for duty and experience his first taste of military life. Once at Fort Bliss, Joe and his fellow rookie soldiers awoke to their first reveille at 5:15 a.m. On that first day they received multiple shots, took a battery of tests, did

241

K.P. for thirteen hours, and, if that wasn't enough, got their first GI haircuts. "You should see me," wrote Joe. "My hair stands straight up." Joe reported that the weather in El Paso was hot, "especially with these fatigue clothes on." All civilian clothes had been shipped home in boxes.

Joe Tondre, Jr.—then and now

After a short period at Fort Bliss, Joe was transferred to Fort Knox, Kentucky, for boot camp. All went well until the young soldier suffered a freak accident on a tank and was confined to an army hospital for the next three months. Once released, Joe finished his basic training, served at several camps in the United States, enjoyed a brief furlough in Los Lunas, and was finally shipped overseas from Brooklyn, New York, on January 18, 1945. Through all of his travels, Joe learned more and matured faster than he had ever done in his young life. He certainly saw many new sights.

In San Antonio, Texas, Joe visited the Alamo. At Brownsville, local citizens rang bells and blew horns with the news on June 6, 1944, that D-Day had begun in Europe. Joe crossed the impressively large Mississippi River and saw his first riverboats on the Ohio River—quite a contrast to the Rio Grande. In New York City Joe fit in visits to as many sites as possible, from Times Square to the Radio City Music Hall, but ran out of time and vowed to return to see much more someday. The Statue of Liberty and the vast New York skyline were the last scenes of the United States Joe recalled as his ship left port for Europe.

Cultural Encounters

Joe Tondre also matured by meeting new people from other states and cultures. A Chinese solider in Joe's barracks couldn't speak a word of English and, to Joe's surprise, sang in his native language while sleeping. Joe was particularly close to the men in his eight-man squad. These men remained together from May 1944, when the squad was formed at Camp Bowie, Texas, until the last days of the war. The squad's leader was from Illinois, while other squad members came from Missouri, North Carolina, New York, and Virginia. Joe's closest friend was a man named Holmes ("we called each other by our last names only") from Chicago.

Other soldiers were less appreciated, to say the least. During his earliest days in the Army at Fort Bliss, Joe and his fellow New Mexicans shared their barracks with "guys from New York—Brooklyn—ugh, what an accent [who were always] bragging about their tall buildings, population, etc., [while we were] bragging about the Indians, mountains, etc." of New Mexico. Another soldier came from Texas and "he really lets us all know he is from there. He's always bragging about the horses and cows on his ranch…. He's getting on everybody's nerves."

With so many men from so many places, friction was bound to occur, especially when some fellows were thoughtlessly disrespectful and prejudiced. The rancher from Texas, for example, "made some crack about 'niggers,' and I thought it would lead to a race riot" when five black soldiers heard his remarks. The blacks "wanted to punch the Texan in the nose, but they were just talking."

Joe met many talented men in his travels, but he also encountered many individuals who were uneducated and even ignorant about the war itself. One soldier in Joe's barracks was a coal miner from Pennsylvania. "He doesn't know how to read or write very well and never reads a newspaper." In mid-1944, when several soldiers talked about the fall of Rome to the Allies, this fellow asked where Rome was. "We told him Rome was in Italy, and he didn't even know that we were fighting in Italy. He said, 'I never pay any attention to the war'—and I guess he doesn't."

Once in Europe, Joe met many civilians as his squad passed through the countryside. In France, he was struck by the number of kids "everywhere you go." They all pled for "cigarettes for papa or for gum or candy." A French family invited Joe and one of his army buddies into their home where they served cognac. "Of course, they didn't know any English, but we had our French Language Guidebook" and conversed the best we could.

Hardships

Like all soldiers, Joe faced his share of hardships. Army meals were seldom good, and Joe frequently asked his family to send food by mail. He "craved a good Mexican dinner" and envied a trip to a Belen bakery that his mother described in one of her letters. "That sounds so good…. You don't realize how good stuff like that is until you can't get it anymore." In Europe, Joe mostly ate C rations, placing these Army-issued cans of food on the engine of his truck in an admirable attempt to heat them as the vehicle drove along. Writing from France in early 1945, Joe declared that "It seems that all we talk about is food."

Joe was also hungry for news about practically everything, including his family, his friends, his town, his state, the country, politics, and the progress of the war. Like millions of soldiers overseas, Joe told his family that he was often "not able to keep up with the war news as well as you are" back home. Joe especially enjoyed his father's informative letters and his kid sister Ruthie's homemade newspaper, the *Weekly Trumpet*. The *Weekly Trumpet* made Joe laugh so hard that "the boys thought I was going crazy when I read it," so "I had to read it to them."

Joe was grateful for copies of the *Albuquerque Journal*, although he confessed that he used old copies to start campfires. The *New Mexico Magazine* helped Joe stay grounded in his roots. And he appreciated books about his home state, including Eugene Manlove Rhodes's *Proud Sheriff*, which he read in a day.

Joe was glad to describe New Mexico and its many cultures to those who inquired about his background. A Catholic chaplain, for example, wanted to know about the Hispanic people, how they lived, and if they were "good about going to church." When a fellow soldier jokingly asked if Joe was a sheriff "out West," Joe said no, but proudly announced that his dad was. The soldier "was so surprised and asked me about everything."

Of course Joe experienced his greatest hardships and dangers on the battlefields of Europe. Once within artillery range of the enemy, Joe and his squad members "willingly dug our fox holes." They survived German shelling, although "quite a few shells fell in our vicinity" and one hit so close to Joe's position that his friends were amazed that he had not been killed, or at least badly injured. Joe wrote home, "It's very nerve wracking. You can hear the shell screaming—it gets louder and louder, closer and closer—of course, you think it's coming right at you—then you hear it burst—a loud explosion—then you hear the flying shrapnel. Then you look out of your hole to see where it hit. Then you wait until you hear another shell coming and dive into your fox hole again."

German planes also strafed Joe's unit, causing his group to screech their truck to a stop and dive into a ditch along the road for safety. The going was especially difficult when it rained or when they had to move forward in the "pitch dark." Bathing in a small stream was "pretty cold," but a welcome relief after days of stress, dirt, and fatigue.

Into Germany

Joe and his company crossed into Germany on March 26, 1945. Staying in a recently captured small town, the Americans "had to search every house for weapons, explosives, military equipment, etc." Fortunately, little was found, although the GIs had to repeat this dangerous procedure at each town they entered along the way.

As the war drew to a close in the spring of 1945, Joe experienced some of the most stirring moments of his war years—and life. With their country's fate sealed, over two thousand German soldiers surrendered to Joe's unit en masse. The prisoners were searched, with their weapons and anything of value confiscated. As a result, some Americans acquired "full German uniforms as well as pistols, cameras, watches," and similarly coveted "souvenirs." Officers granted permission for GIs to take any confiscated weapons they wanted. Joe was not present at the time, but a buddy saved him a new German pistol in a leather holster, an item that Joe still owns and treasures today.

Once the Germans were searched, "We put them in the [local] church, which was quite large, and had a guard on each of the three entrances—only three guards!" Joe was one of the three guards that first night and was kept busy doing nothing more dangerous than allowing prisoners to go to the church's only bathroom, one at a time. The Germans had clearly lost their will to fight. In Joe's words, "Villages were full of white flags as we entered them, and German soldiers carried white handkerchiefs overhead as we approached."

Joe and his unit were glad to receive thousands of German prisoners, but they were overjoyed to help liberate several hundred American POWs near Burghausen, just over the German border in Austria. Joe reported that these Americans "hadn't been treated too badly," having regularly received Red Cross packages and having gotten healthy exercise while working on German farms during their six to seven months in custody. Despite such relatively good treatment, Joe described the GIs as "the happiest bunch of guys I've ever seen" when they were finally liberated.

Joe and every American soldier shared a similar joy when the war in Europe finally ended on V-E Day, May 8, 1945. At last Joe could "write just about anything" because all censorship of letters had been lifted. He now proudly announced to his family that his "Black Cat" 13th Armored Division was part of General George Patton's famous Third Army.

By late May, Joe and other men in his company received permission to enjoy some much deserved rest and relaxation at a large lake near the Alps. The men swam, rowed boats, admired their beautiful surroundings, and began the long process of healing from the horrors of war. Days later Joe was one of only three men from his company given passes to spend time at a rest camp in France. The camp boasted a swimming pool, a beer garden, a PX, a chapel, and a large dining room where over a hundred French girls served good meals. The facilities also included a movie theater where Joe, a big movie fan, watched "Thunderhead," one of more than a hundred movies he watched in the course of his service in the Army. Joe described his brief trip to France as "like returning to civilization again."

In perhaps the most unusual experience in his six-month tour of duty in Europe, Joe and hundreds of his fellow American GIs were given the opportunity to visit Adolf Hitler's former mountain retreat near Berchtesgaden. Ascending a "steep grade," Joe found the "once beautiful, modern place" to be "practically in ruins from bombings." Joe walked through the many buildings and went so far as to send a "diagram of the place" home to Los Lunas.

Going Home

Joe and his company began their triumphant journey home by traveling from Germany to France in freight cars. Although the men had to place boards across open freight car doors "so that no one would fall out" and "cut a hole in the floor for the toilet," they had plenty of food and water and were happy to be heading west toward home. And the French people were glad to see them. In Joe's words, "as we went through the French towns, the people "were really celebrating. They gave us wine and food, and the women wanted to kiss every one of us."

Once in Le Havre, Joe and his company embarked on the *USS General William Black*, sailing on Friday, July 13, 1945. They arrived at Newport News, Virginia, about a week later. Joe received four medals for his six-month duty overseas and received an honorable discharge from the Army on February 14, 1946. He was home in Los Lunas within days.

Joe Tondre and millions of soldiers like him survived World War II because they were brave, loyal American citizens who were determined to serve their country and "get the job done" in defeating our country's enemies. Their burden was made more bearable in several ways, not the least of which was the exchange of letters with loved ones back home. Powerful guns, individual skills, and military strategies were essential to winning the war as a whole. But letters to and from the front lines helped sustain soldiers with a lifeline and a will to fight one day at a time until their work was done and they could return home, victorious and safe at last.

First Lieutenant Frank Holcomb in Korea, the Forgotten War

Jim Boeck

Historians often call the Korean Conflict America's forgotten war. Today's generation generally thinks of this war as ancient history and probably not relevant to the current world. But to older residents of Valencia County, the Korean War brings memories of a time when many of our finest youths lost their lives in a faraway land in a cause to stop the spread of communism. Lieutenant Francis A. Holcomb was one such youth.

The son of Mr. and Mrs. Earl A. Holcomb, Frank (as everyone called him) was born in Texas. In 1941, his family moved to Belen where he attended Belen High School. Once World War II began, Frank joined the Marine Corps. Participating in many invasions of the Pacific Theater, Frank faced great dangers in some of the most famous battles of the war. He earned several battle ribbons, including a Purple Heart after suffering severe back injuries in combat.

Learning to Fly

After World War II, Frank returned to Belen where he was employed as a fireman by the Santa Fe Railway. Seeking to further his education, he also attended the University of New Mexico for two years. In addition, his brother Earl convinced Frank to take up flying. A veteran pilot of World War II, Earl was convinced that Frank was a natural-born flyer. The future would prove him right. Under Earl's watchful eye, Frank learned to fly at the Mesa Airport west of Belen.

Frank loved soaring like a great eagle in the skies over Belen, and he longed to become a pilot in the Army Air Corps. He joined the corps in 1948, was commissioned at Williams Air Field in Arizona, and received his flight training at Goodfellow Air Field Base in Texas.

Frank had at least two close calls during his days at Goodfellow. While completing practice rolls at 8,000-feet altitude, the rudder on his plane suddenly jammed. Only his iron-nerved composure enabled him to pull his plane out of trouble. Avoiding almost certain death, Frank somehow landed his plane safely.

On another occasion in 1949, Frank was seriously injured in a car accident near Lowell, Massachusetts. The young New Mexican suffered a concussion and broken arm, but survived this second brush with death and continued his pilot training. In July 1949, Frank received his Air Force commission at Williams Air Force Base. He received additional jet training at Otis Air Base in Korea.

By 1950, the "winds of war" were blowing over the Korean Peninsula. North Korea had been making threatening moves along the 38th parallel that separated the divided nation. Clashes along the border occurred almost daily by the spring of 1950. Then, without warning, the North Korean army invaded the south on June 25, 1950.

Frank was dispatched to help fight back the communist incursion. He was assigned to the 18th Fighter Bomb Wing as a P-51 fighter pilot. The P-51, or Mustang, was considered one of the finest fighter aircraft of its time. Christened in World War II, it was used primarily for air-to-ground attacks during the Korean War.

Meanwhile, Frank had found time to fall in love with a young lady from Lowell, Massachusetts. They married in 1950. A child was on the way when Frank was sent to Korea.

Back home in New Mexico, the *News-Bulletin* featured far different issues regarding Lieutenant Holcomb. The newspaper's March 20, 1951, headline read, "Belen Pilot Missing in Korea." A War Department telegram to Frank's parents conveyed the same message. Brigadier General John H. McCormick's telegram stated, "It is with deep regret that I officially inform you that your son, First Lieutenant Francis Holcomb, has been missing since March 18, 1951 (Korean time), as a result of participating in a Korean operation. A letter containing further details will be forwarded to you at the earliest possible date. Please accept my sincere sympathy during this time of anxiety."

Ironically, the Holcombs had recently received an upbeat letter from their pilot son. He mentioned that he had completed more than 60 combat missions and had been awarded the Distinguished Flying Cross with two

250

clusters. His unit had also been presented with a presidential citation. Frank added that he would be finishing his tour of duty in two months. Serving on the southern tip of Korea, he wrote that the food was good and "we have it rather nice." In addition, Frank claimed that he was working with "the finest bunch of fellows I ever saw." Only the thought of his first child, a son, made him happier about his life and his future.

But now Frank was missing in action. Having just given birth, his wife's condition was considered to be so delicate that she wasn't told of her husband's indefinite status. The Holcombs, on the other hand, were conditioned by the anxiety caused by war. Their three sons had all seen action and had all been wounded in combat during World War II. One son had been missing for a considerable length of time in the Italian campaign. Only the brave work of Italian insurgents led to his rescue and eventual return to American lines. A strong, resolute woman, Mrs. Holcomb remembered that "Frank has always said he is ready to go when his time comes and has urged us not to worry too much if he is killed in the war. Our boys always felt that if they had to die for their country, it couldn't be helped."

Newspaper article on the loss of Frank Holcomb in Korea

A Second Telegram

A second, sadder telegram from General McCormick arrived at the Holcombs' house on March 20. The telegram read, "It is with deep regret that I officially inform you that your son, First Lieutenant Francis A. Holcomb, who was previously reported missing, was killed on March 18, 1951, as the result of participation in the Korean operation. A letter containing further details will be forwarded to you at the earliest possible date. Please accept my sincere sympathy in this hour of grief." Frank Holcomb was buried in Korea beside his buddies who had also fallen in the cause of freedom.

The promised letter with further details arrived in April 1951. Captain David K. Skelton, wing chaplain of Frank's fighter bomber wing, stated that it was the general consensus that Frank died in a gallant effort to save the lives of his fellow airmen. Captain Skelton went on to say,

> Lieutenant Holcomb was liked by everyone who knew him and he was held in especially high regard by those with whom he worked closely. It is the belief of those who witnessed the tragic mishap that he made a decision to try to fly around after his aircraft developed engine trouble rather than jeopardize the lives of his fellow airmen who might be injured by the explosives which he had aboard if he crash landed on the runway. A ground loop on the runway might have averted fatality for him, but it would probably have meant certain death for many who were working in the area. Because we who knew him intimately know that he was always interested in others, we are prone to accept this belief as the facts in his case. I was at the scene of the accident within minutes after the crash, and I can assure you that all was done that could have been done to save his life.

Frank Holcomb was only 26 when he was killed on his 67th mission over Korea. His body was later shipped back to the United States, and was reburied in the National Cemetery in Santa Fe, as his wife had hoped it might be. Without fanfare or parades, final services were held in Santa Fe on October 25, 1951, for the brave pilot from Belen who now surely soars in the great beyond among the angels.

The Last Full Measure of Devotion: Daniel Fernandez in Vietnam

Jim Boeck

It was February 18, 1966, in Cu Chi, Hua Nghia Province, South Vietnam. Specialist 4 Daniel Fernandez of Los Lunas and his seven-man fire team lay quietly, waiting to ambush "Charlie," Viet Cong Communist troops, on the 25th Division, 2nd Brigade's perimeter. Suddenly, the Viet Cong opened fire with automatic weapons. Fernandez's squad heard the heavy thud sound of a .50-caliber machine gun, the steady staccato blasts of a light machine gun fire, and the blasts of grenades near the Americans' position. Fernandez and his buddies hugged the ground.

This was Daniel Fernandez's second tour of duty in the Republic of Vietnam. During his first tour in 'Nam, Daniel had been wounded as he helped three of his fellow soldiers under heavy enemy fire. Despite incredible danger, he had also volunteered to ride "shotgun" on Army helicopters. His job was to protect the slow-flying aircraft by firing potent .50-caliber machine guns at the enemy from the helicopter's side doors. For his wounds and heroism in action, Fernandez had received the Purple Heart in March 1965 and the Air Medal in May of that same year.

After a short recovery period in Hawaii, Fernandez was given a one-month leave to spend with his family in Los Lunas. Following his time at home in June 1965, he and his unit were stationed at Schofield Barracks, Hawaii. There he indulged in his favorite pastime, horseback riding.

But in January 1966, Fernandez's unit received orders to leave its lush paradise in Hawaii for duty back in the steaming jungles of Vietnam. As Daniel shipped out, he no doubt thought of his future plans once his latest "hitch" in the Army was up in November. He hoped to get a job as a heavy equipment operator and live in a place where he could enjoy his horses.

Withering Enemy Fire

Thoughts of his family, his girl in New Mexico, and his future must have

253

weighed heavily on his mind on February 18, 1966, as he crawled under withering enemy fire. The Viet Cong's first burst of fire hit one of Daniel's fellow squad members. Daniel and three of his buddies tried to reach their fallen friend under a hail of lead and exploding grenades. An Army sergeant was also hit in the knee by deadly .50-caliber machine gun fire.

Fernandez was trying to rally his squad when a grenade suddenly hit his foot. Spotting the live grenade, Daniel hollered, "Move out, you people," and, without hesitation, lunged himself on it. The grenade exploded, its fragments ripping into his groin, his abdomen, and his right leg. Fernandez bled badly as Private David R. Massingale, a medic, worked feverishly on "Dan," as he was called by his buddies. As they waited for the medical evacuation helicopter, Massingale realized that Daniel's wounds were life-threatening. Besides wounds inflicted by the exploding grenade, Daniel had been hit by a stray enemy bullet. "Hang on, Buddy," the medic told Fernandez. In great pain, Daniel replied, "I'm going to hang on," but added, "I never believed it would hurt so much."

A helicopter soon arrived. With the aircraft's blades still rotating, medics rushed Daniel on board. Sergeant Ruben Perkins, nicknamed Sergeant Rock by Fernandez, had spoken to "Old Dan" (Perkin's nickname for Daniel) before the helicopter took off. Still in good spirits despite his serious condition, Daniel kiddingly asked Perkins, "Who's going to take care of you now?" Sadly, Sergeant Perkins was to die in combat within weeks.

Daniel was airlifted back to his brigade's hospital where Army doctors on duty fought for two hours to stop the internal bleeding. Their hard work was to no avail. The damage to Daniel's body was too great. He died that day in the hospital. He was only 21.

Returning Home

Daniel Fernandez's body was flown to the United States and then transported by train to Belen, arriving on board the Santa Fe Railway's San Francisco Chief on February 25, 1966. Brigadier General Burton R. Brown and other high-ranking officers from Sandia Army Base in Albuquerque were present to accord military honors for Daniel. Seven hundred county residents also braved a snowy day to pay tribute to Valencia's finest. His body

254

Private First Class Daniel Fernandez

was viewed at the Gabaldon Mortuary in Albuquerque later that evening.

On Saturday, February 26, Father Francis Schuler celebrated a Requiem High Mass in Daniel's honor at the Los Lunas High School gymnasium, the only building large enough to hold the 1,500 in attendance. Among the flowers was a wreath ordered all the way from Vietnam. Badly shaken by the loss of their fallen friend, the men of his platoon had chipped in to buy a wreath for "Dan's" funeral service.

The essence of Father Schuler's funeral message was from John 15:13 in the New Testament: "Greater love than this no one has, that one would lay down his life for his friends." The Catholic priest told Daniel's grieving parents, "My prayers are with you. I grieve over the pain of your loss, but be consoled in this, that without liberty, life is worthless, and your son died for liberty." Father Schuler added that "As parents you must be proud to have such a son. And as an American, I am indeed proud to say that he was

255

my fellow countryman. While my sympathy goes out to you, I ask you to remember that what we do for self never lasts, but what we do for others is never forgotten." Following mass, Daniel's body was taken to Santa Fe where, before his parents, Mr. and Mrs. Jose I. Fernandez, his 19-year-old sister Rita, and an estimated crowd of 2,000, Daniel was laid to rest at the National Cemetery.

Later that day, back in Valencia County, several dignitaries paid homage to this hero of Homeric bearing. U.S. Senator Joseph M. Montoya spoke to an audience of about 200 in Belen after visiting with the Fernandez family in Los Lunas. The senator described the Fernandez home as "sad but proud." Montoya declared that "The whole country feels our loss in New Mexico for this boy who died to save his comrades." The senator concluded his remarks with the simple words, "I salute Daniel Fernandez." Los Lunas Mayor Howard Simpson declared Saturday, February 26, as Daniel Fernandez Day. He requested that every home and business in town fly an American flag at half-staff in honor of the local hero.

Highest Honor

Meanwhile, the commander of the Army's 25th Infantry Division recommended Daniel for the Medal of Honor. The recommendation underwent a ponderous review, going through a dozen headquarters in the Army chain of command before it reached the desk of Secretary of Defense Robert McNamara in Washington, D.C. McNamara approved the recommendation in October 1966 and sent it on to the Joint Chiefs of Staff. The Joint Chiefs concurred that Daniel deserved our nation's highest military honor.

On April 6, 1967, President Lyndon B. Johnson posthumously awarded the Medal of Honor to Daniel's parents in a solemn ceremony held at the White House. Daniel's sister, Rita, and his two brothers, James and Peter, were also present. James McKeoh and Ray E Sue, two of the grateful soldiers whom Daniel had saved on the battlefield of Vietnam, were on hand for the ceremony in the White House Rose Garden. In his eulogy, President Johnson said that Daniel "died a martyr in the search for peace." A White House press release noted that Daniel was the first Spanish-American to be awarded the nation's highest military decoration in the Vietnam conflict.

256

Presentation of the Congressional Medal of Honor to the parents of Daniel Fernandez by President Lyndon B. Johnson

Back in Los Lunas, the Daniel Fernandez Memorial Park was named in his honor, as was a local school, and VFW Post 9676. Buildings were dedicated in his name at Kirtland Air Force Base in Albuquerque and at Schofield Barracks in Hawaii, where he had served briefly. His name is inscribed on the granite walls of the Vietnam Memorial (panel 5E, row 46), along with the other 57,661 American soldiers killed in action in Southeast Asia from 1959 to 1975.

Who was Daniel Fernandez and why was he willing to sacrifice his life for others? The answers lie with those who knew him best. His mother described him as "a normal child, no different from any other. He loved animals and was in the 4-H. His dream was to buy a horse ranch where he could raise a lot of horses." An avid rider, Daniel participated in many amateur rodeos. He had saved money from the sale of apples and livestock to buy western-style clothes. In short, he was a cowboy.

Rebecca Lutz, Daniel's high school English teacher, remembers him as a bright, kind boy. She recalls the day he came by her classroom to tell her that he was dropping out of school to join the Army. Dr. Lutz urged Daniel to finish school before entering the military. A few weeks later, Daniel returned to tell her that he had enlisted because the war in Vietnam was heating up and he wanted to get there to serve his country.

Daniel's father made a salient comment when interviewed about his son by a *News-Bulletin* reporter: "I would say he evidently had a love for his fellow men." Jose I. Fernandez also mentioned, "Daniel was a man who didn't have any hatred. He had lots of friends among the South Vietnamese. He also had respect for the Viet Cong. He considered them very brave people, very tough." But then Jose Fernandez related, with a mixture of pride and sorrow, "When I heard it [that Daniel had died], I just couldn't believe it. It's so unreal. I can say that I feel humble to know that my son did such a thing."

Daniel was also known for his generosity and friendship. "Daniel was the sweetest boy we ever knew." That is how a young woman from Los Lunas described him after she heard the tragic news of his death. "He was dedicated to all his friends. If you ever made a friend in Daniel, he was a friend forever." This grateful friend went so far as to name her first child after Daniel. When asked if Daniel's act of bravery was typical of him, this same woman replied, "Absolutely. Daniel would do anything for anyone."

Daniel's Army buddies had their own opinions. The consensus was that "he was a friend to everyone, generous with his money when others had run out, a likable guy." A fellow platoon member said that everyone was Fernandez's friend. Second Lieutenant Joseph D'Orso said, "He was always volunteering. He was in the same spot [where he was killed] the night before and volunteered to go out on patrol again, even though he had only slept for four hours." Lieutenant D'Orso added that Fernandez "was one of the best men in the platoon. He was ready to do anything. And he was always cheerful, even when he came out of a swamp covered with leeches."

To his family: Valencia County's heartfelt sympathy will always be with you. Daniel Fernandez's unselfish love and sense of duty for his fellow countrymen and his country as a whole will always be remembered.

Daniel, you were a friend to us all.

Father Martin Jenco:
A Captive in Lebanon

Richard Melzer

I only met Father Lawrence Martin Jenco once. It was on a warm Sunday morning in July 1995. Father Jenco was in Belen to sell and autograph copies of his memoirs, which had just been published. He was also in town to renew old friendships, having served as a priest at Our Lady of Belen Catholic Church from 1979 to 1982.

I remember walking into the parish hall to find Father Jenco seated at a long table, surrounded by admiring members of his former parish. I bought a copy of his book and sat at a respectful distance. As the crowd thinned, I introduced myself and asked him several questions. I felt rather foolish asking my questions, sure that he had answered them all a thousand times, including in the book I had just purchased. But, as a curious historian, I had to be sure. So I asked my questions and awaited his replies.

As expected, Father Jenco had answered my questions a thousand times before and, yes, they were clearly answered in his book as well. But this kind gentleman answered my questions patiently and thoroughly, as if they were brand new and original. In other words, he answered this stranger's questions gently and peacefully. In fact, these are the very words that described him best and the same words he used to sign my book: "Gentle peace!"

It shouldn't have surprised me that a devout man of God would be so gentle and full of peace. Most priests, ministers, and rabbis seem to share these exceptional qualities to one degree or another. But Father Jenco wasn't just any clergyman, and the experiences of his life were hardly typical.

Early Years in the Church

Lawrence Martin Jenco had been born on November 27, 1934, in Joliet, Illinois. He came from a large Czechoslovak family, steeped in traditional Catholic beliefs and values. The family lived next to the parish church, making it convenient for them to frequently participate in local religious and social activities. When old enough, Lawrence became an altar boy, regularly serving at Masses and filling in for other boys who were unable to serve for one reason or another.

Given his strong religious background, it was perhaps predictable that Lawrence felt called to the priesthood as a young man. He studied at seminaries and universities on the east and west coasts of the United States and in Rome, Italy. Ordained in 1962, he was assigned to various parishes, starting in an Italian neighborhood in Denver and, eventually, in Belen. By all accounts, Father Jenco was a popular, effective priest in Belen. He made many close friends while ministering to his flock in countless ways. Parishioners like Rupert and Filomena Baca described him as humble, soft-spoken, sincere, and gentle.

But he was never truly happy in Belen because, as he told some members of his parish, there was no great misery or loss of freedom to deal with here. He felt sure that his services were needed in far less fortunate corners of the world.

As a member of the Servite Order, Father Jenco had already worked in India through Catholic Relief Services (CRS). From Belen, he went on to work in North Yemen and Thailand. He faced his share of hardships abroad. In India, there had been so many rats in the place where he lived that several would run over his bed while he tried to sleep each night. He also fell seriously ill with hepatitis.

In North Yemen, where Catholic Masses were forbidden, members of his church held "parties" at which Mass was said while lookouts watched for intruders. In Thailand his heart was broken when the handicapped in refugee camps were denied evacuation to safe havens elsewhere. Despite such adversity, Father Jenco felt sure he was doing meaningful work as a Christian and as a Catholic priest.

Father Jenco had agreed to yet another difficult overseas job in 1984. He had been asked to become the CRS director in Beirut, Lebanon, then a center of turmoil and violence in the ongoing Middle East crisis. After a 10-day visit to Beirut, he accepted the job, knowing that it would be both challenging and potentially dangerous.

Crisis in Beirut

Father Jenco arrived in Beirut in October 1984, moving into his predecessor's vacated apartment to use the remaining months on the apartment's lease. It was hardly a peaceful city in which to live. Warring factions exchanged gunfire, fired mortars, and exploded bombs all night. Father Jenco feared for his life, but remained determined to help the victims of the chaos that surrounded him.

The stress was already taking its toll. In January 1985, 50-year-old Father Jenco felt ill enough to undergo a series of medical exams, ever mindful of

Father Lawrence Martin Jenco, OSM

his father's death of a massive heart attack at the age of 53. Father Jenco was scheduled for additional tests on Tuesday, January 8. That morning, Khaled, his driver, arrived outside his apartment at 7:30 a.m., soon after Father Jenco had celebrated daily Mass. They drove through a crowded section of Moslem-dominated West Beirut and were stopped in traffic when the American priest sensed that something was very wrong: a shop owner was directing traffic while four policemen stood talking on a nearby corner. But it was already too late to react. As Father Jenco later wrote, "Within seconds, a tremendous crash of automatic weapons fire shattered the morning. I looked up and saw men rushing the car, guns shooting wildly to the heavens. People all around were fleeing, terrified. 'Khaled,' I said, turning to him, 'I'm going to be kidnapped.'"

Father Jenco was right. Two men pulled the priest and his driver from the front seat of their car and pushed them into the back seat. Father Jenco's captors soon transferred him to a second car, forcing him into its trunk before driving on. Remembering the case of a Catholic priest who had been abducted and savagely beaten to death in Poland just three months earlier, Father Jenco was sure that he was about to die. He prayed as he prepared for the end.

But he was not killed. Instead, his kidnappers drove to an isolated building, released him from the trunk, led him into a building, and began to question him. They started their interrogation by asking, "Are you Mr. Joseph Curtin?" As Father Jenco assured them he was not Joseph Curtin, he suddenly realized that his kidnapping had been a tragic case of mistaken identity. Joseph Curtin had been Father Jenco's predecessor at CRS and the man whose apartment the priest had agreed to occupy for the remainder of its lease. Seeing him coming and going from the apartment, the kidnappers had wrongly concluded that he was Joseph Curtin.

Father Jenco hoped that, having realized their mistake, his abductors would release him within hours. But this would be the first of countless frustrated hopes during Father Jenco's long captivity. The priest who had come to Lebanon to help serve the victims of that nation's civil war had now become a victim himself. He was to be held hostage for the next 564 days.

Hostage

Father Jenco's kidnappers were Shiites, a fundamentalist Islamic sect that believed that western influences were steadily corrupting the Middle East and its people. They had planned to kidnap Joseph Curtin to use him as a hostage in an attempt to free a Shiite terrorist accused of bombing the U.S. and French embassies in Beirut. Failing to abduct Curtin, the kidnappers opted to use Father Jenco as substitute "bait" for the exchange. When Father Jenco asked how long it might take to complete this prisoner exchange, he was told "soon." But soon became days and weeks and months. The word "soon" became an empty word, according to the disappointed priest. "Strange to imagine that one syllable could be so painful."

Life as a hostage was traumatic, to say the least. Father Jenco was moved from one terrible prison to another, usually transported while wrapped in tape from head to toe and with a gag placed in his mouth. Each new prison had its own set of miserable conditions. He was often chained to radiators with only a thin mat to sit on in the day and sleep on at night. He was constantly made to wear a blindfold, especially when his kidnappers were present so that he would be unable to identify them later. He was only allowed one trip to the bathroom each day, and water was often scarce or freezing cold or both. In one primitive mountain house, the toilet on the second floor leaked through the ceiling directly above him. During several months, he was not even allowed to wash. Later, he had to bathe in the same water and share a single towel with five other hostages.

In one location, Father Jenco was chained inside a three-by-six-foot clothes closet near where his guards cooked their meals. The heat became unbearable, as did the odor in his cramped, unventilated space. The priest later recalled that his guards "solved this problem by opening the door and spraying me with an aerosol can of room deodorizer. Then they'd spray the closet."

Father Jenco remembered that his days were filled with equally "absurd and pointless indignities" imposed by his fanatical guards. Consumed with hate for all Westerners, they played the same cassette tape over and over. Its lyrics called for the death of all Americans. In one savage attack, a guard wearing heavy boots with stones embedded in the soles stood at the priest's forehead while he lay prone on the floor. Father Jenco recalled that the man "pressed his foot on me like he might squash an insect or a cigarette butt."

At other times, the guards would order him to stand in a painful position with his hands over his head for seemingly endless periods of time. Beatings were also typical. When his guards accused him of concealing a spoon to use as a weapon against them, they beat him about his head so badly that he suffered a permanent loss of hearing in his left ear. And, as a result of not washing and wearing the same filthy blindfold for months, Father Jenco developed a serious eye infection.

In another absurd moment, the guards accused Father Jenco of being a CIA agent whose teeth fillings were actually tiny radio transmitters. They gave the priest 30 minutes to remove the transmitters from his month and hand them over or they would do it themselves. Their threat was a cruel bluff meant to inflict panic and unbelievable stress.

Free Father Jenco button

Worse yet, the brutal guards sometimes led Father Jenco to believe that he was about to be executed. After more stress and anguish the terrified prisoner would learn that, like the teeth filling extractions, these were only empty threats and unpredictable acts of terror.

Survival Skills

How could Father Jenco, or any human, survive such repulsive conditions over many weeks and months? Determined to survive, this courageous American priest used many effective coping skills and defense mechanisms. First, Father Jenco did everything he could to defy his tormentors. Convinced that at least two of his guards were mentally ill, Father Jenco secretly nicknamed them "Sicko" and "Psycho." The priest also removed his blindfold whenever possible and tried to determine his prison locations for possible identification once he was freed.

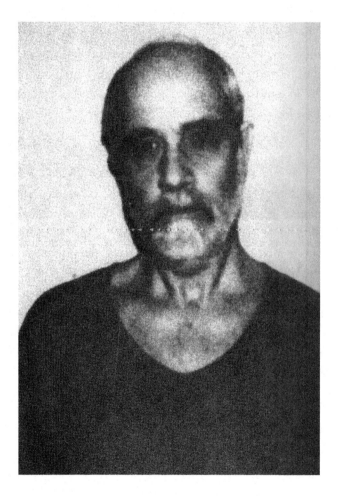

Father Jenco as a hostage

In the face of even his worst torture, Father Jenco boldly asserted his humanity and maintained his dignity. As his head was being "squashed like an insect," Father Jenco yelled, "I am not an insect. I am a person of worth, a person of dignity. I am loved and redeemed and I do have a destiny."

In order to keep track of time and his place in it, Father Jenco used his saliva to mark the passing days in the dust on the tile walls in one prison. As days grew into weeks, he later wrote that he tied "a knot in a potato sack string for each day, with a larger knot to indicate the end of the week. As the months passed, I doubled the size of the larger knot to indicate the end of each month."

Over languishing months of solitary confinement, Father Jenco also maintained his sanity by taking what he called "mental pilgrimages into my past ... recalling the details of existence prior to captivity." Alone in thought, he returned to Joliet, to his family, and to his happy childhood. He retraced his early days in seminary school and as a young priest assigned to outposts around the world.

Later, when Father Jenco was released from solitary confinement and was allowed to meet with as many as five other Western hostages, the men would lead each other on similar mental pilgrimages based on their diverse lives and travels. In this way, the group walked the beaches of southern California, explored the streets of Tokyo, and, with Father Jenco in the lead, saw the famous sights of Rome. As a result, the priest wrote that "each of us occupied worlds much larger than our nine-by-twelve-foot room."

The prisoners did anything they could to distract and encourage one another. Terry Anderson made a deck of cards out of scraps from magazines, Daniel Jacobson read tea leaves, and Tom Sutherland recited poetry by Robert Burns. Yes, they sometimes argued and got on each others' nerves, but the hostages provided essential moral support for one another. All but one, William Buckley, a U.S. embassy diplomat, survived their terrible ordeal.

Father Jenco and several of his fellow prisoners possessed one more critical advantage in their resolve to survive and remain sane: their strong religious faith. From the beginning, Father Jenco prayed almost constantly, using his chain as rosary beads. He recalled favorite verses of scripture, taking particular solace from the book of Psalms. He also found himself singing favorite hymns he had learned as a child. Unable to say daily Mass, he at least celebrated Eucharist from his ration of Arabic bread. He later wrote that he always kept "a piece of Eucharistic Christ, clinging to the Lord especially in moments of violence, sadness, boredom, or fear." Father Jenco sometimes complained to God, "Why this? I am not Job!." But, in the end, it was undoubtedly his faith in God that saw him through, much as it has seen countless millions through other unspeakable trials in history.

Father Jenco's final source of support came from a completely unexpected group. Even during the worst periods of his captivity and increasingly over his final months, some Islamic guards were capable of isolated, simple acts of compassion. One guard, for example, secretly passed cookies and pieces of candy to the priest when he was sure his fellow guards weren't looking. Learning that Father Jenco liked popcorn, a few guards got some corn and began to heat it in a pot, never consulting their prisoner on the best way to prepare the snack. Father Jenco remembered the comical scene when the hot corn kernels began flying in all directions and his guards scattered for cover.

On Christmas Day 1985, the guards went so far as to give Father Jenco and his fellow Christian prisoners a birthday cake, topped with candles and inscribed with the words, "Happy Birthday, Jesus." After this, the prisoners told their guards about other small and large events (such as the anniversary of Father Jenco's priesthood) in hopes of receiving treats.

Some guards also showed a bit of humanitarian kindness (or political self-interest) by bringing a doctor to check on the prisoners' deteriorating health. A kidnapped Lebanese doctor examined Father Jenco's heart and blood pressure and prescribed terramycin for his infected eyes. The guards faithfully put the terramycin in the priest's eyes, although this meant that he could plainly see their faces.

Guards were capable of other acts of unexpected benevolence. After long denying Father Jenco the use of his glasses, the guards finally brought them to him and allowed him to keep a journal and read certain literature. They even let the prisoners watch television, although TV shows like "Dallas" and "Knot's Landing" were considered another "exquisite form of torture," in Father Jenco's opinion.

With time, the prisoners engaged in occasional discussions with their young guards. According to Father Jenco, "We discussed religion, politics, the need to love and be loved, mothers and fathers, wives and marriage, children, health, all normal topics in an abnormal setting. I really believe they wanted to be my friends. Strangely, they wanted approval for their acts of kindness and their acts of cruelty."

Eyes of Love and Forgiveness

His guards' most unexpected moment of kindness came on July 26, 1986, Father Jenco's final day in captivity. On the day of his kidnapping, one of Father Jenco's abductors had looked him in the eyes with hatred and announced, "You are dead!" Now this same young man stood behind Father Jenco, massaging his shoulders with what the priest described as a "gentle touch - not one of violence but of compassion." Although Father Jenco could not lift his blindfold and look into the man's eyes, he was sure of what he would have seen if he was allowed. Eager to see the good in his former tormentor's face, he felt confident that he "would not see the eyes of hatred as I did that first morning. This was his way of apologizing and I believe I would have looked into the eyes of love. ..."

Even after months of torture, misery, and anxiety, Father Jenco would have looked back at his guard with eyes filled with love too. Through his nightmarish journey, Father Jenco had maintained his inner strength and enormous capacity to love. He had maintained the same gentle peace he had exuded on that warm Sunday morning when I met him many years ago in Belen. I will always treasure his memory and the heartfelt inscription he wrote in my copy of his book, *Bound to Forgive*.

(Father Jenco died of natural causes a year to the month after I met him. Terry Anderson, a fellow former hostage, delivered the eulogy at Father Jenco's funeral Mass. Father Jenco was buried in the Queen of Heaven Cemetery in Hillsdale, Illinois.)

MYSTERIES

A Muerto *on the* Jornada del Muerto: *Bernardo Gruber*

Richard Melzer

It was Christmas morning, 1667. As Fray Francisco de Salazar said Christmas Mass in the crowded mission church at Quarai pueblo, two men climbed the choir loft ladder and mingled with members of the parish choir. One of the two, Bernardo Gruber, offered choir members little pieces of paper (*papelitos*) on which he and his companion, Juan Martin Serrano, had written "+ABNA+ADNA+."

Gruber whispered that whoever ate one of the slips of paper would from that hour until the same hour of the next day "be free from any harm," whether it be caused by knives or swords or bullets or Apache arrows.

A 19-year-old resident of Quarai named Juan Nieto accepted Gruber's offer, although he did not eat the strange paper until Mass had ended and he had entered a *kiva*, or sacred Indian center, elsewhere in the pueblo. As older Indians looked on, Nieto swallowed a piece of Gruber's paper and proceeded to stab himself in his hand and wrist with the sharp point of an awl. Amazingly, no blood flowed and he showed no sign of pain. Later, in another part of the pueblo, Nieto swallowed another of Gruber's *papelitos* and began to stab his legs with a knife. Many watched in amazement. It appeared that Nieto was indeed "free from any harm" and showed no sign of bleeding.

But then Nieto admitted that he did not really believe that Gruber's *papelitos* had saved him from the pain of self-mutilation. He confessed that he had only pretended to stab himself in his hand, wrist, and legs. Urged by his wife, who saw no humor in her husband's hoax, Nieto reported the entire incident to Fray Jose de Paredes of the San Buenaventura mission at Las Humanas (now known as Gran Quivira).

269

A German Merchant

Who was the strange man who instigated the hoax to which Juan Nieto confessed? Bernardo Gruber was a German merchant who had come to New Mexico from Sonora, Mexico, to trade goods and raise livestock. Arriving in Quarai with a large pack train in 1667, his merchandise included stockings, gloves, cloth, skins, tools, and weapons. Compared to most of his neighbors, Gruber was quite prosperous, with an estate that included 10 mules, 18 horses, three oxen, two female Apache slaves, and one male Apache slave, about 15 years of age. Gruber wore a doublet (short-waist jacket), pantaloons (with woolen stockings), and an elk skin coat. He owned a sword, a harquebus, a knife, and a small ax. Several people, including his paper-writing companion, Juan Martin Serrano, owed him considerable amounts of money. So what would motivate such a man to offer strange powers to people who ate his *papelitos* on one of the holiest days of the Catholic calendar?

One explanation was that he had learned the custom (or his confused version of it) in his native Germany and simply practiced what he had always done at Christmas, without knowing what it actually meant. If he had known, Gruber would have realized that writing symbols on small bits of paper was a tradition in Germany dating back hundreds of years. According to tradition, different letters (known as runes) and different actions on different days had different meanings. For example, writing the letters "C+M+B" on your doorway on Christmas Eve meant "Christ, bless this home." The Catholic Church had banned runes in 1639, but, like many ancient customs, their use had continued in the hands of many traditional Germans, including Bernardo Gruber.

Gruber may have also used this German custom to help protect his neighbors in Quarai. The foreigner might have known that the runes he wrote and the paper he urged others to eat were used in Germany to shield soldiers going into battle. The pueblo Indian and Spanish residents of Quarai, Abo, and Las Humanas were under increasingly heavy attack by Apache raiders in the 1660s and 1670s. These attacks, plus droughts and epidemics, became so prevalent in the 1670s that Quarai, Abo, Las Humanas, and three smaller pueblos would be completely abandoned by 1680. Could Gruber have simply attempted to aid his neighbors in their defense against the Apaches?

But the Franciscan friars of New Mexico had little patience with Gruber and whatever cultural defense he might offer. To the priests, Gruber's mysterious *papelitos*, strange words, and impossible promises of protection bordered on sorcery and witchcraft.

Gruber's case was definitely in the realm of the Mexican Inquisition, an institution of the Catholic Church created to eliminate just such behavior, even if it required long periods of imprisonment and torture to reveal guilt. Of the 20-odd cases brought before the Inquisition from New Mexico, most had had to do with witchcraft. Thus began one of the earliest, most bizarre cases of the Inquisition in all of New Mexico history.

Arrest and Incarceration

Fray Juan de Paz, chief agent of the Holy Office of the Inquisition in New Mexico, soon left Abo to arrest Bernardo Gruber. Fray Paz was accompanied by Fray Gabriel Torija of Abo, Captain Jose Nieto, Jose Martin Serrano, and Juan Martin Serrano, the same man who had accompanied Gruber to the choir loft and owed the German money. The five riders arrived in Quarai and found Gruber quite easily. Gruber was arrested without incident, peacefully surrendering his harquebus, sword, and knife. Mounting their horses, the men and their prisoner rode in the dark, getting to Abo after midnight.

Gruber was placed in a small room, which was to become his cell for the next month. Guards watched the room's door and single window 24 hours a day; they were threatened with excommunication if the prisoner escaped. Captain Francisco de Ortega eventually offered a larger, better secured cell (with a barred window) at his *estancia* (landed estate) near Sandia Pueblo. Guards transported Gruber to Ortega's home in April 1668.

Although Gruber requested that he be taken to Mexico City to clear his name as soon as possible, he remained a shackled prisoner for over two years. His captors explained to their superiors that Apache raids, drought, and bureaucratic complications had prevented them from moving Gruber south to face trial before the Inquisition. While incarcerated, Gruber lost much of his livestock and his Apache slave, Atanasio, ran away. The German grew increasingly desperate.

Daring Escape

Rather than languish in his cell forever, Gruber began to plot his escape. Two unlikely accomplices came to his aid: Juan Martin Serrano and Atanasio. Serrano may have helped Gruber as a means to pay off the debt he still owed the German. Atanasio may have helped for fear of the strange powers Gruber once possessed.

Gruber planned carefully. On Sunday, June 22, 1670, he feigned illness and convinced his guards to remove his shackles. Juan Martin Serrano assisted by sneaking in supplies, including a harquebus at the last moment. Atanasio provided several horses for Gruber's dash to freedom.

Gruber's daring escape took place at midnight. A negligent guard slept as Gruber and Atanasio removed a wooden bar from his window, a difficult job that took far longer than expected. With the bar gone, Gruber climbed through the window and made his escape by horse, accompanied by his Apache slave and three spare mounts. The fugitive and his slave rode south down the Rio Grande Valley.

As the sun rose over the Manzano Mountains, the pair suddenly encountered a lone rider coming toward them from the south. The rider was Francisco Dominguez de Mendoza, a son of Tome Dominguez de Mendoza, one of the most powerful men of the Rio Abajo.

Fearing that his escape would be foiled, Gruber asked Francisco not to tell anyone that their paths had crossed. Francisco agreed and, in fact, offered fresh horses, if Gruber and his slave needed them. They refused the kind gesture.

So far it was as if Gruber had swallowed his own *papelitos*. No harm had come his way. But whatever magical power the *papelitos* had was good for only one day. Gruber seemed to know this as he hurried south on the *Camino Real*, or Royal Road, toward New Spain (today's Mexico).

Pursuit

Meanwhile, Captain Francisco de Ortega had awoken at his *estancia*, only to find that the bar on Gruber's window had been removed and his prisoner had broken out in the night.

Galloping south, Ortega picked up Gruber and Atanasio's trail. The captain made good progress and soon approached Tome Dominguez de Mendoza's house, in today's Tome. Ortega asked for assistance in his pursuit, but Dominguez de Mendoza refused to help, asserting that Gruber had suffered enough for his seemingly small indiscretion. Dominguez de Mendoza had undoubtedly shared this opinion with his son, leading to Francisco's vow of secrecy and generous offer to provide fresh horses for the fugitive earlier that day.

Only members of a powerful family could defy a Spanish officer in hot pursuit of an escaped prisoner. The Dominguez de Mendoza family's power was based not only on wealth, but also on military prowess. Tome's ambitious, controversial son, Juan, was considered the strongest military leader of his day. Fearing and respecting him, Spanish governors relied on Juan's fighting skills, while his enemies testified that his reputation was "worse than the devil's." Tired and with no aid from Tome Dominguez de Mendoza, Ortega went no further.

It took another nine days before a search party was organized and on the road. New Mexico's governor, Juan de Medrano y Mesia, ordered Captain Cristobal de Anaya Almazan, accompanied by eight Spanish soldiers and 40 Indian allies, to pursue Gruber as far south as El Paso del Norte (today's Ciudad Juarez), if necessary.

Captain Anaya and his party got as far as the pueblo of Senecu, near today's Socorro, before they learned of Gruber's fate. Their source was none other than Gruber's Apache slave, Atanasio.

Trail's End

Atanasio described Gruber's escape in some detail. After leaving Francisco Dominguez de Mendoza, the German and his slave had passed Senecu and had camped at a *paraje* (campsite) on the north end of the worst 90-mile stretch of the *Camino Real* in New Mexico. The date was Tuesday, June 24, just two days into their journey.

The pair traveled the next day, but had found no water by late afternoon. Exhausted, Gruber sent Atanasio to search for whatever water he could find. After several mishaps, the slave finally returned to where he had left his

273

German master. But Gruber was gone. It was now Friday, June 27. Unless Gruber had found water on his own, he had gone thirsty for over two and a half days.

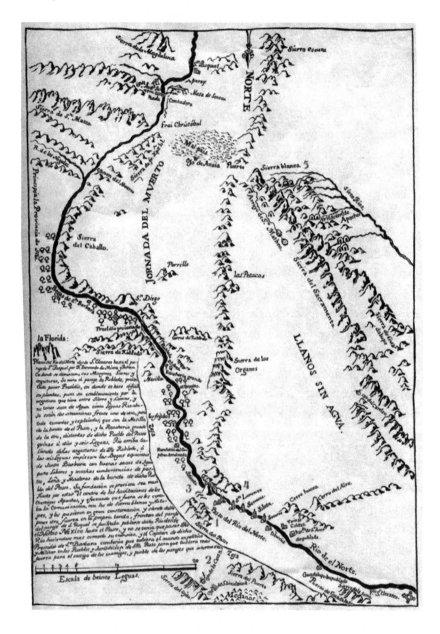

1758 Map of the Jornada del Muerto *by Bernard Pacheco y Miera*

Atanasio had returned to Senecu to report Gruber's disappearance. After being questioned in Senecu and, later, in Sandia, Atanasio wisely disappeared. Some said that he ran as far away as Sonora, where Gruber had originally purchased him as a slave. Many said that Atanasio had made the whole story up and that he had killed Gruber in the desert wilderness.

Search parties sent from Senecu were unable to find any trace of the missing German. Then, about three weeks after Gruber's escape, five Spanish merchants heading south to Chihuahua came across a dead horse, scattered clothes, and bones that had been gnawed on by animals. One of the Spaniards, who had known Gruber earlier, thought he recognized the rather expensive clothes as the German's. The travelers erected a *descanso* (roadside cross) to mark the spot. The date was July 13, 1670.

Gruber's remains were taken to El Paso del Norte where they were buried by a mission priest. Nine years later all charges against Gruber were officially dropped. His belongings in Quarai were auctioned off, with the proceeds used to say a Mass for the German's departed soul.

Bernardo Gruber is not remembered in Quarai where he lived or in Sandia where he was held captive for over two years. Instead, a *paraje*, or campsite, near where his body was found was named Aleman, which is Spanish for "German."

Aleman is located about half way through a treacherous stretch of the *Camino Real*, originally known as *El Despoblado*, or the Uninhabited Trail, and later known as the *Jornada del Muerto*, or the Journey of the Dead Man. Gruber was one of many unfortunate men and women who perished on this road and gave the route its eerie name.

In an odd twist of fate, New Mexico's wilderness, not the Mexican Inquisition, Spanish soldiers, Apache raiders, or his former Apache slave, had killed Bernardo Gruber, finally administering whatever justice he may or may not have deserved for his strange behavior on Christmas, 1667.

A Mistake, a Murder, and a Marriage

John Taylor

This could be a Shakespearean tragedy or a Tom Clancy thriller. It starts with a fateful decision by a member of one of the leading families of the area. A murder is committed which leads to international intrigue. A trial is held, men are hanged, and a twist of fate brings a widow and a widower together. But unlike Shakespeare's or Clancy's tales, this story is true and has its roots right here in the Rio Abajo.

The first characters to cross our page are members of one of the most prominent families in the Mexican province of New Mexico. Francisco Xavier Chavez, the first governor of New Mexico after Mexican independence from Spain, his wife Ana Maria Alvarez del Castillo, and their nine children lived in Los Padillas, a small settlement on the west bank of the Rio Grande about ten miles south of Albuquerque. In a series of transactions starting in about 1819, Chavez had purchased a tract of land on the east side of the Rio Grande known as Los Pinos (now Bosque Farms) from the heirs of Clemente Gutierrez, one of the original grantees. Francisco's oldest son, Jose Mariano Chavez, built a *hacienda* on the Los Pinos land and moved there in 1837 or 1838 with his wife, Dolores Perea, daughter of Don Pedro Perea, the patriarch of the wealthy Bernalillo Perea family, and some or all of their three children. Like his father, Jose Mariano would also serve, for a short time, as governor of New Mexico.

The Mistake

The protagonist in the first part of our plot is Jose Mariano's younger brother, Antonio Jose Chavez. He grew up in Los Padillas and married Barbara Armijo, the niece of New Mexico Governor Manuel Armijo. The Santa Fe Trail had opened a trade route from Missouri to Santa Fe in 1821, and Antonio Jose, along with his older brother, had joined the lucrative trade along the famous east-west pathway. This route of commerce ran from Independence, Missouri, to Santa Fe. Trade goods flowed west from the United States, and silver, gold, and furs flowed east and were used to purchase more

276

A view of Los Pinos from the north

goods to send west. Although some of the merchandise remained in New Mexico, much of it was transshipped to destinations in Mexico and California. Traders commonly plied the trail in the spring, summer, and early fall in order to avoid the fearsome blizzards that roared down the plains during the winter months. However, by choosing this time frame, they did expose themselves to raids by Plains Indians who resented the intrusions of the Americans and Mexicans into their traditional homelands.

So, we come to the fateful year of 1843. For reasons that we will address later, Antonio Jose decided to leave for Independence in February, much earlier than the normal April departure. In addition, he took a very small train—only 20 men, two wagons, a carriage (for himself), and 55 mules. In late March, somewhere between the Cimarron and Arkansas Rivers in what is now southwest Kansas, the winter weather hit with a vengeance. Mules died and men suffered from frostbite. Some men even deserted, but Chavez was determined to forge on to Independence with only one wagon and five remaining men.

Chavez's mistake was to leave so early—but why? Did he hope to be the first trader of the year to reach the merchandise in the East? Did he worry more about the Indians who were still in their winter camps than he did about the weather? Was he concerned about the rumors of Texas raiders along the trail and hoped to get to Missouri before they started their seasonal raiding? Or was it simply a case of hubris—a flawed belief in his own invincibility? We will never know the reason, but we do know the tragedy that unfolded as a result.

The Murder

In 1836, the Republic of Texas won its independence from Mexico with stated (but not accepted!) boundaries of the Rio Grande on the west and the Arkansas River on the north, thus claiming parts of New Mexico, Colorado, Oklahoma, and Kansas. An abortive 321-man expedition in 1841 attempted to solidify the Texan claims to New Mexico east of the Rio Grande and to divert some of the lucrative Santa Fe Trail commerce south into the nearly-bankrupt Republic. However, a 1,500-man Mexican army captured the ill-equipped Texans, put them in chains, and forced them to march 2,000 miles to imprisonment in Mexico City.

By 1842, the Republic of Texas was still struggling financially and continued to feel the sting of embarrassment for their inglorious attempt to reach the Rio Grande. Texas Governor Sam Houston was approached by a friend who suggested that Houston authorize another attempt to overthrow the provisional governments in both Santa Fe and Chihuahua, bringing New Mexico and its lucrative trade into Texas and avenging the treatment of the members of the 1841 expedition. Houston agreed and authorized Colonel Charles Warfield to recruit an army to conduct the operation. Among the early recruits were two Missouri brothers, John and David McDaniel, who were reputed to be outlaws and perhaps even murderers. John McDaniel, the elder of the two, was commissioned as a captain in the service of Texas. McDaniel and his brother were directed to continue recruiting efforts in and around Westport, Missouri, and to meet Warfield in western Kansas on May 15, 1843, to begin the invasion of New Mexico.

The McDaniels did not have much luck recruiting soldiers, but did manage to find 13 men who were ready for an adventure in the West. While one

278

could argue that the effort authorized by Houston could be thought of as patriotic from a Texas point of view, there was no such thought in the mind of the McDaniels and their crew. They were out for booty, and their plan was to intercept Mexican wagon trains heading for Independence as they passed through the area of Oklahoma and Kansas claimed by Texas. On April 1, 1843, their fifteen-man contingent headed west from Westport, Missouri, looking for victims along the Santa Fe Trail.

It is not clear whether or not the McDaniels knew in advance that Don Antonio Jose was undermanned and in dire straits heading east, but sometime between April 7 and 10, the two parties "collided" north of the Arkansas River near a small gully called Owl Creek (now named Jarvis Creek—an Anglo misrendering of Chavez). The international implications were significant—a group of Republic of Texas mercenaries had encountered a Mexican citizen in land that belonged to the United States.

Chavez and his five men were bound while their wagon was ransacked. The furs and gold in the wagon were divided among the thieves, but a debate ensued about what to do with Chavez and his retainers. After three days, it was decided that the retainers would be released and sent west, presumably to die in the wilderness, but Chavez would have to be killed. Half of McDaniel's crew objected and headed east toward Independence with their loot. The remaining men drew lots and five of them—the McDaniel brothers, Joseph Brown, Thomas Mason, and Thomas Towson—took Chavez off, allegedly to allow him to relieve himself. Several gunshots were heard, and the five men returned, carrying only a money belt stuffed with silver coins that they removed from the body before unceremoniously throwing it into a gully.

It didn't take long for word to spread about the murder and robbery. Tavern braggadocio, reports by the men who had left the McDaniels before the murder and by the four retainers who had been rescued by another wagon train, and reports by other travelers soon reached Westport and Independence. The murder of Chavez and the theft of his money took on real significance. Not only did this potential international incident involve three countries, but it challenged the entire Santa Fe Trail trading model. Mexico threatened to stop all American traders from entering New Mexico, thereby strangling the trade which the residents of western Missouri had come to

279

depend on. In addition, theft of goods or money that were destined to move along the trail was almost unheard of. Traders would leave their valuables essentially unprotected on loading docks or wagons while they took care of other business. Thus, the incident at Owl Creek captured the attention of merchants and bureaucrats from Washington to Santa Fe to Mexico City.

Posses were assembled and the miscreants were rounded up a few at a time. By mid-May, most of the gang was incarcerated, and most of the stolen furs, money, gold dust, and specie had been recovered. Chavez's abandoned wagon was found but was severely damaged, so only the cargo trunk was returned as evidence. All that was left of Chavez's body was a few tufts of hair; it was assumed that wolves had disposed of the rest.

There would seem to be no honor or loyalty among thieves because soon all of the prisoners were telling their own stories and pointing fingers of blame at their erstwhile friends. Arguments were made that the killing was not murder but some sort of justified reprisal (read vengeance) for the treatment of the men from the abortive Texas-Santa Fe expedition. It was also claimed that the U.S. courts did not have jurisdiction. However, confessions were taken; plea deals were made; and indictments were handed down.

Finally, on April 1, 1844, just one year after the murder and robbery, the trial of the main perpetrators began. Defense attorney Edward Bates did his best for his clients by assailing the character of the witnesses, especially Thomas Mason who had turned state's evidence, and accusing them of being "perjured villains" and "vile miscreants who unscrupulously fabricated the basest falsehoods." Nonetheless, by the end of April, the verdicts were all in—the four men were found guilty of murder and sentenced to hang. June 14, 1845, was set as the date for their executions.

The convicted men—the two McDaniels, Joseph Brown, and Thomas Towson (Thomas Mason had been spared by turning state's evidence)—appealed for clemency to President John Tyler, claiming that the court in St. Louis had no jurisdiction for a crime committed in Indian Country. Stays were granted until August 16 for the elder McDaniel and Brown, and the younger McDaniel and Towson were pardoned, the former because of his age and the latter because he was deemed to be "mentally deficient." On August 16, 1845, at 2:00 p.m., the two remaining condemned men, John McDaniel and Joseph Brown, were led to the gallows. They protested their innocence to the assembled crowd of over a thousand men, women, and children; but the nooses were placed around their necks; blindfolds went over their heads; and the gallows traps were sprung.

The Marriage

This might well be the end of the story—the murderers paid for their crime and the good guys rode off into the sunset. But we are not finished. We now introduce the last member of our cast of characters—Henry Connelly. Connelly was born in 1800 in Kentucky and received a medical degree from Transylvania University. He practiced medicine in Missouri for a short time before giving up that profession for the more lucrative one of merchant and trader along the Santa Fe Trail. He moved to Chihuahua, Mexico, in 1828, where he bought a store and continued his mercantile endeavors. He married a Mexican woman in 1838, and had three children. His wife died just before the outbreak of the Mexican War, and, after a brief imprisonment by Mexican authorities, Connelly moved to New Mexico and resumed his mercantile activities.

The money and possessions that had belonged to Don Antonio Jose Chavez had been taken to St. Louis to serve as evidence in the trials of the McDaniels and others. The county clerk, who had custody of the material and who also was a trader, asked his friend, Henry Connelly, if he would take the material back to Barbara Chavez, Antonio Jose's widow, on his next trip west. Connelly agreed.

Meanwhile, in May 1845, while awaiting the execution of the murderers, Antonio's brother, Mariano, had died, leaving his wife, Dolores, a widow at the family hacienda in Los Pinos. When Connelly returned to New Mexico with the material from the trial, he was smitten by Mariano's 34-year old widow. After a suitable courtship, they were married in the Isleta church on January 1, 1849. Together, they moved into the Los Pinos estate and went on to have three children of their own.

Connelly was appointed governor of the New Mexico Territory by President Abraham Lincoln in 1861, and led the territorial response to the Confederate invasion of 1862. He was reappointed as governor in 1864, but resigned in July 1866 due to failing health. He died of an accidental opium overdose in August 1866, and is buried in the Rosario Chapel in Santa Fe.

And so we come full circle—a trader, the son of a governor and brother-in-law of another, makes the dubious decision to leave the Mexican province of New Mexico during the winter. He is hit by a blizzard and is murdered in the United States by mercenaries from the Republic of Texas. The murderers are tried and two are executed. Antonio Jose's money and other materials

Governor Henry Connelly

are returned to his widow by another trader who marries the first widow's widowed sister-in-law and goes on to become governor of the United States Territory of New Mexico.

Although the body of Antonio Jose Chavez was never recovered, a marker on private property near the Jarvis Creek crossing in Rice County, Kansas, marks the site where he was killed and dumped. It is a simple, rough-hewn plinth with a single word—Chavez—engraved on one side.

Dolores Perea de Chavez de Connelly

The Chavez-Connelly home in Los Pinos was torn down around the turn of the century and their land eventually became the Village of Bosque Farms, a flourishing bedroom community for Albuquerque. The legacy of Dolores and Henry Connelly is represented by their descendants who still live in the Peralta area.

The Chavez memorial on Jarvis Creek in Rice County, Kansas

Charles Lummis in Isleta, 1888-1892

Richard Melzer

A small, muscular stranger entered Isleta Pueblo in December 1884. Twenty-five-year-old Charles Fletcher Lummis was in no particular hurry in his travels, but he was hardly on a casual stroll through the New Mexico countryside. A journalist born in Massachusetts and educated at Harvard, Lummis had set a personal goal to hike no less than 3,507 miles from Cincinnati, Ohio, to Los Angeles, California, writing short newspaper reports about the people and places he observed along the way. His newspaper columns were later compiled in his most famous book, *A Tramp Across the Continent*, published in 1892.

Charles Lummis's first visit to Isleta was brief. He entered the pueblo about sunset simply to buy tobacco. According to the newspaper column he wrote about the experience, he "walked around pretty extensively," finding the Indian village "tolerably interesting." At the St. Augustine Catholic Church Lummis watched a man climb a ladder to the east tower where he rang a church bell with rapid blows of a hammer. After dark, two teams of youths staged a "grand firefight," pelting each other with "blazing brands, a pretty sight in the darkness." And that was all that Lummis wrote of Isleta. After his few hours in the pueblo, Lummis continued west. He could not have predicted what impact the small village would have on the rest of his life. Nor could the village have imagined the impact this traveler would have on its future.

Illness and Wrath

On February 1, 1885, Lummis reached his destination in California and began work as the city editor of the *Los Angeles Times*. He remained at his job for nearly three years, working day and night, with little time for rest or relaxation. But the stress and demands of newspaper work soon caught up with him. In late 1887, Lummis suffered a stroke that left his left arm paralyzed. Like thousands of health seekers of his time, Lummis thought of New Mexico as an ideal place to recover. Lummis spent several months with Don

285

Amado Chaves at the Chaves *hacienda* in San Mateo, renewing a friendship that had begun on Lummis's earlier "trek" across the country.

Interested in Hispanic culture, Lummis became particularly curious about the rituals and beliefs of the Brotherhood of Our Father Jesus the Nazarene, better known as the Penitentes. As part of a secretive Catholic organization, Penitente brothers frowned on Lummis's inquiries and especially on his photographs of their activities during Holy Week.

Lummis drew additional wrath from the powerful Baca family of western Valencia County. Having written scathing articles about the family's corrupt influence in the election of November 1888, Lummis was said to be on Don Ramon A. Baca's hit list to be killed. Lummis recalled the sound of more than one bullet whizzing by his head as he rode on isolated trails. No longer welcomed in San Mateo, Lummis sought refuge in the Rio Grande Valley and, specifically, in Isleta Pueblo by late 1888. The village he had visited with little comment in 1884 was about to become his home and the center of his growing interest in Indian culture for the next four years.

Return to Isleta

At first Isleta citizens were less than enthusiastic about Lummis's arrival and residence. After centuries of uneven relations with outsiders, few Anglos were welcomed as residents of Isleta unless they played specific roles, such as schoolteachers, trading post operators, or parish priests. Pueblo elders ordered Lummis to leave, but he managed to ignore them and remain.

Lummis's relations with his new neighbors soon improved. An honored pueblo leader had recently died after suffering from paralysis during the last years of his life. Many pueblo residents saw a spiritual significance in the arrival of the similarly afflicted Lummis. Many called the newcomer "*Kha-Tay-Deh*," or withered arm or branch. Lummis was also eventually welcomed into the community because he was so generous. Sharing candy with children and tobacco with adults, Lummis's second nickname became "*Por Todos*," meaning "for everyone" in Spanish.

This unusual Anglo was accepted in Isleta because of the friendship of one family in particular, the Abeitas. The Abeitas were among the most influential, progressive families in the village, owning flocks of sheep, a herd of cattle, a horse-powered threshing machine, and a thriving store. Juan Rey Abeita, his wife Marcelina, and their son Pablo were especially kind and helpful to Lummis. For $2.50 a month, the newcomer rented a room in their large adobe house, located northwest of the pueblo's plaza.

Charles Lummis

Lummis repaid the Abeitas' kindness with more than cash. Juan Rey had sent three of his young sons off to a government boarding school in Albuquerque, but had regretted his decision when the boys were not allowed to return home, even for holidays or during the summer months. Juan Rey could not even visit his sons at the Indian school; he was thrown off the school's grounds with such force that he suffered bruises on both arms. It was increasingly clear what the government was attempting to do in its boarding schools: destroy Indian culture and values by teaching Indian children white culture and values from an early age. As a Taos Pueblo boy said, "They told us that the Indian ways were bad; they said we must get civilized. I remember that word. It means 'be like the white man.' After a while we also began to say Indians are bad. We laughed at our own people and their blankets and cooking pots."

Fearing a similar transformation of his children, Juan Rey had resisted sending his youngest son, Tuyo, to the government school in Albuquerque. But the boy had been forced from his home before he was four years old. And Tuyo was not alone. Dozens of other Isleta children, and thousands from other tribes, suffered the same fate.

Although he had originally favored Indian boarding schools, Lummis now recognized that they did more harm than good. Offering to help the Abeitas, Lummis secured a lawyer and filed a writ of *habeas corpus*, charging the government school in Albuquerque with kidnapping and abduction. The former *Los Angeles Times* editor also wrote letters to newspapers across the country to rally public support for the Indians' cause.

Lummis's efforts bore fruit in July 1892. Not only were the Abeita children freed from the boarding school, but three days later, another 35 boys and girls were released to their parents who led them home in triumph and joy. It was said to be the first successful "rescue" of Indian children from a government boarding school in the United States.

Over a thousand pueblo residents greeted the *cautivos* (captives) in a celebration held in the Isleta village plaza. "There wasn't a dry eye in the crowd," wrote Lummis. Forever grateful, Tuyo went so far as to name his own son after Lummis when he later married and had a family of his own. Later generations of Isleta children returned to the Albuquerque Indian School when its rules and policies changed. In 1925, 139 children from the pueblo attended, representing 30 percent of the school's enrollment. Only Laguna with 38 percent had a higher percentage of students at A.I.S.

At Home in Isleta

Now accepted by the pueblo, Lummis lived much like other members of his adopted community. When not eating wild fruits that he gathered or ducks that he shot along the Rio Grande, he ate with the Abeitas, enjoying a steady diet of chile, beans, and mutton stew. He even dressed much as adult males did in Isleta, with moccasins on his feet and a red sash around his waist. Lummis was allowed to participate in most social events and was even permitted to enter the pueblo's *kivas*. Few, if any, Anglos had ever been granted permission to enter these sacred religious centers. The athletic white man ran with the pueblo's young men in their annual spring race, although his physical weakened condition caused him to collapse after one lap around the village. In the winter, he listened as village elders told their ancient tales to the tribe's children, passing on important values the Indian schools had tried to replace.

Eager to learn more about his neighbors and their ways, Lummis attempted to learn the Isleta language. For 25 cents an hour, Domingo Jiron, a young graduate of the famous Indian school in Carlisle, Pennsylvania,

A Charles Lummis photo of Isletans

taught the inquisitive Lummis, starting in March 1890.

Although more traditional members of Isleta believed that their spirits would be lost if their images were taken in photographs, others granted Lummis permission to photograph them as they performed everyday tasks. Lummis took hundreds of photos; at least one "progressive" pueblo leader later wrote to Lummis, asking for a photo of his father. Many of Lummis's photos still exist in Western archives and libraries, including at the University of New Mexico.

Assassination Attempt

Lummis had settled into his new home and surroundings when his past suddenly caught up with him in a life-threatening event. Accustomed to writing late into the night, Lummis had left his room for a breath of fresh air at about 1:00 a.m. on February 14, 1889. While Lummis stood near his door, a lone assassin shot from behind a low adobe wall about twenty yards away. Wounded in his hand, scalp, and cheek, the ambushed victim fell to the ground. Struggling to his feet, Lummis tried to pursue his attacker, but collapsed after a short distance.

Hearing the gun shot, Lummis's neighbors rushed outside and carried their wounded friend to his room. Lummis almost died from a loss of blood. Only a small book of poetry in his shirt pocket had stopped the potentially lethal buckshot's path to his heart.

Lummis's would-be assassin was never found, much less arrested and brought to justice. But most agreed that the powerful leaders Lummis had alienated in San Mateo were behind the violence that nearly took the writer's life. Some suspected that the shooter had been brought all the way from Mexico to commit the crime.

Lummis refused to go to Albuquerque for medical attention, preferring the care of his friends in Isleta. He received particular attention from a young woman who had come to teach at the village's day school while living with her sister and brother-in-law, who operated a local trading post. Twelve years his junior, Eva "Eve" Frances Douglas of Lime Rock, Connecticut, was attracted by Lummis's kindness and talents. Although still married to his first wife, Dorothea, who lived in Los Angeles, Lummis reciprocated Eve's attention. It came as no surprise when Lummis divorced Dorothea and announced his engagement to Eve.

The couple married on March 27, 1891. Ten days later Lummis wrote in his diary, "*Estoy enteramente feliz por la primera vez.*" ("I am entirely happy for the first time.") The newlyweds set up housekeeping in two rooms Lummis rented from the Abeitas and remodeled for his bride. With little income, they hardly had enough for their next meal. But they did not seem to mind. As Lummis later wrote, "The less Eve and I had, the more we valued." A new part-time job as Isleta's postmaster and compensation for his poems and articles, published in various magazines and newspapers, helped the couple survive. To supplement their earnings, "Charlie" and Eve sold thousands of the photographs Lummis had taken in New Mexico, including in Isleta. They also sold Indian handicrafts to a curio dealer in Los Angeles.

Lummis valued not only his new marriage, but also the many lasting friendships he made in New Mexico. His circle of friends widened to include Isleta's French priest, Father Anton Docher, the Hunings of Los Lunas, and the most famous anthropologist in New Mexico history, Adolf Bandelier. Lummis visited these and other New Mexicans for days at a time.

Despite the paralysis in his left arm, Lummis enjoyed many outdoor activities. He rode his favorite horse, hunted, trapped, fished, and even rolled his own cigarettes with his good right hand. He often hiked for miles, carrying his heavy camera and other photographic equipment. It was after one such trip with Eve that "the great thing happened" on July 5, 1891. With Eve kneeling beside him, Lummis began stroking her hair—with his formerly paralyzed left hand. The couple and their friends were overcome with joy. Many in Isleta were convinced that Lummis must have paid a *bruja* (witch) because he had healed so suddenly.

A second "great thing" happened to the Lummis family a year later when Charles and Eve's first child was born on June 8, 1892. They named the infant girl Dorothea, after Charles's first wife. Neighbors brought gifts of silver, pottery, calico, and chocolate. Doña Marcelina Abeita asked to be the child's *madrina* (godmother), an offer the new parents accepted readily. In Isleta, a *madrina* fasted for four days while she prayed to be shown her godchild's true Indian name. On the fifth day, the godmother would rise and watch for a sign to indicate what the child's Indian name should be. After

291

praying for four days, Doña Marcelina awoke on her fifth day of fasting and, seeing the sun rise over the Manzano Mountains, decided that Charles and Eve's daughter should be named Turbese, meaning sunburst or "sun halo."

Meanwhile, the newborn's father had a large responsibility of his own. A father had to be sure to keep the fire in his fireplace burning for four days and nights. The Isleta Indians believed that if a father let his fire die out at any time in these four days and nights, his child would die before his or her first birthday. Lummis successfully kept his fire burning all four days and nights. Turbese survived her first year and, in fact, lived an additional 74.

Leaving Isleta

Eight years after his first visit to Isleta and four years after he had first made it his home in 1888, Charles Lummis left the pueblo on October 2, 1892. Lummis had accepted an offer to accompany Adolf Bandelier on an archeological expedition to Bolivia and Peru. Ever the adventurer, Lummis traveled with Bandelier for nearly a year.

Lummis never returned to Isleta to live, but remained in contact with many of his former *vecinos* (neighbors). After returning from South America and settling with his family in Los Angeles, he recruited several Isletans to help build his large new house, called *El Alisal*, and serve in various roles, from nannies to house boys. At Lummis's request, Isleta dancers also performed at annual *fiestas* held in Los Angeles.

But Lummis's ties to Isleta were strained by two tragic events. First, traditionalists at Isleta resented Lummis's inclusion of their ancient stories in his many books and articles. They had shared these stories with a trusted friend in the privacy of their adobe homes. They accused Lummis of violating their sacred trust. As a result, several of Lummis's sources in Isleta were summoned by the pueblo's council to explain their indiscretions. Largely based on its experience with Lummis, the council no longer permitted outsiders to rent rooms in the pueblo.

Great tragedy also struck when an older house servant at *El Alisal* murdered a youth from Isleta named Procopio in August 1907. The two men had been good friends, but violence ensued following a brief argument. The older man, Francisco Amate, never forgave himself for Procopio's death; Amate soon died of stomach cancer. Few Isletans came to work for Lummis after Procopio's murder. And Lummis did not return to Isleta for many years.

Working as an editor, librarian, and author, Lummis became nationally famous, although his life was marred with controversy, including a bitter divorce from Eve in 1912 and a disastrous third marriage, to Gertrude Redit, that began in 1915 and ended in 1923. But Lummis renewed his ties to Isleta late in his life, visiting the pueblo in 1919 and staying in the community for short periods on his last two visits to New Mexico, in 1926 and 1927. As Lummis wrote to his old friend Amado Chaves, "Every year makes Los Angeles crazier and more crowded, but New Mexico is a bit of God's Grace in making a land so spacious (and so dry) that the hand of man shall never destroy it, nor much disfigure."

Lummis's escape from California's craziness in 1927 was to be his last. Diagnosed with brain cancer in November 1927, doctors told him that he had less than a year to live. His health grew steadily worse. Lummis's friends in Isleta and throughout New Mexico learned the sad news of his death on November 25, 1928. He was 69 years old.

Years later, old wounds had healed and mostly fond memories of Lummis at Isleta remained. Pablo Abeita summarized Lummis's life in the pueblo, writing, "He was so well-liked here that he was allowed to set his camera any place he chose. No man can write enough of his good standing in the pueblo of Isleta, and I say elsewhere too." Charles Lummis could not have asked for a finer epitaph by the people he loved and admired most in the Rio Abajo.

Did Teddy Roosevelt Visit Isleta in 1903?

Richard Melzer

Thousands of men and women have visited Isleta Pueblo. Many have come to see the native dances, tour the mission church, or shop at local craft stores. Some visitors have been quite famous, including the king and queen of Belgium in 1919. According to some sources, Teddy Roosevelt was the first and only U.S. president to ever visit the pueblo, if only briefly and in secret on May 5, 1903.

Teddy Roosevelt at the Rough Riders' first reunion, Las Vegas, New Mexico, 1899

294

Teddy Roosevelt had visited New Mexico once before. As the most famous Rough Rider in the Spanish-American War of 1898, he had attended his regiment's first reunion, held in Las Vegas, New Mexico, in June 1899. Thousands of well-wishers welcomed Roosevelt to Las Vegas, including Valencia County's most honored Rough Rider, Captain Maximiliano Luna. No less than thirty percent of all Rough Riders had been recruited from New Mexico. The Rough Rider reunion drew newspaper coverage from across the country. Always eager for attention, Roosevelt enjoyed his stay in the territory, even promising to support New Mexico's goal of statehood however he could.

Teddy Roosevelt at the Rough Riders' reunion in Las Vegas, New Mexico, 1899

The following year Roosevelt used his wartime fame to secure the Republican Party's vice-presidential nomination on a ticket led by incumbent president William McKinley. Tragically, an assassin shot McKinley on September 6, 1901. A grieving Roosevelt was sworn into office within hours of the president's death. Roosevelt had been in office for two years when he ventured to New Mexico a second time.

Roosevelt's Western Tour

Teddy Roosevelt visited New Mexico on Tuesday, May 5, 1903, as part of an extensive Western tour that took him to 25 states and territories, covering 14,000 miles in just nine weeks and three days. No president had ever attempted such an extensive tour of the country in a non-election year. Greeted by large crowds wherever he went, Roosevelt made 262 speeches, averaging about four a day, undoubtedly a record in American history. The people of New Mexico were excited to be included on the tour because Roosevelt and his Rough Riders remained enormously popular in the territory. In fact, a new county on the east side of the territory had just been named after the president on February 28, 1903, about two months prior to his arrival in New Mexico.

On the 35th day of his tour, the president's special 6-car train pulled into Santa Fe where Roosevelt addressed a crowd estimated at 10,000. Although in town for less than four hours, Roosevelt found time to visit San Miguel Church, the oldest church in the U.S., and attend the baptism of the month-old son of one of his favorite fellow Rough Riders, George Washington Armijo, at St. Francis Cathedral. Showing his admiration for his former commander and following his parents' example of naming their son after a patriotic American, Armijo had named his son Theodore Roosevelt Armijo. The president also met local dignitaries at the Governor's Mansion where newspapers reported that "several bottles of champagne were served to cool the parched throats of the party." Governor Miguel Otero gave Roosevelt the unusual gift of a rifle once owned by the notorious New Mexico train robber, "Black Jack" Ketchum.

Another huge crowd greeted Roosevelt in Albuquerque later that same day. City leaders had declared a holiday to roll out the red carpet for their famous guest. A towering arch inscribed with Roosevelt's name stretched across Railroad Avenue (now Central) near 2nd Street. Historian Marc Simmons writes that "Young ladies clinging precariously to the top of the arch showered the president with flowers as he passed underneath." American flags and patriotic bunting adorned homes and businesses throughout the city. A military band escorted the chief executive on a tour of the town, with stops at the Albuquerque Indian School, the Commercial Club, and the

296

newly opened Alvarado Hotel, where Roosevelt gave a five minute speech to a crowd of 15,000 admirers. It might well have been the shortest speech of his entire tour. To remind the president of his earlier promise to support New Mexico statehood, 46 little girls, representing the nation's 46 states, stood before Roosevelt, while a 47th girl, representing New Mexico, appeared in the foreground pleading for the territory's admission to the Union. Some wondered if begging was the best tactic to use in the statehood campaign.

Roosevelt also met the famous Navajo weaver Elle of Ganado at the Alvarado's Indian Building. Albuquerque's Commercial Club had commissioned Elle to weave a Navajo saddle blanket as a special gift for Roosevelt. Although she was given less than a week to complete the job, Elle finished her beautiful red, white, and blue blanket in time for the president's arrival. The local press reported that Roosevelt gave Elle a "hearty shake and told her how much he appreciated her work."

Visiting Isleta

President Roosevelt had hoped to visit another famous Native American during his stay in New Mexico. According to legend, President Roosevelt first met Isleta's Pablo Abeita in Washington, D.C., during one of the Indian leader's 18 trips to lobby in his pueblo's behalf in the nation's capital. After one long meeting with Abeita, the president reportedly declared that he would someday like to visit Abeita's home in Isleta.

Abeita remembered the president's interest in Isleta when he heard that Roosevelt was in Albuquerque on May 5, 1903. Knowing that it would be nearly impossible to rearrange Roosevelt's tight schedule to allow time for a trip to Isleta, Abeita, nevertheless, devised a plan to honor the president's wishes. Abeita drove a buckboard wagon from Isleta to Albuquerque, tying his horses outside the Alvarado. Stepping inside the hotel, he asked to see the president. Especially cautious after President McKinley's assassination, Roosevelt's security guards refused the request. But Abeita persisted, eventually drawing such a crowd that Roosevelt himself came out to see what all the commotion was about. Spotting Abeita, the president ushered his friend into his private quarters. Step one of Abeita's plan—how to get to see the president—had worked.

The next problem was how to get Roosevelt out of the hotel and off to Isleta. Abeita reportedly asked the president to place an Indian blanket over his head and shoulders. Doing the same for himself, Abeita ushered Roosevelt down the hotel hall and through its crowded lobby. Once outside the Alvarado, Abeita and his guest boarded Abeita's waiting wagon and rode south to Isleta. The two friends enjoyed a good visit in the Abeita home. Unfortunately, we know nothing of what they discussed, ate, or saw. We can only be sure that the Abeitas would have extended every form of Isleta hospitality to their honored guest.

Abeita soon accompanied Roosevelt back to the Alvarado, with both men still wearing the Indian blankets they had worn to make their original escape. As they entered the hotel lobby, Abeita reportedly relished the moment by pulling off Roosevelt's blanket and shouting a loud war cry. Security men ran to the president's side, not sure what to make of his sudden appearance. Roosevelt quickly reassured his guards, declaring, "Boys, I was just as safe in Pablo's hands as I am with anybody in the world." Roosevelt

Pablo Abeita

298

undoubtedly described his adventure as a "bully good time," a phrase he often used to describe his favorite experiences.

Roosevelt's train departed from Albuquerque that same evening, stopping in Gallup for five minutes and reaching the Grand Canyon, which he toured for the first time the following day. His whirlwind tour continued through California and other Western states before he finally returned to the White House in early June 1903.

Fact or Fiction?

Now, more than a century after Roosevelt's visit to New Mexico, we must wonder if the story of his trip to Isleta is true or simply a legend invented to embellish Roosevelt's fame and popularity. Would it have been possible to spirit the president of the United States past his guards and everyone else in a crowded hotel lobby? Would it have been possible to drive a wagon to Isleta and return to Albuquerque in a few hours, before anyone noticed that the president was gone and before his train was scheduled to depart?

Teddy Roosevelt certainly craved such stories about his adventuresome spirit, independent nature, and strenuous life. Stories abound regarding his driving a train in California, hunting wild game in Africa, exploring the jungles of Brazil, and of course charging up San Juan Hill in the most famous battle of the Spanish-American War. Adding, or at least not denying a story about evading his security guards (symbolizing authority) and visiting a pueblo (symbolizing adventure) was certainly in the realm of possibilities in Roosevelt lore.

And what of Pablo Abeita? Like his friend the president, Abeita enjoyed his reputation as an independent, adventurous leader who did not hesitate to defy authority or break with tradition through unconventional acts of bravery. As historian Marc Simmons has written, Abeita "loved a joke, especially if he could put one over on the Anglos."

If the story of Roosevelt's trip to Isleta was not true, maybe telling this tale was a joke Abeita played on Anglos gullible enough to believe him. If true, this story was only one of many famous incidents in the life of one of the most respected Pueblo leaders in New Mexico history.

At one time or another Abeita met and shook hands with every U.S.

president from Grover Cleveland to Franklin D. Roosevelt, with only one exception, Calvin Coolidge. And he may or may not have taken one very willing president to his home. There is no wonder why the people of his Pueblo still refer to Pablo Abeita as the Grand Old Man of Isleta.

The Belen Bank Robbery, 1904

Richard Melzer

The first major motion picture made in Belen was about a bank robbery. Released in 1971, "Bunny O'Hare" featured the escapades of an older woman (played by Bette Davis) who robbed a bank to seek revenge against a bank that had repossessed her house. She teams up with a veteran bank robber (played by Ernest Borgnine) who teaches her the tricks of his criminal trade.

It is ironic that the first major movie made in Belen was about a bank robbery because there had been only one bank robbery in Belen's long history.

The first heist occurred shortly after the First National Bank of Belen was incorporated on February 15, 1903, with merchant John Becker as its first president. First National remained open until its sale to Norwest Bank on March 10, 1995, but never experienced another robbery. Nor did the bank close during several severe economic crises, including the Great Depression, when most banks in the nation failed. Few banks could claim such an impressive record of safety and security.

Robbery at the Depot

Although the First National Bank of Belen was robbed only once in its 92-year history, its money was not always safe. On June 23, 1905, the bank sent $2,000 in a package to be delivered to the First National Bank of Albuquerque via the Santa Fe Railway.

The mail carrier inserted the package into a mail pouch and brought the valuable cargo from the bank to the depot on South 1st Street. In those days the mail train didn't stop for the mail, but simply grabbed the waiting mail pouch from a large hook located along the tracks.

The mail carrier had just placed the mail pouch on the ground and prepared to put it on its hook when a stranger suddenly approached, cut the bottom of the bag, and stole the enclosed money. The thief ran off before he could be apprehended. Some believed that he was so brazen that he took the next passenger train to Albuquerque.

301

The police alerted authorities in towns near and far. After several weeks on the case, Santa Fe Railway police chief Ben Williams arrested a veteran hold-up man, safe cracker, and "all-around bad man" in Kansas City. Williams brought William S. Lewis back to New Mexico for trial.

Two early interior views of the First National Bank of Belen

Newspapers reported the brash act and subsequent arrest in states as far west as Washington and as far east as Ohio. Some believed that Lewis was the leader of a gang that had planned a series of similar robberies, if the first one had been a success. Officer Williams vowed to pursue the gang until all of its remaining members joined Lewis behind bars.

Embezzlement

John Becker's bank faced theft of another kind some five years later when a formerly trusted employee was accused of embezzling $1,166 (equal to over $28,000 in today's money). Assistant cashier John Fewkes, a married man with two children, absconded with the cash and headed west, supposedly to visit relatives in Arizona. Fewkes was arrested in Flagstaff, Arizona, on September 21, 1910.

According to the *Albuquerque Journal*, Fewkes had "strong hopes of squaring things up" with the bank, but apparently failed in his efforts to convince Becker or the police of his innocence. He pled guilty to his white collar crime in December 1910 and was sentenced to five years in the territorial prison. With good behavior, his term could have been reduced to ten months.

Fewkes asked for clemency from President William Howard Taft in mid-1911, but his request was denied on the same day that a man convicted of land fraud and a married couple convicted for their involvement in the white slave trade received clemency from the chief executive.

The Heist at Becker's Mercantile

Thieves chose to break into John Becker's store, rather than his bank, on December 15, 1910. Described in the press as "expert cracksmen," the robbers entered the store about 2:00 a.m. and opened the store's two safes, using combinations they had somehow previously obtained. The outlaws also blew up a large vault with dynamite. The robbers escaped into the night with $800 in cash (worth $19,708 today), several gold watches valued at $100 each and checks, and papers that were of no value to the crooks.

The *Albuquerque Journal* reported that the crime was committed "quietly, quickly, and with a daring possessed by professional burglars." Not even

H.E. Davis, a Becker employee who slept on the store's second floor, heard any sound. Nearby neighbors said they heard an explosion but did nothing because it sounded like a rifle shot, an apparently normal nocturnal sound.

Other Belenites said they had seen two men loitering in town, "having the dress and appearance of persons who would undertake such a job without great urging." Although they thought that the pair looked suspicious, no one had alerted the police to be on the lookout. As with the sound of a rifle shot in the night, the presence of suspicious looking characters was apparently quite normal in town.

Newspapers noted that the robbery at Becker's store stirred a "great deal of excitement" in Belen. Most residents were confident that the thieves would be captured within hours.

But no one was arrested and only one bit of evidence was ever collected. Newspapers reported that the checks and papers that had been taken from Becker's (and were of no value to the thieves) were found on the steps of the Lutheran church where the robbers evidently held an "executive session" after their late night "safe-cracking expedition."

Unfortunately, the thieves' "donation" was of no value to the church. At least Becker, a leading member of the Lutheran congregation, recovered his checks and papers, although his stolen $800 and several watches were lost forever.

Some old-timers remember when the Becker store created a unique security system to discourage additional thieves. Bill Gore reports that it was well known that the store kept bull snakes in its basement to catch rats of both the two-legged and four-legged varieties. Becker offered 25 cents a snake for anyone brave enough to capture the slithering creatures and add them to the snake pit's population. Bill prudently refused to participate in these snake hunts, no matter what the compensation.

On a Personal Level

The 1910 robbery of John Becker's Mercantile Store was adjacent to the First National Bank, but the bank went untouched. The same could not be said for the bank's cashier (manager) L. C. Becker, John Becker's second oldest son.

On July 11, 1913, 31-year-old L.C. Becker had just arrived at his office at the bank when he received news of a robbery at his residence on North 4th Street. Apparently two "tramps" had come to the house looking for a handout. An unidentified household member let the pair into the kitchen where they spied a valuable watch lying on a table. The pair managed to steal the watch and make good their escape.

The best L.C. Becker could do was to contact the police in Albuquerque with the tramps' descriptions in case they headed north from Belen. We are left to wonder if the tramps really stole Becker's watch, if Becker simply lost it, or if someone else made off with the expensive item and conveniently blamed it on the homeless men.

Becker experienced another spell of bad luck 25 years later while visiting the famous Alvarado Hotel near the train depot in Albuquerque. Now 56 years old, Becker was washing his hands in a hotel bathroom when an unknown assailant attempted to rob him by attacking him with a brick inside a sock.

Miraculously, the blow did not knock Becker out. Instead, the holdup man demanded money from the banker as the pair grappled in the small space. Becker claimed that he had almost overpowered his attacker when he (Becker) suddenly slipped and the would-be robber escaped. Perhaps remembering the fate of his watch 25 years earlier, Becker was strongly motivated to retain his property—and his pride—in 1938.

The Bank's Only Robbery

But what of the First National Bank of Belen's first and only robbery? When did it happen and who attempted the crime? How much did they steal? Were the bank robbers ever caught and brought to justice?

The First National Bank of Belen was located in the rear of John Becker's mercantile store until a territorial law of 1903 decreed that banks and mercantile stores could not coexist in the same building. Complying with the law, Becker moved his new bank to a building just north of his large store. The move took place on January 4, 1904. The robbery took place eleven days later.

Exterior of the new First National Bank of Belen building after 1914

The crime was clearly well planned and executed. Two bandits waited until everyone but the bank's cashier, Al Frost, had left the building for lunch just before noon.

In a scene straight out of a Western movie, the strangers rode up to the bank's front door and calmly hitched their horses. With masks on and guns drawn, the outlaws entered the bank to find Frost standing at his cashier's window with between $600 and $1,000 (worth $15,000 to $25,000 today) on the counter before him.

Frost grabbed a revolver from below his counter, but the well-armed thieves demanded that he hand it over "on pain of being perforated with bullets." Frost wisely complied.

Reporters later asked Frost how many six-shooters the robbers pointed at him, to which he answered, "They didn't have any six-shooters at all."

"Then did they have any Winchesters?"

"No, sir," replied the cashier.

"Well, what then? They didn't hold up the bank with a pleasant smile, did they?"

"No, no smiles. When I looked up all I saw was the business end of a battery of artillery and I didn't look into it very deep. I feared I'd fall in."

Clearly intimidated, Frost had handed over the cash without hesitation. The outlaws backed out of the building, mounted their waiting horses, and rode off at a "rapid speed," according to the press. The entire escapade had taken less than five minutes. Frost only remembered that both outlaws were Anglos and that one was quite a bit taller than the other.

News of the robbery spread quickly. Fifty men soon organized a posse to follow the outlaws' trail. The situation was far different than the 1898 robbery when "Bronco Bill" Walters and his gang stole thousands of dollars from a Santa Fe train traveling south from Belen. Although deputy sheriff Francisco Vigil called for men to form a posse, only Daniel Bustamante stepped forward to pursue the thieves. None of the stolen loot belonged to anyone in Valencia County and only Bustamante and Vigil were willing to risk their lives in pursuit of out-of-town assets.

Fifty local men were more willing to volunteer for a posse in 1904 because many of them probably had deposited money in their hometown bank. They were personally determined to do whatever it took to recover what might well have been their own cash. Members of the posse need not have worried. The bank was insured and no depositors lost their savings.

Although led by Sheriff Carlos Baca and divided into four highly motivated, well-armed groups, the posse never caught the elusive outlaws. They were last seen riding in the direction of Ladron (Thieve's) Mountain, the notorious hangout for thieves in the Rio Abajo.

For years the First National Bank of Belen hung a yellowed copy of the *Albuquerque Daily Citizen*, which reported the 1904 robbery, on a prominent wall in the bank. Perhaps bank officials hoped to remind customers of its enviable track record in avoiding thefts in the ensuing decades.

Valencia County did not experience another bank robbery until January 1980 when a lone thief robbed $15,000 from the Rio Communities branch of Ranchers' State Bank. Los Lunas's Sandia Federal Savings and Loan was also stuck-up by a man who matched the description of the thief who had robbed the same bank's Los Lunas branch in November 1989. Police arrested a robber while he attempted a heist at Sandia Federal's Rio Communities' branch in March 1990. But none of these crimes took place in Belen.

Jim Foley, who had become the First National Bank of Belen's fourth president in 1981, recalls that a string of similar bank robberies in Albuquerque made his employees so nervous that he hired extra security. Foley soon let his additional guards go when no thefts were attempted and he realized that the male guards were spending most of their time flirting with his female cashiers.

Pasó Por Aqui (He Passed Through Here)

In 1927 the famous Western author Eugene Manlove Rhodes published *Pasó Por Aqui,* his most famous and most popular novel. Some readers believe that the novel's plot was based on the Belen bank robbery of 1904.

There are similarities between the novel and the crime, including the scene of the crime, the large posse sent in pursuit, and the outlaws' successful getaway. But there are many more differences than similarities. Ross McEwen, the novel's outlaw, acted alone, robbed a store rather than a bank, and escaped with the help of a lawman, none other than Sheriff Pat Garrett.

Garrett was willing to assist in the outlaw's getaway because the robber chose to help an isolated, bed-ridden Mexican family rather than save himself by continuing his flight. In the novel's last scene, a main character concludes that "We are all decent people," when given a chance.

It would be nice to believe that the criminals who robbed the First National Bank of Belen performed a similarly selfless, decent act, but Rhodes's novel is pure fiction and does nothing to help us solve the real mystery.

The best we can say is that two strangers *pasarón por aqui* and then disappeared into history as quickly as they had first appeared. Belen lost a bit of its innocence on January 15, 1904, but, with the exception of a Hollywood movie, the Hub City would be left undisturbed by bank robbers to the day of the First National Bank's sale to Norwest in 1995.

Exiled from Isleta:
Monsignor Frederick Stadtmueller's Expulsion from the Pueblo, 1965

Richard Melzer

A 42-year-old German priest sat quietly in a rear pew of the St. Augustine Catholic Church in Isleta. Monsignor Frederick A. Stadtmueller had been the parish priest in the Indian community for ten of his 25 years in the priesthood. As he watched the 11:00 morning Mass on June 27, 1965, Monsignor Stadtmueller reflected on all that he believed he had accomplished over the last decade. Monsignor Stadtmueller recalled that when he arrived in Isleta in July 1955 there was only one Sunday mass, at 8:00 a.m. Now, with many more local residents attending, three Masses were scheduled each Sunday. The church had become so active that Monsignor Stadtmueller had required a second priest, Father Del Thomas, to help out.

Remodeling the Church

Work had also progressed in and around the church itself. Built in the early seventeenth century, largely destroyed in the Pueblo Revolt, and rebuilt in the eighteenth century, St. Augustine's ancient roof and *terrón* walls were in urgent need of repair. As was done at several churches in the Rio Grande Valley, Monsignor Stadtmueller had had the exterior walls covered with tons of Portland cement. His intention was to reinforce the structure and preclude the need to replaster its walls each spring. Monsignor Stadtmueller had also removed the church's wooden bell towers, replacing them with towers made of concrete bricks. Telling visitors that the church's two old copper bells "sounded terrible," Monsignor Stadtmueller installed a new bell from Cincinnati that operated electronically.

Reverend Frederick Stadtmueller

The priest had had a new concrete sidewalk built, extending from the church gate on the pueblo's plaza to the front door of the church. By 1960, he had had a circular 30-foot concrete slab built where pueblo residents could dance their ancient dances without disturbing the *camposanto*, or cemetery grounds, in front of the church. He had landscaped the area with cacti. There were rumors that Monsignor Stadtmueller had plans to pave part or all of the plaza so that people could park their vehicles more conveniently on pavement rather than on a dirt surface, especially during New Mexico's windy spring season.

Monsignor Stadtmueller had been so eager to proceed with his restoration plans that he had neglected to secure permission from the Archdiocese in Santa Fe. Architect Van Dorn Hooker recalls the day he and his partner, John McHugh, were called to an urgent meeting at Archbishop Edwin V. Byrne's office to discuss the situation in Isleta. Monsignors Francis Reinberg and Stadtmueller were also present, although Stadtmueller never uttered a word. Clearly upset, Archbishop Byrne arranged for Hooker and McHugh to take over the restoration project as soon as possible.

The architects got to work immediately, measuring every part of the church. Inspecting the structure's leaking roof, Hooker discovered 3" to 4" of pigeon droppings on top of the old asphalt roof. A new roof was installed, as were new mahogany pews, florescent lighting, a loudspeaker, and a modern heating system. McHugh designed a new adobe front, although Stadtmueller was allowed to keep his concrete block bell towers.

Frederick Stadtmueller was proud of all that he had done in Isleta. Promoted to monsignor by Archbishop Byrne's successor, James Peter Davis, he felt sure that his superiors in the Catholic Church were satisfied with the progress he had made, despite his initial, unapproved haste.

Bavarian Roots

Monsignor Stadtmueller was in fact pleased with everything he had accomplished since he had first arrived in the United States on April 2, 1928. Born in Bavaria, he had grown up in a large family that had faced hard times after Germany's humiliating defeat in World War I. Able to grow little more than weeds on their farm, Stadtmueller and his family eventually lost everything they owned. Their father could only find work milking cows. Somehow the Stadtmuellers scraped together enough money to migrate to the United States and start a new life. The voyage across the Atlantic took ten days and was so rough that many fell ill, including two of Frederick's six brothers and sisters. Like millions of immigrants before them, the Stadtmueller family arrived at Ellis Island in New York Harbor.

Family members took any work they could find in their new country. In one instance, Frederick helped a farmer build a new barn after the man's original barn had blown up. With Prohibition still enforced, the farmer had tried to make some extra cash by becoming an amateur bootlegger, making illegal whiskey with a still built in his barn. Things went terribly wrong with the still. The barn had burned quickly.

Frederick attended high school in Columbus, Ohio, but experienced a lot of bullying from classmates who teased him about his inability to speak English. He forced himself to learn English in three weeks "for self-defense," in his words. Despite the Great Depression, Frederick attended four years of high school, four years of college, and four years of seminary before he entered the priesthood in mid-1940. Requesting an assignment in New Mexico, the new priest first served in Santa Rosa and then as the assistant pastor in the Sacred Heart Church in Albuquerque's South Valley.

The Flying Padre

Monsignor Stadtmueller's third parish in New Mexico was far to the northeast, in Harding County. Arriving in November 1943, he discovered that his parish included eleven mission churches spread over 4,000 square miles of desolate ranch land. He tried to travel to his mission churches by car, but soon found that his Model A Ford was too slow and too vulnerable to flat tires to be effective. It was 74 miles to Tucumcari, the nearest large town.

The Flying Padre

Always impressed by modern aviation and high speed vehicles, Monsignor Stadtmueller was determined to learn how to fly and visit his parishioners by air. For $8 an hour, a pilot in Las Vegas, New Mexico, taught him how to fly. A friend lent him $2,200 to purchase a Piper Cub, which he flew and fixed as needed. In his words, he and the plane got to "understand each other." Perhaps inspired by Charles Lindbergh's *Spirit of St. Louis*, the priest called his plane the *Spirit of St. Joseph*, the patron saint of his parish church in Mosquero. Monsignor Stadtmueller flew as many as 12,000 miles per year, traveling to say Mass, preside at funerals, baptize babies, and counsel his mostly Hispanic parishioners. The priest and his plane were also available in emergencies, especially when people on isolated ranches needed immediate medical attention.

News of the flying priest soon spread, attracting notice from across the country. In 1951, a young producer named Stanley Kubrick made an 8-minute movie, titled "Flying Padre," about two typical days in Monsignor Stadtmueller's life in the air and among his parishioners. It was Kubrick's only movie to star an airborne priest, although his most famous film, "2001: A Space Odyssey," featured unusual air travel as well.

Monsignor Stadtmueller served St. Joseph's parish for eleven-and-a-half years. He was content with his life and had no real interest in change. He enjoyed flying, raising canaries, and collecting guns, some of which he used to hunt. His long-time housekeeper, Josephine Haffnet, catered to his cooking and housekeeping needs.

A Clash of Cultures

But then Archbishop Byrne assigned Monsignor Stadtmueller to a new parish, miles, some might say worlds, away from the arid, flat terrain of northeastern New Mexico. Stadtmueller was sent to Isleta in the Rio Grande Valley in July 1955.

Monsignor Stadtmueller knew nothing about Isleta and Isletan culture, no less about Southern Tiwa, the Isletan language. When Archbishop Byrne came for a confirmation ceremony in October 1955, he invited Isleta's governor and the lieutenant governor to socialize with their new priest. The governor asked Monsignor Stadtmueller if he intended to learn Tiwa, as many previous priests had, including the beloved Monsignor Anton Docher, who had served at the pueblo for more than 28 years before his death in 1928. Monsignor Stadtmueller replied that he might learn the language if he was there 28 years. He said that he had been sent to pastor a Catholic church, not necessarily to learn the local language and culture. It was hardly the answer that the governor and lieutenant governor had wanted to hear.

Monsignor Stadtmueller gradually learned about Isleta culture, in his words, "with good ears and good friends" in the pueblo. But his focus was always on the Catholic Church and its needs, even if it meant offending local residents.

The Catholic Church had lived in relative peace with the Pueblo Indians of New Mexico since the Pueblo Revolt of 1680. The revolt, the largest of its kind in all of American history, had been mainly caused by the intolerance of Franciscan missionary priests who did not allow the practice of ancient Indian religious ceremonies. Over 400 Spanish settlers, including 31 priests, had been killed in what some Pueblos still call the first American war for independence.

The Franciscan priests who returned to New Mexico in the Spanish reconquest of the 1690s seemed to have learned their lesson well. They were far more willing to live side-by-side with the Pueblos' religious leaders and their religious practices. The Franciscan goal was to convert the Pueblos' residents over time, and not necessarily all at once. At Isleta, the one Franciscan who still interfered in the pueblo's native customs was asked to leave. He voluntarily moved, "finding himself in such conditions that prevented him from serving the mission" in 1791. A precedent had been established in the pueblo.

If Monsignor Stadtmueller ever read about Isleta history, he did not appear to have learned from it or believed that it was relevant to his work as a priest in the mid-twentieth century. Behaving more like the Franciscan missionaries (and martyrs) of the seventeenth century than those of the eighteenth century and later, Stadtmueller was uncompromising in his stand on many issues. He claimed that he was only doing what was expected of him as a Catholic priest. A clash of cultures was inevitable.

Objections to the Priest

Much of the "progress" that Monsignor Stadtmueller was so proud of in his decade-long service in Isleta was seen as offensive by many village elders and local residents. Many appreciated most of the physical improvements at the church, but objected to the concrete walk built over the *camposanto* to the church door. Even more strenuously, they criticized the new cement slab they were told to dance on, saying that their ceremonies were meant to be performed on bare earth, not artificial surfaces. The slab was never used for dancing. At one point a black swastika was painted on its surface as a symbol of protest.

Other Isletans complained about the money Monsignor Stadtmueller raised to pay for all the objectionable changes he had made at St. Augustine's. The priest required that each family make monthly contributions. Rather than require a tithe, or 10 percent of their income as the Bible instructed, Monsignor Stadtmueller asked for 5 percent, a reasonable amount in his estimation. Many still objected, especially given the pueblo's general poverty. It was said that Monsignor Stadtmueller refused to marry couples or even baptize their babies unless they could "prove" that they were Catholics by regularly attending Mass and regularly contributing money to the church. Some suspected that their hard-earned contributions were going to Monsignor Stadtmueller himself, noting that he visited Europe each year and at one point replaced his Volkswagen with a Mercedes Benz.

Some Isletans voiced concerns regarding Monsignor Stadtmueller's comments from the pulpit, especially when he referred to non-religious issues during Sunday Mass. He often spoke about the need for increased police protection, a new fire truck, and a public library on the pueblo. By 1959, his sermons became more secular and more intense, boldly preaching the "virtues" of assertiveness and competition, alien values in traditional Indian cultures. At other times Monsignor Stadtmueller reportedly ridiculed Pueblo culture by calling traditional Indian costumes "rags." He called women who wore ceremonial shawls the "black shawl people." He even referred to traditional foods as "slop." He denounced Indian beliefs and rituals as "pagan," "heathen," and "stupid." When called to the homes of grieving families, he was accused of being sarcastic, rude, and impatient with those who could not "control themselves" in their sorrow.

Monsignor Stadtmueller even refused to participate in Isletan traditions tied to the Catholic Church. The priest would not participate in the important blessing of the fields each spring and objected to religious processions in which women walked barefoot to show their penance. He was particularly opposed to allowing native dances performed in the church nave at Christmas.

When called before the pueblo council in 1962, the priest was asked directly if his ultimate goal was to destroy Isleta's culture and ancient religion. Without hesitation, he answered, "I will spell it out so that you will not misunderstand me: Y-E-S. It is my duty."

Tensions continued to rise. One Easter Sunday Isleta police barricaded all entries to the plaza to prevent traffic from interfering with the traditional dances scheduled that day. Seeing the barricades, Monsignor Stadtmueller rushed to remove them, saying that they prevented his parishioners from parking on the plaza on their way to Easter Mass. The priest finally relented, but a similar incident occurred in February 1964, when Stadtmueller threatened to get one of his guns if the barricades were not removed. Some residents also grew concerned about Monsignor Stadtmueller's gun collection, questioning why a man of God would need so many weapons and need to kill animals for sport. When a pueblo governor asked Stadtmueller what he intended to do with all his guns, he laughingly replied, "You never know when there is going to be another Indian uprising."

Monsignor Stadtmueller was additionally accused of harassing Isleta residents who went to a Baptist missionary church on the reservation. Mormon missionaries said that many residents refused to talk to them for fear of repercussions from their priest.

Disgruntled by these and other affronts, 127 men and women had signed a petition demanding that the priest be replaced in 1964. Others protested in appeals written directly to the archbishop in Santa Fe. Monsignor Stadtmueller's harshest critics claimed that "He thinks he is God and is respectful of no one."

Monsignor Stadtmueller replied to these many accusations by calling them "out-and-out lies" fabricated by his enemies to discredit his work in Isleta. He dismissed the 1964 petition signed by only 127 of the more than 2,200 residents of the pueblo and even suggested that the 127 thought they were signing a petition for the installation of modern sewers. He called accusations that he interfered in the Baptist mission "the biggest lie" of all. He continued to defend his opposition to Indian religious practices, declaring that the people of Isleta "don't know they can't practice two religions."

Strained Relations and an Ultimatum

Relations between the priest and local political and religious leaders only worsened with time. The long-smoldering feud finally culminated in 1965 when Monsignor Stadtmueller refused to participate in a procession on St. Augustine's feast day. Governor Andy Abeita and his lieutenant governor, Louis Lente, met with Monsignor Stadtmueller on Friday, June 11, 1965, to discuss the procession. According to Governor Abeita, Stadtmueller told the pueblo leaders that he did not feel compelled to participate in the procession simply because it had been a tradition. Stadtmueller reportedly said that Isleta's "traditions were nothing, that they can be changed." Abeita replied that as the governor of Isleta he had the power and duty to protect the religious beliefs of his people, as guaranteed in the Bill of Rights of the U.S. Constitution. In order to protect this religious freedom, Abeita told Monsignor Stadtmueller that he must leave Isleta voluntarily by 6:00 p.m. on Sunday, June 20, 1965.

Defiant, Monsignor Stadtmueller asked Abeita to officially inform him of this decree in writing. The governor obliged the following day, asserting in a letter to the priest, "If you do not leave this Pueblo voluntarily..., I and my officials [of] the Executive Branch will have to take steps in escorting you out of the reservation on June 21."

The governor sent copies of his ultimatum to Archbishop Davis, to New Mexico Governor Jack M. Campbell, to high officials of the United Pueblos Agency in Albuquerque, and to the New Mexico Association of Indian Affairs in Santa Fe.

June 20 came and went without any indication that Monsignor Stadtmueller intended to leave Isleta on his own accord. He in fact refused to leave, contending that only Archbishop Davis had the authority to order him or any priest to abandon his church post. Agreeing to leave in response to Governor Abeita's ultimatum would be like a Catholic priest in Albuquerque agreeing to abandon his parish simply because the mayor of Albuquerque ordered him to do so. June 21 also came and went without Governor Abeita taking more forceful action to evict the parish priest. Each side waited for the other to blink. But nothing happened in a tense standoff that lasted a week.

Finally, Governor Abeita and eight Isleta councilmen were able to discuss their grievances with Archbishop Davis in Santa Fe on Saturday, June 26. The Isleta leaders were encouraged by the cordial session, believing that the archbishop had promised that Monsignor Stadtmueller would be promoted to a new position outside the pueblo within the year. But later that evening an *Albuquerque Journal* reporter contacted Abeita with the news that Archbishop Davis had publically denied that he planned to transfer or promote Monsignor Stadtmueller. Abeita felt like he had played his last hand and had been bluffed. He met with members of the pueblo council and all agreed that they had only one last course of action.

Forced into Exile

And so it was on Sunday, June 27, when Monsignor Stadtmueller left St. Augustine's after the 11:00 a.m. Mass that Governor Abeita, Sheriff Pablo Abeita, and other pueblo officials confronted the priest with orders that he must leave the pueblo immediately and permanently. Monsignor Stadtmueller responded by entering the rectory, retreating to a bedroom near the kitchen, and locking himself inside. The Indian leaders followed, although they were not sure if Monsignor Stadtmueller had gone to the bedroom to arm himself in preparation for a potentially bloody showdown. Shouting through the door, a policeman announced that the priest had five minutes to come out. When Monsignor Stadtmueller shouted back that the governor didn't know what he was doing, Governor Abeita answered, "Oh, yes, I do. I've taken it for nine years, and I'm not taking it anymore."

Monsignor Stadtmueller replied by bursting through the door and shouting, "How dare you. This is brutality. This is totalitarianism," to which Abeita responded, "We have had your totalitarianism for the past nine years." Monsignor Stadtmueller was led into the courtyard where handcuffs were snapped onto his wrists and he was escorted to a waiting police vehicle parked in the plaza. Newspaper photographers captured the dramatic moment on film. Dozens of witnesses watched a small scuffle occur as the priest refused to ride in the police vehicle like a common criminal. Given the option, he chose to walk into exile. With a police vehicle following closely behind, Governor Abeita led Monsignor Stadtmueller to the northern edge of the pueblo. There in the center of Isleta Boulevard with traffic backed up in both directions, the governor bade Monsignor Stadtmueller his official farewell.

Monsignor Stadtmueller led from Isleta in handcuffs

Reaction

News of the unusual event spread across the state, throughout the nation, and around the world. Hearing of his priest's ousting in Isleta, Archbishop Davis responded by closing St. Augustine's and padlocking its large wooden doors. Newspapers, including the *News-Bulletin*, reported the incident with many photos, considerable detail, and lengthy editorials. Within a month *Life Magazine* published a large photo of Monsignor Stadtmueller being led away in handcuffs. The magazine's racist headline read, "White Father Is Heap Bad Medicine."

Reaction to the forced exile varied in Isleta. An elderly resident was quoted as saying that "even in Russia I know damn well they don't tie up and handcuff a religious man, and it shouldn't have happened here. I am ashamed." But other residents applauded Governor Abeita's actions. A crowd of over 300 men and women gave their leader a standing ovation after he delivered a long report on the situation, making his remarks in his Tiwa language. One by one, the tribal elders asserted their support for Abeita's conclusion that he had been left with no other alternative in dealing with the defiant monsignor.

Meanwhile, almost a hundred letters arrived in Isleta from as far as California in the west and New York in the east. The vast majority were supportive. One letter writer said, "We do not want to see your village reduced to a white man's town." Another wrote, "Do not tolerate further destruction of the soul and religion of the American Indian." Some letter writers enclosed as much as a $100 "toward your legal expenses, if needed."

Archbishop Davis visited Isleta a week after Monsignor Stadtmueller's expulsion, saying three Masses on Sunday morning, July 4. Davis criticized Governor Abeita's actions, asserting from the pulpit that only he had the authority to dismiss priests in his diocese. He proclaimed that St. Augustine's would remain a "dead church" until Monsignor Stadtmueller returned and received a formal apology from the governor. The archbishop nevertheless announced that he was willing to negotiate all issues as long as talks were held "on mutual terms." When Governor Abeita requested a meeting to begin such a discussion after Davis's third Mass of the morning, the archbishop said that he was needed back in Santa Fe and did not have time to talk.

Governor Abeita also attempted to resolve the crisis by writing to Pope Paul VI at the Vatican. Abeita asked the pontiff to suggest a compromise acceptable to all sides. The pope did not reply. Growing increasingly impatient, a dozen Isleta residents went so far as to file a civil suit in federal court, charging that they had been denied their religious freedom by the actions of their tribal government. Judge H. Vearle Payne dismissed the case in early 1969, saying that it was a conflict between tribal factions that did not really involve the freedom to worship.

Life in Exile

Years later, Monsignor Stadtmueller remembered the trying days of his early life in exile. The same day he was escorted from Isleta, he was given a "temporary trespass pass" to return that evening and collect his father, who had been staying at the rectory, his housekeeper, Josephine Haffnet, and at least some of his belongings. Three weeks later he sent three trucks to retrieve the balance of his possessions after Governor Abeita gave notice that they would all be confiscated if he did not act by Friday, July 16.

Monsignor Stadtmueller recalled the help he received from several kind people from Isleta and the surrounding communities. Norman "Doc" Phillips, a veterinarian in Los Lunas for 52 years, remained a good friend and provided free care for Stadtmueller and his housekeeper's pet Chihuahua. Others remembered the priest fondly and at least one former Pueblo Council member made a dying wish that the exiled priest conduct his funeral Mass when he died in 1966. The *Albuquerque Journal* reported that the funeral was held "without incident" and the church was "filled to overflowing."

Monsignor Stadtmueller also remembered how the trauma of his exile caused him many sleepless nights and frequent nightmares. Fearing that he was going to be killed, he exhibited symptoms of having suffered a nervous breakdown. He traveled to Germany to stay with a cousin, hoping that long, peaceful walks might help speed his emotional recovery. Eventually, he returned to New Mexico and served at the Church of the Ascension (about 5 miles north of the pueblo) where Isletans were told they could worship until the dispute at St. Augustine was resolved.

On March 1, 1970, Monsignor Stadtmueller was transferred to the Holy Ghost parish in southeast Albuquerque. He served at the church on San Pedro Boulevard for ten years until he moved to Blue Water Lake and was assigned to temporary positions at as many as 26 different churches on the Navajo Reservation. Strangely, given his experience at Isleta, he did not receive any special training in Navajo history or culture to help him relate to his new parishioners. Apparently, he did not serve in any one church long enough to cause friction, as had happened in Isleta.

Church Reopened

Finally, after five years of closure (except for special Masses), St. Augustine's was officially reopened by Archbishop Robert F. Sanchez two weeks before Easter in 1970. Religious services, from Masses to weddings and funerals, resumed under Father John R. Regold of the Ascension Parish in Albuquerque. Perhaps to save face, Monsignor Stadtmueller conducted one Mass on each of three Sunday mornings, although he had now been permanently assigned to the Holy Ghost parish.

Four years later the first full-time priest since 1965 was assigned to Isleta. Monsignor Francis Reinberg had served in New Mexico for 39 years when he was assigned to St. Augustine's. Over the years, Father Reinberg had served as a parish pastor and in several other capacities within the Diocese of Santa Fe, often in troubleshooting roles. He had, in fact, been present at the meeting Archbishop Byrne had called to secure the services of architects Van Dorn Hooker and John McHugh when Monsignor Stadtmueller had begun to restore St. Augustine's without prior permission. Father Reinberg was assigned to Isleta by a young new archbishop, Robert F. Sanchez (ordained in mid-1974) who promised many changes within the diocese. Sanchez would in fact be the first archbishop in the Archdiocese of Santa Fe to apologize to the Pueblo Indians for grievances reaching as far back as the Spanish colonial era.

Changes in attitudes and practices were apparent soon after Father Reinberg's arrival in Isleta. As proof that he respected native traditions, Father Reinberg approved a request that the hated concrete slab that Monsignor Stadtmueller had installed in the church courtyard be removed. Indian dances on sacred ground in the courtyard resumed. In the words of former Governor Abeita, he was "very happy" that the tradition had been restored.

Last Days

Monsignor Stadtmueller finally retired to a home not far from the northeast intersection of I-25 and Isleta Boulevard, the very place where Governor Abeita had left him when he had been escorted from the pueblo in handcuffs in 1965. It would be difficult to be any closer to Isleta without actually living on the pueblo. It was as if the priest still hoped to restore his dignity by defiantly standing his ground so close to where he had been publicly shamed.

I interviewed Monsignor Stadtmueller at his home on May 14, 2005,

St. Augustine Church at Isleta

a week before his 92nd birthday and 40 years after his dramatic expulsion in 1965. Despite a triple by-pass operation in 1979, a quadruple bypass in 1990, cataracts, and the use of a hearing aid, the former priest's mind was as sharp as ever and he said he "couldn't complain." He lived with his dachshund, Fritz (which means Fred in German) and with the help of several able aides. His loyal housekeeper, Josephine Haffnet, had died several years earlier. Monsignor Stadtmueller still liked speedy vehicles, including a powerful motorcycle that he proudly showed me, but did not attempt to drive that day. Given his experience of 40 years earlier, the monsignor may never have wanted to be caught again without a fast means of escape at his disposal.

Monsignor Stadtmueller described the events of his life to me in remarkable detail. He made no apologies for his attitude or behavior in Isleta, still believing that he had done nothing wrong during his ten-year tenure. When I asked if he would do anything differently, he declared in a clear, firm voice, "There was nothing I would do differently at Isleta because I acted as a Catholic priest in a Catholic parish."

Monsignor Frederick A. Stadtmueller died of cancer at age 95 on August 22, 2008. In his final months he had moved to Rocky Mount, Virginia, to be near relatives. His funeral was held at Albuquerque's Holy Ghost Church; his remains were buried in an Albuquerque Catholic cemetery. His obituary in the *Albuquerque Journal* said nothing about the turmoil in Isleta, no less his controversial role at St. Augustine.

New Days

Meanwhile, the Catholic Church in Isleta has thrived with a succession of pastors who have worked well not only as Catholic priests, but also as respected—and respectful—members of the Isleta community. Father James T. Burke revealed his respect for Isleta's culture and history by collecting, copying, and distributing old photos of the pueblo at each of a hundred Sunday Masses. Father Burke compiled the photos in a bound volume titled *100 Sundays at Isleta*, printed in 1979. A later priest, Father Bernard Loughrey, was so admired for his work at Isleta from 1985 to 1999 that his image is preserved in a stained glass window on St. Augustine's west wall.

The church building itself has undergone a comprehensive restoration, planned over a period of five years and completed in 2012 after 16 months of intensive, careful labor. The original church, in all of its historic detail, has been restored as a Cornerstone project with the support of Governor Frank Lujan, chair of Isleta's Restoration Committee. Over 375 tons of cement, applied to cover the old *terrónes* in 1959, have been removed. Rather than preserve the original *terrónes* as intended, the cement had actually weakened the old bricks and would have destroyed the entire structure if nothing had been done to rescue the walls. Over 75,000 new adobes, plus thousands of recycled ones, were used in the enormous project.

Symbolically, the rigid concrete that Monsignor Stadtmueller had used to cover the church in 1959 had damaged the traditional adobes, much like the rigid ideas that Monsignor Stadtmueller had tried to implement had harmed Isleta's traditional culture and values. Isleta's church has now been restored to its former beauty, the product of sincere appreciation and cultural cooperation at last.

Bibliography

Adams, Charles and Andrew I. Duff, eds. *The Protohistoric Pueblo World A.D. 1275-1600*. Tucson: University of Arizona Press, 2004.

Alberts, Don E., ed. *Rebels on the Rio Grande*. Albuquerque: University of New Mexico Press, 1984.

Anaya, Rudolfo, Juan Estevan Arellan, and Denise Chavez. *Descansos: An Interrupted Journey*. Albuquerque: Del Norte, 1995.

Bayer, Laura. *Santa Ana—The People, the Pueblo, and the History of Tamaya*. Albuquerque: University of New Mexico Press, 1994.

Burke, Father James T. *100 Sundays at Isleta*. Isleta Pueblo, 1979.

Chavez, Fray Angelico. "A Nineteenth-Century New Mexico Schism," *New Mexico Historical Review*, vol. 58 (January 1983): 35-54.

Chavez, Tibo J. *New Mexican Folklore of the Rio Abajo*. Portales: Bishop, 1972.

Cordell, Linda S. *Prehistory of the Southwest*. San Diego: Academic Press, 1984.

Dawson, Katharine. "Coal, Community, and Collective Action in McKinley County, New Mexico, 1900-1935." Unpublished Ph.D. dissertation, State University of New York at Binghamton, 2004.

De La Vega, Roberto. *Three Centuries of Tome, New Mexico*. Los Lunas: San Clemente Church, 1976.

Ellis, Florence Hawley. "Tome and Father J. B. R," *New Mexico Historical Review*, vol. 30 (April 1955): 98-114.

_____. "Tome and Father J. B. R. (concluded)," *New Mexico Historical Review*, vol. 30 (July, 1955): 195-220.

Ellis, Florence Hawley and Edwin Baca. "The Apuntes of Father J. B. Ralliere," *New Mexico Historical Review*, vol. 32 (January 1957): 10-35.

_____. "The Apuntes of Father J. B. Ralliere (concluded)," *New Mexico Historical Review*, vol. 32 (July 1957): 259-273.

Espinosa, Gilberto and Tibo J. Chavez. *El Rio Abajo*. Portales: Bishop, 1967.

Frazier, Donald S. *Blood and Treasure*. College Station: Texas A&M University Press, 1995.

Gregg, Andrew K. *New Mexico in the Nineteenth Century—A Pictoral History*. Albuquerque: University of New Mexico Press, 1998.

Guggino, Patricia. "Pablo Abeita: Cultural Broker Between Isleta Pueblo and the United States Government." Unpublished Masters thesis, University of New Mexico, 1995.

Horgan, Paul. *The Great River*. New York: Rinehart and Company, 1984.

Houlihan, Patrick T. and Betsy E. Houlihan. *Lummis in the Pueblos*. Flagstaff: Northland Press, 1986.

Jenco, Father Lawrence Martin, OSM. *Bound to Forgive: The Pilgrimage to Reconciliation of a Beirut Hostage*. Notre Dame, Indiana: Ave Maria Press, 1995.

Julyan, Robert. *The Place Names of New Mexico*. Albuquerque: University of New Mexico Press, 1996.

Kessell, John L. *Kiva, Cross and Crown*. Washington, D.C.: National Park Service, 1979.

_____. *Pueblos, Spaniards, and the Kingdom of New Mexico*. Norman: University of Oklahoma Press, 2008.

_____. *Miera y Pacheco*. Norman: Univerrsity of Oklahoma Press, 2013.

Lummis, Charles. *A Tramp Across the Continent*. Lincoln: University of Nebraska Press, 1982.

Ortman, Scott G. *Winds from the North—Tewa Origins and Historical Anthropology*. Salt Lake City: University of Utah Press, 2012.

Marshall, Michael P. and Henry J. Walt. *Rio Abajo—Prehistory and History of a Rio Grande Province*. Santa Fe: New Mexico Historic Preservation Division, 1984.

Melzer, Richard and Margaret Espinosa McDonald. *Valencia County: History Through a Photographers Lens*. Virginia Beach: Denning, 2002.

Melzer, Richard and Phyllis Ann Mingus, "Wild to Fight: The New Mexico Rough Riders in the Spanish-American War." *New Mexico Historical Review*, vol. 59 (1984): 109-36.

Melzer, Richard and John Taylor, eds. *Murder, Mystery, and Mayhem in the Rio Abajo*. Los Ranchos: Rio Grande Books, 2013.

Phillips, David A. Jr. "Agriculture at Pottery Mound," in *Southwestern Interludes—Papers in Honor of Charlotte J. and Theodore R. Frisbie*. Wiseman, Reggie N.,

Thomas C. O'Laughlin, and Cordelia T. Snow, eds. Archeological Society of New Mexico, No. 32, 2006.

Phillips, David A. and Jean H. Ballagh. *The Pottery Mound Monitoring Program, 2009*. Maxwell Museum Technical Series Number 13. Albuquerque: Maxwell Museum of Anthropology, 2010.

Prince, L. Bradford. "The Rev. Hiram Read—Baptist Missionary to New Mexico." *New Mexico Historical Review*, vol. 17 (April 1942): 113-147.

Ralliere, Father Jean Baptiste. *Cánticos Espirituales*.

Rhodes, Eugene Manlove. *Pasó Por Aquí*. Norman: University of Oklahoma Press, 1973.

Robb, John Donald. *Hispanic Folk Songs of New Mexico*. Albuquerque: University of New Mexico Press, 2014.

Roberts, David. *The Pueblo Revolt*. New York: Simon and Schuster, 2004.

Rodriguez, Father Arnold L., OSM. "New Mexico in Transiton—Chapter IV: The Churches," *New Mexico Historical Review*, vol. 24 (April 1942): 284-299.

Roosevelt, Theodore. *The Rough Riders*. New York: Charles Scribner's Sons, 1899; New York: New American Library, 1961.

Sanchez, Joseph P. *The Rio Abajo Frontier*. Albuquerque: Albuquerque Museum, 2000.

Schaafsma, Polly, ed. *New Perspectives on Pottery Mound Pueblo*. Albuquerque: University of New Mexico Press, 2007.

Silverman, Robert. *The Pueblo Revolt*. Lincoln: University of Nebraska Press, 1970.

Simmons, Marc. *Albuquerque*. Albuquerque: University of New Mexico Press, 1982.

_____. *Murder on the Santa Fe Trail*. El Paso: Texas Western Press, 1987.

Stuart, David E. *Anasazi America*. Albuquerque: University of New Mexico Press, 2014.

Taylor, John. *Dejad a los Niños Venir a Mí*. Los Ranchos: LPD Press, 2005.

_____. *Catholics Along the Rio Grande*. Charleston: Arcadia Press, 2011.

Thompson, Mark. *American Character: The Curious Life of Charles Fletcher Lummis and the Rediscovery of the Southwest*. New York: Arcade Publishing, 2001.

Valencia County Historical Society. *Rio Abajo Heritage: A History of Valencia County*. Belen: Valencia County Historical Society, 1981.

Valencia News Bulletin: February 19-20, 2000; May 27-28, 2000; March 17-18, 2001; April 21-22, 2001; March 16, 2002; September 21 & October 19, 2002; December 20, 2003; April 17, 2004; July 17, 2004; July 16, 2005; July

21, 2007; March 22, 2008; November 29 & December 6, 2008; July 18, 2009; December 15, 2012; February 16, 2013; April 18, 2013; October 17, 2013; Feb. 20, 2014; April 3, 2014; April 17, 2014.

Warner, Michael J. "Protestant Missionary Activity Among the Navajo—1890-1912," *New Mexico Historical Review*, vol. 45 (July 1970): 209-232.

Weber, David J., ed. *What Caused the Pueblo Revolt of 1680?* Boston: Bedford/Saint Martins, 1999.

About the Authors

JIM BOECK of Belen studied at the Center for the American West at the University of New Mexico. He earned a Masters degree in Southwest Studies from New Mexico Highlands University. He was a regular contributor to *La Historia del Rio Abajo* until his death in 2014. This book is dedicated to his memory.

MARGARET ESPINOSA MCDONALD was raised in Albuquerque. After obtaining a B.S. in Elementary Education, she taught in Kansas City, Kansas. Returning to New Mexico, McDonald taught in the Belen Public Schools. She received her doctorate from UNM in American Studies. Dr. McDonald authored *Through the Photographer's Lens: A Photographic History of Valencia County* with Dr. Richard Melzer. She has continued to write and lecture on numerous topics on Valencia County and the Rio Abajo. Dr. McDonald is past president of the Historical Society of New Mexico and the Valencia County Historical Society. She is also past chair of the New Mexico Humanities Council.

RICHARD MELZER is a professor of history at the University of New Mexico-Valencia Campus, past president of the Valencia County Historical Society, and past president of the Historical Society of New Mexico. He is the author or co-author of many books and articles about New Mexico and the Southwest.

FRANCISCO SISNEROS is a retired educator and a life-long student of New Mexico history and culture. His research interests are in lesser known figures of the New Mexico Spanish Colonial and Mexican periods and on the origins of the first Hispanic families of New Mexico. He and his wife, Inez, live in Casa Colorada, New Mexico.

JOHN TAYLOR is retired from Sandia National Laboratories. He has

329

a Masters Degree in Nuclear Engineering from Stanford University and was a member of Sandia's Technical and Management Staff from 1975-2010. He has published over 50 technical reports and papers. He is the author or co-author of five books on New Mexico history, one on physics of soccer for youth players, and one on a high school in southern California. In addition, he has published numerous articles in various books and journals on Civil War and Catholic history topics.

Photo Credits

Cover image: "River's Edge," photograph courtesy of Bill Tondreau, bill@unit16.net.

p. iii: Jim Boeck, courtesy Richard Melzer.

p. 5: Father Ralliere as a young man, Tome Church Museum.

p. 6: Tome's Immaculate Conception Church circa 1915, Museum of New Mexico Photo Archives, 163771.

p. 15: Father Ralliere in later years, Tome church museum.

p. 19: Father Jose Antonio Zubiria, Bishop of Durango, Museum of New Mexico.

p. 21: Father Jean Baptiste Lamy, Archbishop of Santa Fe, Archdiocese of Santa Fe.

p. 22: Reverend Hiram Read, Albuquerque First Baptist Church.

p. 24: Methodist (formerly Baptist) mission in Peralta, New Mexico. Museum of New Mexico Photo Archives, 124378.

p. 25: Ambrosio Gonzales grave marker in old Methodist Cemetery in Peralta, courtesy John Taylor.

p. 27: Don Felipe Chavez, National Park Service.

p. 30: Felipe Chavez house, Belen, New Mexico, Valencia County Historical Society.

p. 33: Joe and Ruth Tondre, courtesy Anne T. Williams.

p. 39: Dennis Chavez as a young man, courtesy Chavez family.

p. 45: Senator Dennis Chavez, courtesy Chavez family.

p. 48: Statue of Dennis Chavez in the National Statuary Gallery in Washington, D.C., Library of Congress.

p. 51: Tibo J. Chavez, Sr., as a young man, *Valencia News-Bulletin.*

p. 54: Tibo Chavez campaign button, image from Kenneth Burt blog.

332

334

Index

340

343

344

346

CPSIA information can be obtained
at www.ICGtesting.com
Printed in the USA
FSOW04n0041260615
8258FS

9 781936 744503